EARTHQUAKES

A Teacher's Package for K-6

Produced by

The National Science Teachers Association
1742 Connecticut Avenue, N.W.
Washington, DC 20009

Supported by the

Federal Emergency Management Agency
Washington, DC

NSTA/FEMA Earthquake Curriculum

Project Director:

   Phyllis R. Marcuccio, Director of Publications, National Science Teachers Association

Project Coordinator:

   Marie McClintock Barry, Administrative Associate, National Science Teachers Association

Editor:

   Mary Liston Liepold, Washington, DC

Authors:

   Jeffrey C. Callister, Earth Science Teacher, Newburgh Free Academy, Newburgh, NY

   Lenny Coplestone, Second Grade Teacher, Wyngate Elementary School, Bethesda, MD

   Gerard F. Consuegra, Elementary Science Specialist, Montgomery County Public Schools, Rockville, MD

   Sharon M. Stroud, Earth Science Teacher, Widefield High School, Colorado Springs, CO

   Warren E. Yasso, Science Coordinator, Department of Mathematics and Science Education, Teachers College, Columbia University, New York, NY

Consultants:

   Jane H. Hall, President, Board of Directors, Environmental Volunteers, Palo Alto, CA

   Lynne Stietzel, Science Teacher, Environmental Volunteers, Palo Alto, CA

Design Director:

   John Sinnett, John Sinnett Associates, Arlington, VA

Illustrator:

   Forrest Plesko, Superior, WI

Project Officer:

   Marilyn P. MacCabe, Earthquakes and Natural Hazards Programs Division, Federal Emergency Management Agency

Single copies of the publication may be obtained from the Federal Emergency Management Agency

   FEMA SL-NT, Earthquake Program
   500 C Street, S.W.
   Washington, DC 20472

This product was developed by the National Science Teachers Association (NSTA) with financial support from the Federal Emergency Management Agency (FEMA) under Contract No. EMW-87-C-2573. NSTA is solely responsible for the accuracy of statements and interpretations contained herein.

ISBN 0-87355-082-X

Contents

Unit I: Defining an Earthquake

Unit II: Why and Where Earthquakes Occur

Unit III: Physical Results of Earthquakes

Unit IV: Measuring Earthquakes

Unit V: Recognizing an Earthquake

Unit VI: Earthquake Safety and Survival

Appendix
Earthquake Background

Book of Legends

Earthquake Curriculum, K-6 List of Line Masters

UNIT I

Master 1.	U.S. Map
Master 1.	U.S. Map (without state names)
Master 2.	The Turtle Tale
Master 3.	Draw and Write
Master 4.	Turtle Dot-to-Dot
Master 5.	World Map
Master 6.	World Map with Legend Sites
Master 7.	World Map with Epicenters
Master 8.	Elastic Rebound
Master 9.	Dresser Drawers
Master 10a.	Earthquake Terms
Master 10b.	Earthquake Terms Worksheet
Master 11.	U.S. Map with Epicenters

UNIT II

Master 12.	Layers of the Earth
Master 13.	Earth Plates
Master 14a.	Earth Plate Puzzle Pieces
Master 14b.	Earth Plate Puzzle Pieces
Master 15.	Earth Layers Worksheet
Master 16.	Earthquake Words
Master 17.	A Pizza the Earth
Master 18.	Graph of the Earth's Layers
Master 19.	Plate Boundaries Map
Master 20.	Convection Currents and Plate Cross Section
Master 21.	Formation and Breakup of Pangaea

UNIT III

Master 22.	Fault Movements
Master 23.	Rural Community After an Earthquake
Master 24.	Fault Model
Master 25.	Fault Worksheet
Master 26.	Earthquake Math Facts
Master 27.	Fault Planes
Master 28a.	Landscape Regions Worksheet
Master 28b.	Landscape Regions of U.S.
Master 28c.	Landscape Regions Key
Master 29.	Ocean Bottom

UNIT IV

Master 30a-e.	Earthquake Damage Set
Master 31.	Modified Mercalli Scale
Master 32.	Several Seismographs
Master 33.	Seismogram Worksheet
Master 34.	Richter Scale
Master 35.	P-Wave Motion and S-Wave Motion
Master 36.	The S-Wave Machine
Master 37.	Student Seismograph
Master 38.	Seismogram Showing Amplitude

UNIT V

Master 39a-e.	Where Earthquakes Happen Set
Master 40a.	Living Room
Master 40b.	Bedroom
Master 40c.	Neighborhood
Master 40d.	Downtown
Master 40e.	Tsunami
Master 40f.	Landslides
Master 41.	Earthquake Simulation Script
Master 42.	Drop and Cover
Master 43.	Earthquake Feelings
Master 44.	Shimmy—Shimmy—Shake
Master 45.	Earthquake Risk Map
Master 46.	Earthquake Severity Worksheet
Master 47.	Killer Earthquakes
Master 48.	Coalinga Schools Report
Master 49.	Selected U.S. Earthquakes of the 20th Century
Master 50.	U.S. Map with 14 Epicenters
Master 51.	Isoseismal Map, San Fernando, CA 1971
Master 52.	Isoseismal Worksheet
Master 53.	Tsunami Facts
Master 54.	A Cascade of Disasters

UNIT VI

Master 55.	Fourth Grade Classroom
Master 56.	Classroom Hazard Hunt
Master 57a.	Home Hazard Hunt Worksheet
Master 57b.	Home Hazard Hunt Worksheet
Master 57c.	Home Hazard Hunt Worksheet
Master 58.	Quake-Safe Home Checklist
Master 59.	Neighborhood Hazard Hunt
Master 60.	Safety Rules for Shoppers
Master 61a-c.	Community Hazard Hunt
Master 62.	Drill and Evacuation Checklist
Master 63.	Home Earthquake Safety

NATIONAL SCIENCE TEACHERS ASSOCIATION

1742 Connecticut Avenue, NW,   Washington, DC 20009   (202) 328-5800

October 1988

Dear Colleague,

The National Science Teachers Association is proud to join the Federal Emergency Management Agency (FEMA) in presenting a curriculum on earthquakes for you to use with your elementary school children. The material offers science content and processes that are designed with children's abilities and needs in mind.

Like your students, the science of earthquakes is young. What we know about earthquakes is particularly intriguing to study because many of the great discoveries in the field are still ahead of us. Perhaps one day one of your students will contribute to our understanding of these powerful phenomena, so we can be even better prepared for earthquakes in the future.

Earthquakes are a danger to the entire nation, not just a few states--a fundamental concern throughout the development of this curriculum. The writing team included teachers, scientists, curriculum specialists, and consultants from six states with a wide range of educational experience. Teachers in eleven states tested the material, and offered the kind of feedback that only classroom teachers can provide. Expert reviewers at FEMA, the United States Geological Survey, and several major universities provided constructive criticism from their own perspective. Our colleagues in Arkansas, California, and other states generously shared materials they have developed, and allowed us to benefit from their experience. And our own NSTA staff of editors, graphic designers, and consultants worked tirelessly to make the end product accurate and appealing. To all of them, my thanks and congratulations.

Sincerely,

Bill G. Aldridge
Executive Director

Introduction

NSTA/FEMA Earthquake Curriculum

This K-6 curriculum has been developed by the National Science Teachers Association under a contract with the Federal Emergency Management Agency. Its twofold purpose reflects both sides of this partnership: to introduce you and your students to a fascinating new field of science; and to prepare students, teachers, and, by extension, their communities to cope in the event of an earthquake emergency.

Take some time to familiarize yourself with this curriculum before you introduce the first lesson to your students. The overview covers all the science concepts treated in the lessons. If you read this section first, then read the summary and introduction that precedes each unit as you prepare to teach it, you will have all the background you need to use this curriculum, no matter what grade you teach and what kind of science preparation you've had before.

The authors have taken pains to scale a complex subject to a level suitable for elementary school students without sacrificing scientific accuracy. This has necessarily entailed some simplification. Volumes have been written on topics that are passed over here, or dealt with in a paragraph. The science of earthquakes is an active and exciting field, where every day brings new discoveries and challenges to old hypotheses. You will find it well worth your while to consult the references at the end of each unit whenever you are interested in greater detail on a particular topic.

Organization

This teacher's manual has six units. Each of the first five units is divided into three levels: Level 1, for grades K-2; Level 2, for grades 3-4; and Level 3, for grades 5-6. Since classes and individuals vary widely, however, you may often find the procedures in the other levels helpful for your students. Sometimes the manual specifically refers you to another level. Even when it doesn't, though, it would be wise to glance at all three levels in each unit before you prepare the lessons for your own class.

Overview

Unit I, Defining an Earthquake, builds on what students already know about earthquakes to establish a working definition of the phenomenon. Legends from near and far encourage children to create their own fanciful explanations, paving the way for the scientific explanations they will begin to learn in this unit.

Unit II, Why and Where Earthquakes Occur, presents the modern scientific understanding of the Earth's structure and composition, and relates this to the cause of earthquakes.

Unit III, Physical Results of an Earthquake, provides greater understanding of the processes that shape our active Earth. Earthquakes are put in the context of the large- and small-scale changes that are constantly at work on the continents as well as on the ocean floor.

Unit IV, Measuring Earthquakes, explains earthquakes in terms of wave movement and introduces students to the processes by which their effects are measured.

Unit V, Recognizing Earthquakes, deals with the events that surround an earthquake and dispels some common misconceptions about earthquake damage.

Unit VI, Earthquake Safety and Survival, focuses on all the things students and teachers can do to protect themselves before, during, and after an earthquake.

Units I through VI are intended to be used in the order presented. Since students may raise questions about earthquake safety at any point in the program, however, you may want to at least scan the introduction to Unit VI before you begin to teach the first unit.

The lessons in Unit VI, Earthquake Safety and Survival, are an exception to the general pattern. Although the unit has three parts, the lessons in all three parts are recommended for students in kindergarten through sixth grade.

Features of This Package

Because young students learn best by doing, the lessons in this teaching package are primarily a series of hands-on experiences. You will need to locate simple materials for some of the lessons. Others require only things that are already in your classroom, in addition to those provided in this package. A materials list is given at the beginning of each set of lessons. At the end of each unit you will find master pages ready to reproduce for transparencies, handouts, and worksheets. Masters are identified in the text by name and number. A reference list at the end of each unit suggests readings and other resources that you and your students may use to go beyond the information given.

Because students learn holistically, these lessons include methods and materials from language arts, mathematics, social studies, music, and the other fine arts, as well as physical science. Learning Links, found in the left-hand column near the beginning of each set of activities, summarize some of these interdisciplinary connections.

Extensions, provided near the end of each set of activities, suggest ways for your students to learn more about that topic. You may want to use the Extensions for individual enrichment or to provide additional experiences for the entire class. Defining of terms, teaching tips, and illustrations will also be found in the left-hand columns of the lesson pages.

A Teaching Note

Students find the topic of earthquakes fascinating. Take advantage of their enthusiasm. The knowledge, attitudes, and skills that you promote will not only help your students academically, but may one day save their lives.

Be aware, however, that their fascination will almost certainly contain an element of fear. As you progress through this curriculum with your students, be alert to their reactions, and be attuned to the verbal and nonverbal cues they're sending. Be honest about your own fears and accepting of theirs. Don't exaggerate the danger of earthquakes, but don't minimize it either. Make your message clear: We can't do anything to prevent earthquakes, but we can prepare ourselves to cope with them. We can learn what causes them. We can dispel some of the myths and misinformation that cause needless concern. We can help ourselves and others to do many things that will make our homes, schools, and communities safer.

Acknowledgments

The National Science Teachers Association (NSTA) and the Federal Emergency Management Agency (FEMA) acknowledge with gratitude the valuable contribution of the following individuals:

Technical Reviewers:

Margaret Hopper, Engineering Geology and Tectonics, U.S. Geological Survey

Ann Metzger and Susan Nava, Center for Earthquake Research and Information, Memphis State University

Randolph Updike and Ross S. Stein, Office of Earthquakes, Volcanoes and Engineering, U.S. Geological Survey

James Tingey, Division of Comprehensive Emergency Management, State of Utah Department of Public Safety

Curriculum Reviewers and Field Test Facilitators:

Larry Ash, Roosevelt Elementary School, Olympia, WA. Joyce Bagwell, Earthquake Education Center, Charleston, SC. Diane Beu, Bayside Middle School, San Mateo, CA. William Blair, Clay County Emergency Management Agency, MO. Sandra Bryant, Shelby County Schools, Memphis, TN. Dan Cicirello, Office of Emergency Services, Conway, AR. Peggy Cowan, Alaska Department of Education, Juneau, AK. Robert Gibson, Eastgate Elementary School, Helena, MT. Beverly Hunter, Christian Academy of Chula Vista, CA. Ann Lampkins, Holy Spirit School, Evansville, IN. Laura Podaras, Bells Mill Elementary School, Potomac, MD. Annette Saturnelli, Newburgh City School District, NY. Steve Sellers, Excelsior Springs Public Schools, MO. Paul Spengler, Lewis and Clark County Disaster and Emergency Services, MT. Patricia Sweeney, Montgomery County Public Schools, MD.

NSTA and FEMA are especially grateful to the teachers and approximately fourteen hundred students who participated in the field test of this curriculum. These teachers include:

Peggy Acord, Don Agatep, Marian Barney, Melba Board, Paul Bowen, Laura Canuteson, Julia Carpenter, Mary Cate, Marna Collins, Gail Connelly, Lisa Duckworth, Mary Kay DuBois, Jenny Farrell, Jane Fisher, L. C. Fisher, Connie Ford, Susan Fry, John Garzione, Patti Hahn, Jean Hamlin, Barbara Heath, Deborah Hill, Jennifer Kempf, Ann Lampkins, Mary D. Lee, Martin Leska, Laura Longo, Paula Mataraza, Carol Mehm, Bonnie Miller, Joseph Millner, Joann Mitchell, Barbara Morris, John McCabe, Patricia Parrish, Catherine Plumstead, Lois Powers, J. Quinlan, Ilene Rabinowe, Deborah Rahn, Charles Rapalje, Marcia Rehm, Joyce Rollins, Jan Seder, Roberta Spengler, Mary P. Stone, Betty Templeton, Ann Thompson, Tammy Uetrecht, Patricia Wein, Marlayna Wiley, and Karen Wolner

Defining an Earthquake

EARTHQUAKE CURRICULUM, K-6
SCOPE AND SEQUENCE CHART

Unit I: Defining an Earthquake

Level	Concept	Laboratory	Mathematics	Language Arts	Social Studies	Art
K-2	An earthquake is a sudden, rapid shaking of the Earth caused by the release of energy stored in rocks.	Sand and box demonstration of earthquakes		Vocabulary development of earthquake words	Effects of earthquakes on model buildings	Illustrations of legends
	Legends are traditional narrative explanations of natural phenomena which evolve when scientific explanations are not available.			Original earthquake legends	Effect of earthquakes on people	Illustrations of Earth's interior
					Cultures and legend origins	Mural making
3-4	An earthquake is a sudden, rapid shaking of the Earth caused by the release of energy stored in rocks.	Silicone putty rocks		Earthquake legends	Map study of cultures associated with earthquake legends	Illustrations of earthquake causes
	Legends are traditional narrative explanations of natural phenomena which evolve when scientific explanations are not available.	Gelatin simulation of earthquakes		Paragraph writing	Map study of epicenters	Illustrations of earthquake legends
	Earthquake energy is released in the form of waves.			Class discussion		
5-6	Earthquakes result from the build-up and release of energy stored in rocks.	Stick and erasers simulation of earthquakes	Map scales to measure distances	Vocabulary development of earthquake words	Map study of earthquake locations	Sign making
	Earthquakes occur over much of the world and the United States.	Fault action game		Earthquake legends	Map study of cultures associated with earthquake legends	Diagram making
	Various societies have produced earthquake legends to explain these natural occurrences.			Oral reading and note taking	Map study of state locations	

I

Defining an Earthquake

An earthquake is a natural phenomenon like rain. Earthquakes have occurred for billions of years. Descriptions as old as recorded history show the significant effects they have had on people's lives. Long before there were scientific theories for the cause of earthquakes, people around the world created folklore to explain them. In simple terms, earthquakes are caused by the constant motion of Earth's surface. This motion creates buildup and release of energy stored in rocks at and near the Earth's surface. Earthquakes are the sudden, rapid shaking of the Earth as this energy is released.

At half-past two o'clock of a moonlit morning in March, I was awakened by a tremendous earthquake, and though I had never before enjoyed a storm of this sort, the strange, thrilling motion could not be mistaken . . . Both glad and frightened, [I shouted]: "A noble earthquake! A noble earthquake!" feeling sure that I was going to learn something.
John Muir, 1872

Defining an Earthquake

An earthquake is a natural occurrence, like rain. Earthquakes affect almost every part of the Earth, and like rain, they can be either mild or catastrophic. Over the course of geological time, earthquakes, floods, and other natural events have helped to shape the surface of our planet.

An earthquake may last only a few seconds, but the processes that cause earthquakes have operated within the Earth for millions and millions of years. Until very recently, the cause of earthquakes was an unsolved mystery. It was the subject of fanciful folklore and equally fanciful learned speculation by peoples throughout the world.

> In a legend from Siberian Kamchatka, a god named Tuli drives an Earth-laden sled pulled by flea-infested dogs. When the dogs stop to scratch, the Earth shakes.
>
> ***
>
> Some say the Earth was fevrous [feverish] and did shake.
> Shakespeare, Macbeth, III

In the mid-1960s, many scientific observations and explanations of earthquakes came together in the theory of plate tectonics. We'll be exploring that subject in later units. In this unit we consider both scientific and popular explanations for the phenomenon, and look at the patterns of earthquake occurrence worldwide.

An Earthquake Is . . .

An earthquake is a sudden, rapid shaking of the Earth caused by the release of energy stored in rocks. This is a brief definition which students of all ages can master. A full definition of the term, however, would need to include a good deal more information.

Students may be surprised that we speak of rocks and rock layers, because in many places the rock material of the Earth's crust is covered by accumulations of sand or soil. Remind them that even beneath the sediment in river valleys, plains, and beach areas, some kind of rock is always present.

Pressure Direction

Deformed Rocks

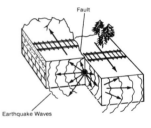

Fault

Earthquake Waves

Earthquake shaking may cause loss of life and destruction of property. In a strong earthquake the ground shakes violently. Buildings may fall or sink into the soil. Rocks and soil may move downhill at a rapid rate. Such landslides can bury houses and people.

Folklore and Scientific Theory

Because strong earthquakes have such disastrous effects, it is not surprising that people have always looked for ways to explain their origin. We find many nonscientific explanations of earthquakes in the folklore of civilizations around the world. We call these traditional narratives earthquake *legends*. Some of them are still being told today.

What we have learned in recent years, however, largely from the study of earthquakes, is that the Earth around us is not static, like a stage set for a play. The Earth's rock layer is broken into large pieces. These pieces are in slow but constant motion. They may slide by smoothly and almost imperceptibly.

From time to time, the pieces may lock together, and energy that accumulates between the pieces may be suddenly released. This sudden release of energy, like the snapping of a rubber band that has been stretched too far, is what we call *elastic rebound*. Energy is released and travels through the Earth in the form of waves. People on the surface of the Earth experience an earthquake.

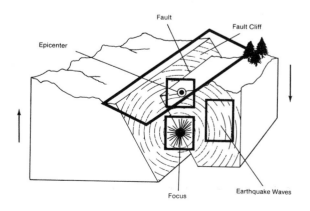

Fault

Fault Cliff

Epicenter

Focus

Earthquake Waves

Earthquake Epicenters

The *epicenter* of an earthquake is the place on the Earth's surface directly above the *focus* (or *hypocenter*), the place inside the Earth where the quake originates. Earthquake foci are usually somewhere between the surface and 100 km in depth. In some areas, however, foci may be as deep as 700 km.

Even a glance at an earthquake epicenter map shows that most earthquakes have occurred in certain well-defined regions of the Earth. Because these regions tend to be relatively long and narrow, they are sometimes referred to as earthquake *belts*.

One large belt of epicenters runs through the Mediterranean Sea, Asia Minor, and the Himalaya mountains, and into the eastern Indian Ocean. A second large belt runs northward through the western Pacific Ocean, the Japanese islands, the Aleutian islands, and the west coasts of North and South America. The longest belt of earthquake epicenters runs through the central regions of most ocean basins. The world epicenter map also shows some shorter belts of epicenters.

Chances are, even if your school is far from any earthquake epicenter, your students already have some ideas about earthquakes and what causes them. In the lessons that follow, you will invite them to tell you what they think.

Master 7, World Map with Epicenters. The dots represent only a fraction of the 5,695 epicenters recorded in 1968 by the National Earthquake Information Center, USGS.

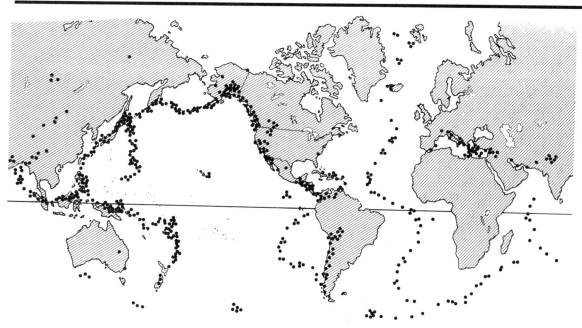

What Is an Earthquake?

Content Concepts

1. An earthquake is a sudden, rapid shaking of the Earth caused by the release of energy stored in rocks.

2. Legends are traditional narrative explanations of natural phenomena that evolve when scientific explanations are not available.

Vocabulary

quake
tremble
vibrate
earthquake
legends
San Gabrielino

Objectives

Students will

—describe personal experiences with earthquakes.

—construct an earthquake model.

—observe effects of a simulated earthquake.

—define the term *legend*, and listen to a legend.

—suggest possible causes of earthquakes.

—write and illustrate original legends.

—draw pictures to illustrate their ideas about the Earth's interior.

Learning Links

Language Arts: Writing a description of a demonstration (older students), sharing ideas about the possible causes of earthquakes, building vocabulary, listening to a legend, creating an original legend, sequencing letters of the alphabet

Social Studies: Observing the effects of a simulated earthquake on model buildings, predicting the effects on people's lives, discussing a Native American legend, locating San Gabriel on a U.S. map

Art: Illustrating the legends, expressing ideas about the Earth's interior in drawing, contributing to a mural

Activity One: Tremors and Turtles

Materials for the teacher
- An audiovisual cart on wheels, or a small table or desk that moves easily
- Wall map of the United States, or transparency made from Master 1, U.S. Map
- Overhead projector
- Master 2, The Turtle Tale

Materials for each small group of students
- A shallow box partially filled with sand or soil
- An assortment of paper plates, cups, and small boxes that can be stacked to represent a building

Materials for each student
- Handout made from Master 3, Draw and Write
- Handout made from Master 4, Turtle Dot-to-Dot

earth • quake

An earthquake is a sudden, rapid shaking of the Earth caused by the release of energy stored in rocks.

leg • ends

Legends are traditional narrative explanations of natural phenomena that evolve when scientific explanations are not available.

Procedure

1. Introduce the topic with a class discussion based on the following questions:

What does the word *quake* mean?

What do we mean when we say people are "quaking in their boots"? (Invite students to imitate a person trembling.)

Have you ever been on a bridge when it shook from heavy traffic, or near the railroad tracks when a train passed over? (Invite students to demonstrate shaking and vibrating.)

What do you suppose is happening to the Earth when there is an earthquake?

Has anyone here ever felt an earthquake? (Allow students time to express their observations and feelings.)

2. Tell students they are going to make a model to demonstrate what happens during an earthquake. Follow these steps:

a. Invite a small group of students to pile plates, cups, and small boxes on top of each other in the filled box to form a tall structure. (Either have enough materials for each group to construct one model, or have the groups take turns.)

b. Place the large box on the cart, table, or desk.

c. Shake the cart, table, or desk until the structure topples.

d. Ask the students to comment on what they see.

What does the sand or soil represent? (the Earth)

What do the plates, cups, and boxes represent? (a tall building)

What moves? (the Earth and the building)

What happens to the building? (various degrees of damage)

What would happen to people in or near the building? (They would be frightened and possibly hurt.)

3. Hand out a worksheet made from Master 3 on which students can draw the simulation. Older students can also construct a brief written description.

4. Discuss the origin of legends.

How can we understand about earthquakes? (from science)

Yes, but earthquakes have been happening for a long time, and we have only been studying them with scientific instruments for a short time. How do you suppose people explained them before that? (with stories)

These stories are called *legends.*

Teacher Take Note: See the Appendix, Earthquake Legends, for more tremor tales from around the world.

Children who have experienced an earthquake will especially love playing the role of that powerful force.

5. Point out the San Gabriel Valley on a U.S. map. (Indicate the southwestern part of California, in the neighborhood of Los Angeles—see map.)

6. Introduce the story on Master 2, The Turtle Tale, and read it aloud. This is a story that was told by a group of Native Americans who lived where earthquakes are common, in the San Gabriel Valley. People call them the *Gabrielinos* (ga • bree • uh • leé • nos).

7. Discuss the story.

Did you enjoy the story? Why or why not?

Do you think the story is true? Why or why not? (Students will give a variety of reasons why it is not: Turtles are not that big. Turtles are not that strong. Turtles can't talk.)

Why do you think the Indians developed this story? (When an earthquake or any other frightening event occurs, people want to understand what causes it. Understanding helps them to be less afraid.)

Have you ever asked an older person to explain something that frightened you, and felt better afterwards?

8. Distribute the turtle dot-to-dot exercise (Master 4) with a brief explanation, and allow time for students to complete it.

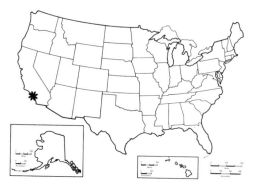

Master 1. U.S. Map
San Gabriel is marked with an asterisk.

Activity Two: Earthshaking Ideas

Teacher Take Note: Oil pastels are easy for young children to use, and produce bright, satisfying colors.

Materials for the teacher
• A large roll of paper for the mural

Materials for each small group of students
• Drawing paper and crayons or oil pastels
• Scissors
• Writing paper and pencil (optional)

Procedure

1. Review the turtle legend with the students to recall how some people have explained earthquakes.

2. Invite the students to share what they think causes earthquakes, or rapid vibrations of the Earth. Ask: What could possibly be going on with the Earth that would cause it to shake or vibrate?

3. Ask students to create their own legends to explain earthquakes. If turtles don't make the Earth shake, what does? Have them dictate, draw, or write their stories.

4. Next, ask each student to draw a large circle representing the Earth and to draw a picture of what there might be inside to make it move.

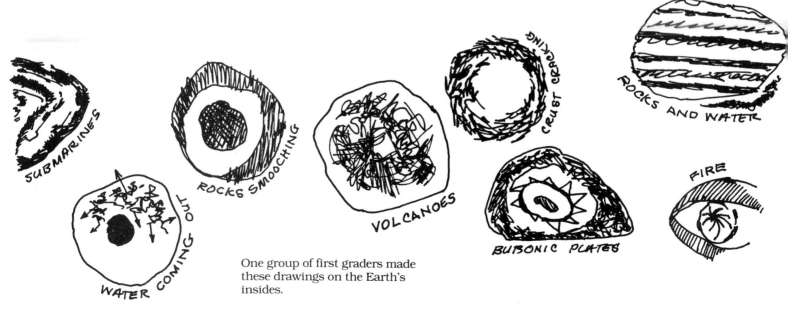

One group of first graders made these drawings on the Earth's insides.

5. Create a class mural by directing the students to cut out their drawings and paste them to a large piece of paper. The explanations students have written or dictated may be displayed beside the drawings.

6. Share all the student stories and the legends. Accept all ideas without evaluation. End the lesson without providing any further information as to the actual causes of earthquakes. (Direct curious students to children's encyclopedias and other classroom or library reference materials. When the discussion resumes in the next lesson, you may find that students have gained some information on their own.)

Extensions

1. Act out the turtle story. Choose seven students to portray the turtles and one for the Great Spirit. Attach green paper to the turtle students' backs, and provide the Great Spirit with brown paper for each one, to represent the land. Students can mime the action and dialogue as the teacher reads aloud.

2. Act out the original legends with paper bag puppets. Provide lunch bags and art materials. Give the students time to make their puppets and rehearse before the final presentation.

3. Ask the children to describe an imaginary journey to the center of the Earth. What might they find there that could cause earthquakes?

People Explain Earthquakes

Content Concepts

1. An earthquake is a sudden, rapid shaking of the Earth caused by the release of energy stored in rocks.

2. Legends are traditional narrative explanations of natural phenomena that evolve when scientific explanations are not available.

3. Earthquake energy is released in the form of waves.

Vocabulary

earthquake
legend
culture

Objectives

Students will

—describe personal experiences with earthquakes.

—write and illustrate a paragraph about what they think causes earthquakes.

—read and illustrate earthquake legends.

—locate the cultures that developed the various legends on a world map.

—compare these locations to the major areas of earthquake activity around the world.

—state what scientists now believe is the cause of earthquakes.

—observe the effects of a simulated earthquake.

Learning Links

Language Arts: Class discussion, writing expository paragraphs, sharing ideas

Social Studies: Locating countries on the world map

Art: Illustrating students' earthquake theories, illustrating legends

Activity One: Earthquake Experiences

Materials for the teacher
- Magazine or newspaper accounts of earthquakes, or books, slides, movies, and other media dealing with the subject

Materials for the students
- Drawing paper
- Crayons or markers
- Tape

Procedure

1. Begin a discussion by asking students what they think an earthquake is. List responses on the board.

2. Ask if any of your students has ever experienced an earthquake. Invite those who have to share their experiences with the class.

3. If the students do not have much personal experience to draw on, use some of the resources suggested above to provide a basis for the unit. You may also want to invite someone who has experienced an earthquake to visit the class.

4. Distribute paper and art supplies. Ask the students to make drawings illustrating what they think causes earthquakes. They may write paragraphs to accompany the pictures, and combine them as a display for the wall or bulletin board. Volunteers can present their ideas to the class. Make no comments about the correctness of their ideas at this point.

earth • quake

An earthquake is a sudden, rapid shaking of the Earth caused by the release of energy stored in rocks.

leg • ends

Legends are traditional narrative explanations of natural phenomena which evolve when scientific explanations are not available.

cul • ture

A culture is the special way of life that holds a group of people together and makes it different from all other groups.

Activity Two: Earthquake Legends

Materials for the teacher
- Large wall map of the world, or transparency made from Master 5, World Map
- Tape or pins
- Colored yarn
- Transparency made from Master 6, World Map with Legend Sites
- Transparency made from Master 7, World Map with Epicenters
- Overhead projector

Materials for each student
- Booklet of earthquake legends (See Appendix)
- Large sheets of drawing paper
- Crayons or markers

Procedure

1. Explain that earthquakes have been happening on Earth for millions of years. Scientists have understood what causes them for less than 30 years. People who experienced earthquakes developed traditional explanations that suited their *culture*, or way of life. We call these explanations *legends*.

Master 6, World Map with Legend Sites

Earthquake Legend Sites Key

1. India
2. Assam, between Bangladesh and China
3. Mexico
4. Siberia
5. Japan
6. Mozambique
7. Greece
8. Belgium
9. Tennessee, USA
10. West Africa
11. Mongolia
12. India
13. Latvia
14. Colombia
15. Scandinavia
16. New Zealand
17. East Africa
18. Central America
19. Romania
20. West Africa

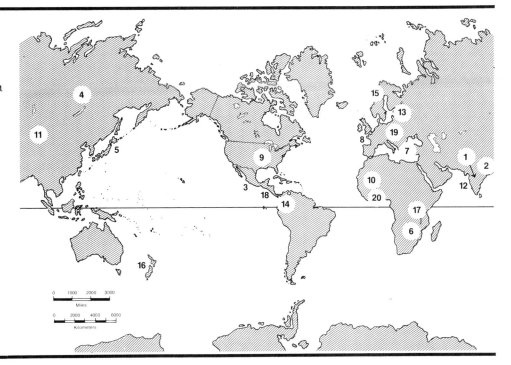

2. Distribute art materials and copies of the legends to every student. Divide the students up into groups and have each group illustrate one of the legends. Label each illustration with the name of the culture or the region of the world it comes from.

3. On a world map, locate the region where each legend originated. (See Master 6. How you approach this part of the activity depends on your students' geography background.)

4. Make a wall display by having students place their illustrations on the wall surrounding the world map. Use the yarn and pins or tape to connect each illustration of a legend to the appropriate spot on the map.

5. Ask each group to read or recount their legend, and tell why they think it does or does not explain earthquakes. You may need to start the groups off by asking such questions as these, for the first story:

Are elephants big enough to hold up the world?

Could an elephant stand on a turtle without crushing it?

Did the early Hindus imagine ordinary animals in this story, or magical ones?

Do you think there are any such magical animals?

Teacher Take Note: You may want to read all the legends with the students before they begin to draw.

Legend Book Assembly

Copy the pages (each one has 2 legends) for the legend book in sequence. Be sure to copy page 2 on the back of the cover page. Repeat this process for the rest of the pages. Fold and staple in the center to form a booklet.

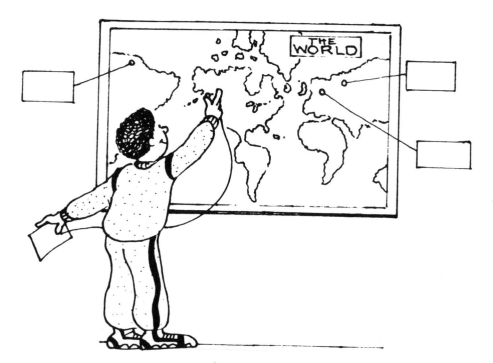

Teacher Take Note: Some of these legends come from parts of the world where quakes do not occur frequently. An earthquake is a highly dramatic, memorable event. Some cultures may have borrowed oral traditions based on events outside their own geographic region. Others may have carried legends with them as they migrated from one part of the globe to another. Be prepared to find a less than exact correlation between legends and earthquake activity.

6. Project the transparency of Master 7, World Map with Epicenters. Explain that each dot shows a place where an earthquake has occurred. You may want to highlight the areas of greatest earthquake activity. Ask students if they can see a relationship between these areas and the places where the legends originated.

Activity Three: Tasty Quake

Materials for the teacher
- A fist-sized rock
- Silicone putty (widely available as Silly Putty ™)
- One pan of prepared gelatin dessert (see recipe)
- Clear plastic wrap
- Sugar cubes or dominoes
- Spoon for serving dessert
- Paper cups and spoons for individual portions

Procedure

1. Prepare gelatin dessert in advance and refrigerate. These ingredients will make one pan. Prepare more if you wish to have several small groups performing the demonstration simultaneously.

2. Write the definition of an earthquake on the board.

3. Explain that under the soil there are rock layers. These layers are under stress because of activity within the Earth.

4. Explain that when these rocks are under extreme stress they react more like a plastic material, such as silicone putty, than like the hard rock we see above the ground. (Show rock and putty.)

Gelatin Dessert

Two 170-g (6-oz) boxes of red or purple gelatin dessert

Two one-serving envelopes of unflavored gelatin

Four cups boiling water

Four cups cold water

One 23 x 30 cm (9 x 12 in.) metal baking pan

Empty the gelatin dessert and the unflavored gelatin into the baking pan. Add the boiling water and stir until all the powder is dissolved, then add the cold water and stir to mix. Chill on refrigerator shelf at least three hours or until set.

Teacher Take Note: This recipe has been carefully tested. To transmit waves that can be seen easily, the pan *must* be metal, and it *must* be full nearly to the top with the gelatin mixture.

5. Demonstrate with Silly Putty™, or distribute several lumps so that each small group can do the activity for themselves. (The putty will be difficult to break if it has been warmed by too much handling, so work quickly.)

a. First, stretch the putty slowly to show how rocks react to slow twisting and pulling.

b. Next, shape it back into a ball and give it a sharp tug with both hands. The putty will snap into two pieces.

c. Explain that this reaction is similar to what happens during an earthquake.

6. Explain that when rocks break in this sudden way energy is released in the form of waves. We can simulate this release of energy by watching what happens to a pan of gelatin.

7. Gently tap the side of the pan of gelatin, while holding the pan firmly with the other hand. Students should be able to see the waves traveling through the gelatin. Compare the gelatin to the ground, the tap of your hand to the rock breaking, and the waves in the gelatin to earthquake waves.

8. Ask the students to predict what will happen when you tap the pan with more force. Tap the pan harder. Is their prediction confirmed? Repeat these two steps several times, and be sure that all the students have a chance to see the waves.

9. Cover the top of the gelatin with plastic wrap so it will be clean enough to eat later. Be sure the wrap touches the gelatin. Ask the students what they think happens to buildings during an earthquake. Then let them distribute sugar cube or domino "buildings" over the plastic wrap.

10. Repeat steps 7 and 8 above. Replace any buildings that are knocked over during the first trial. Allow students to construct different kinds of buildings and predict their resistance to the "earthquake," then test their predictions.

11. Remove the plastic wrap and serve the gelatin to the students. While they are eating, point out their illustrations from Activity One, and discuss. Do any of them come close to what scientists believe about earthquakes?

Extensions

1. Students could act out the legends with a few simple props.

2. Students could survey other students in the school to learn what they think causes earthquakes. Responses can be tabulated on the board or on butcher paper taped to the wall, and become the basis for a class discussion.

3. In an area where earthquakes do not occur frequently, students could survey adults in the community to find out how many of them have experienced earthquakes. Small groups could divide responsibility for a set number of interviews, such as ten per group, and graph their results. No two students may interview the same person.

4. Instead of illustrating the legends on large sheets of paper, students may draw a small symbol for each legend, cut it out, and pin it directly onto a large wall map at the correct location. The Japanese legend, for example, could be represented by a fish.

Energy Waves Cause Earthquakes

Content Concepts

1. Earthquakes result from the buildup and release of energy stored in rocks.

2. Earthquakes occur over much of the world, including the United States.

3. Various societies have produced earthquake legends to explain these natural occurrences.

Vocabulary

earthquake
legend
stored energy (potential energy)
earthquake waves (seismic waves)
fault
fault creep
focus
epicenter

Objectives

Students will

—watch two demonstrations of elastic rebound, and apply the principle to earthquake activity.

—demonstrate the phenomenon of fault creep, and distinguish it from earthquake activity.

—list some events that occur during an earthquake.

—locate their own state on an outline map of the United States.

—determine from the study of epicenter maps if their local area and state have experienced earthquakes.

—read and discuss earthquake legends.

—locate the place where each legend originated on an outline map of the world.

Learning Links

Language Arts: Discussing, oral reading, note taking, following directions

Social Studies: Map reading, correlating different types of maps, discussing effects and explanations of earthquakes in past and present societies

Math: Using map scale to measure distances

Art: Creating signs, coloring on handouts, illustrating activity

Activity One: A Wet Wave Experience

Materials for the teacher
- Transparency made from Master 8, Elastic Rebound
- Overhead projector
- Strip of wood lath the size of a ruler, or a dried stick about 30 cm long and up to 2 cm thick
- Sink or basin large enough to hold wood
- Water to fill basin
- Two large rubber erasers

Procedure

1. Gather students around sink or basin filled almost to the top with water.

2. Hold the wood completely under water. With one hand on each end, bend it slowly until it breaks.

3. Ask students to describe what they see: jerky movement of the water and waves radiating out from the breaking point.

4. Explain that energy was transferred to the stick by the hand movements, stored as potential energy until the stick broke, and then transferred to the water. This concept of build-up and release of energy in rocks is called elastic rebound theory.

5. Direct students to make a drawing of the demonstration in their notebooks.

6. Take two large rubber erasers and push them together end to end until they snap back into their original positions. Have students describe the vibrations they feel in their arms. Explain that this is similar to the way rocks store energy on opposite sides of a fault and then release that energy during an earthquake.

fo • cus

The focus is the place where an earthquake starts.

ep • i • cen • ter

The epicenter is the point on the Earth's surface directly above the focus.

fault

A fault is a crack in rock or soil along which earthquake movement has taken place.

earth • quake   waves

Earthquake waves, or seismic waves, are waves caused by the release of energy in the Earth's rocks during an earthquake.

Elastic Rebound

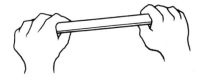

Original position

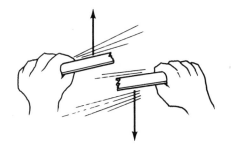

Buildup of potential energy

Breaking stick produces energy release

7. Ask students to explain how both demonstrations relate to an earthquake.

8. Project transparency of Master 8, Elastic Rebound, and use it to illustrate that when pressure from within the earth is exerted on rocks, they bend and store energy until they reach a certain point, like the wood and the erasers.

The stored or potential energy is released, in the form of waves, in an event we call an *earthquake.* The breaking point is the focus of the earthquake. Help students to relate this explanation to the demonstrations.

Activity Two: It's Your Fault

Materials for the teacher
- Transparency made from Master 9, Dresser Drawers
- Transparency made from Master 10, Earthquake Terms
- Overhead projector

Materials for each student
- A sign saying either Block A or Block B (Students can make them and letter them neatly.)
- String or tape for affixing sign

Procedure

1. Project the transparency made from Master 9 and explain that the pieces of Earth's crust often move past each other as smoothly as our dresser drawers move in the morning. Project Master 10 and point out the *fault* on the Earth's surface.

2. Label the area to the left of the fault Block A, and that to its right Block B. Explain to students that they are going to demonstrate what happens when pieces of the Earth's crust move.

3. Take students to a location in or outside the classroom where they will not hit anything but the floor if they fall.

4. Ask them to form into groups of 8 to 10 students, and divide each group into equal halves. (The teacher can participate if necessary to even groups.)

5. Distribute A signs to one half of each group and B signs to the other, and have them tape signs to their chests or hang them around their necks.

6. Line up A and B students facing each other, and explain that each line represents a block of Earth. The area between the two lines represents a fault.

7. Students should stretch out their arms, from both sides of the "fault," so that each is lightly touching the palms of a student on the other side.

Smooth surfaces slide easily.

8. Instruct students on both sides of each fault to shuffle smoothly to the students' right, keeping their palms extended. (The two lines will move in opposite directions, and students will slowly change partners.) Explain that this simulates *fault creep* movement.

9. Line the groups up as before, but this time have them lock fingers across the fault. Again instruct them to move to the right by slow steps, but keep them moving past the point where they can hold on easily. Just before they have to let go or fall, call out "Earthquake!" Ask students to drop hands and stand up straight. The sudden release of energy should cause them to stumble and fall into one another. Explain that this activity simulates an earthquake.

10. Compare and contrast the two events in a class discussion, referring to the Dresser Drawers (Master 9) and Earthquake Terms (Master 10) transparencies. Be sure that students understand the difference between the smooth movement that simulated fault creep and the buildup and sudden release of stress that caused them to stumble in the second demonstration. According to the theory of elastic rebound, it is this buildup and release of stress that causes earthquakes.

A sticky drawer opens with a jerky movement.

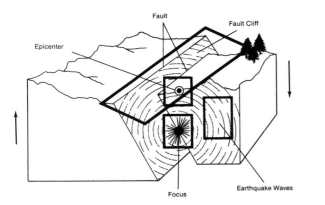

Master 10. Earthquake Terms.

Activity Three: Visual Vocabulary

Materials for the teacher
- Movie clip, video clip, slides, filmstrip, or written eyewitness account(s) of earthquakes
- Transparency made from Master 10a. Earthquake Terms.
- Overhead projector

Materials for each student
- Student handout made from Master 10b
- Colored pencils

Procedure

1. Ask any class members who have experienced an earthquake to describe that event to the class.

2. Use one of the media listed above (movie clip, video, etc.) to give the class some common vicarious earthquake experiences.

3. Brainstorm to create a class list of things that happen during an earthquake (rumbling noises, swaying trees, etc.) on the board or overhead.

4. Project Master 10 and go over the definitions of *focus, epicenter, fault,* and *earthquake waves.* Instruct students to fill in the definitions, then shade over each one in a different color: the first in red, the second in blue, the third in yellow, and the fourth in green. Finally, ask them to color the part of the diagram that each definition refers to in the same color as the definition.

Activity Four: Local Legends

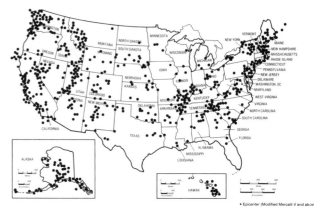

Master 11. U.S. Map with Epicenters

Materials for the teacher

- Standard classroom wall map of the world, or a transparency made from Master 5, World Map
- Transparency of Master 11, U.S. Map with Epicenters
- Transparency made from Master 7, World Map with Epicenters
- Booklet of earthquake legends (See Appendix.)
- Optional: Epicenter map of your state or area (obtain from state geological survey, U.S. Geological Survey, or local college geology department)

Materials for each student

- Booklet of legends
- Worksheets made from Master 11

Procedure

1. Using transparencies and/or student copies of the U.S. Map with Epicenters, Master 11, ask students these questions:

According to this map, which of the states experience a lot of earthquakes?

Which states experience very few or no earthquakes?

Where is our state on this map?

According to the map, does our state experience a small, medium, or large number of earthquakes?

People in states without epicenters, as shown on this map, may still experience earthquakes. How can this be? (Both seismographs and the human senses can register the effects of distant earthquakes, especially large ones. Also, this map only records quakes over a certain intensity. Some states may have quakes below those levels.)

2. Show students how to use the map scale on the U.S. Map with Epicenters to measure the distance from where they live to the nearest epicenter on the map. Use a local or state map if available.

Extensions

1. Ask students to keep a scrapbook log or bulletin board of earthquake reports from newspapers and magazines. Relatives in other parts of the world may be willing to contribute clippings. Make individuals responsible for monitoring specific publications and sharing what they find. Periodically, the class could locate the epicenters of recent earthquakes on a world map and mark them with pushpins.

2. If you live in an area that has ever been affected by an earthquake, check your local library for microfilm copies of old newspapers describing the event. On August 31, 1886, for example, the effects of the Charleston, South Carolina earthquake were felt in most of the states east of the Mississippi and south of New York state.

3. Write the definition of *legend* on the board and invite students to recount some legends they may have heard.

4. Have students read some of the earthquake legends out loud in class. Locate the origin of each on the world map before moving on to the next.

5. Project the transparency of Master 7, World Map with Epicenters, and ask students if they see any correlation between the origins of the legends and the density of earthquake epicenters. (See Unit I, Level 2, Activity Two.)

6. Discuss with students:

Why did these legends develop? (Emphasize that they were creative attempts to explain frightening and puzzling natural occurrences.)

What real facts do these legends contain or reflect? (Siberia: that human beings and animals are interdependent; New Zealand: that the Earth is like a living organism; Romania: that human decency upholds the social world; Mexico: that the evil in the world is hard to understand; etc.)

Master 6. World Map with Legend Sites

Earthquake Legend Sites Key

1. India
2. Assam, between Bangladesh and China
3. Mexico
4. Siberia
5. Japan
6. Mozambique
7. Greece
8. Belgium
9. Tennessee, USA
10. West Africa
11. Mongolia
12. India
13. Latvia
14. Colombia
15. Scandinavia
16. New Zealand
17. East Africa
18. Central America
19. Romania
20. West Africa

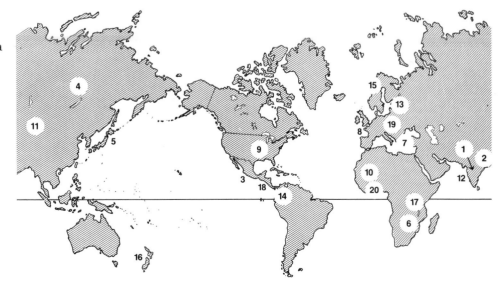

Unit I. Defining an Earthquake

Materials List

Grades K-2	Grades 3-4	Grades 5-6
audiovisual cart on wheels	drawing paper	rubber erasers
shallow box	crayons	wood lath or dried stick
sand or soil	markers	large bowl
paper plates and cups	straight pins	sink or basin
small boxes	colored yarn	colored pencils
writing paper	fist-sized rock	string or tape
pencil	Silly Putty™	overhead projector
overhead projector	tape	
mural paper	red or purple gelatin	
drawing paper	unflavored gelatin	
crayons	boiling water	
oil pastels	metal baking pans	
scissors	clear plastic wrap	
	sugar cubes or dominoes	
	serving spoon	
	paper cups	
	plastic spoons	
	overhead projector	

Instructional Resources (Books, maps, pamphlets, slides)

Asimov, I. (1981). *How Did We Find Out About Earthquakes?* New York: Walker.

Fradin, D. B. (1982). *Disaster! Earthquakes.* Chicago: Children's Press.

Story of the Earth, The, North American Edition. New Rochelle, NY: Cambridge University Press. Geological Museum. pp. 13-14.

References

Bolt, B. A. (1988). *Earthquakes.* San Francisco: W. H. Freeman and Co.

Brownlee, S. (1986, July). Waiting for the big one. *Discover,* 7, pp. 52-71.

Earthquake Country—A Teachers Workshop. (1978, February 25-26). Far Western Section of National Association of Geology Teachers and California Science Teachers Association.

Earthquakes: A National Problem. Washington, DC: Federal Emergency Management Agency.

Leet, L. D. (1948). *Causes of Catastrophe.* New York: Whittlesey House-McGraw Hill.

Mathews, S. W. (1973, January). This Changing Earth. *National Geographic,* 143, pp. 1-37.

Muir, R. (1987). *Earthquakes and Volcanoes: Causes, Effects, and Predictions.* New York: Weidenfeld and Nicolson.

National Oceanic and Atmospheric Administration. (1970). *Catalog of Earthquake Photographs—Key to Geophysical Records, Documentation No. 7.* Boulder, Colorado: National Geophysical Data Center.

San Andreas Fault, The. (1987). Reston, Virginia: United States Geological Survey.

U.S. Map

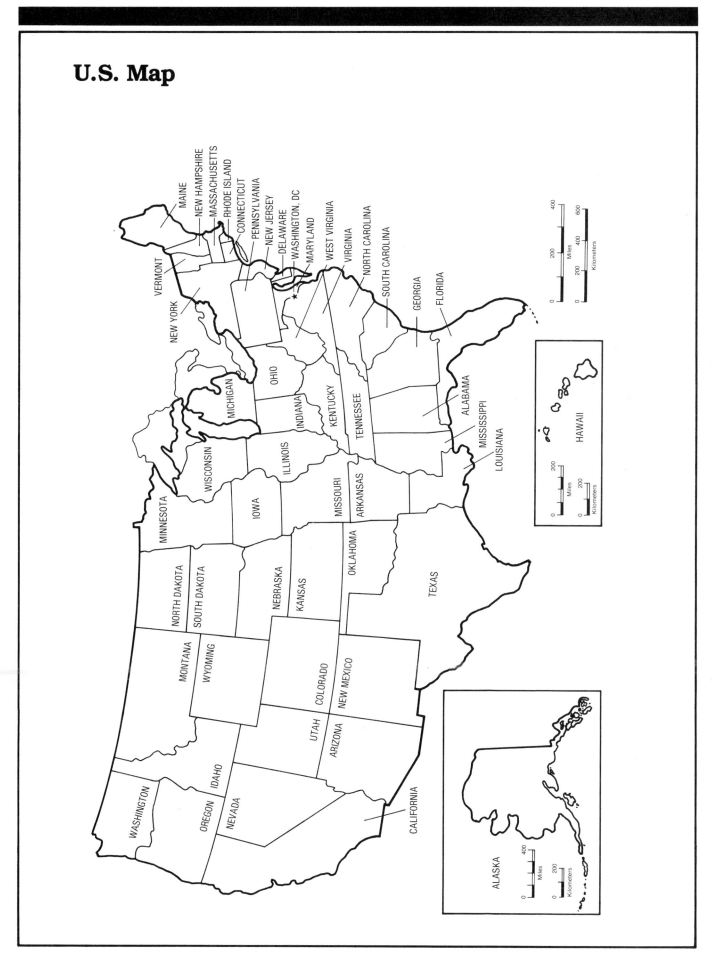

U.S. Map

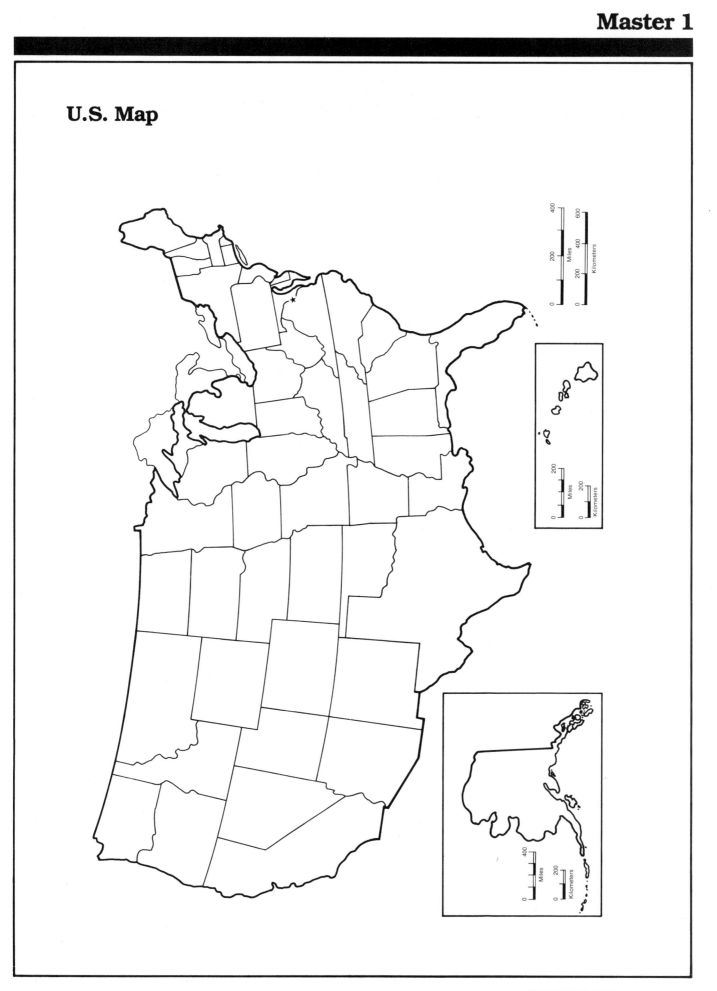

The Turtle Tale

Long, long ago, before there were people, there was hardly anything in the world but water. One day, Great Spirit looked down from heaven. He decided to make a beautiful land. But where could he begin? All he saw was water. Then he spotted a giant turtle. Great Spirit decided to make the beautiful land on the turtle's back.

But one turtle was not big enough. The land Great Spirit wanted to make was very large. So he called out, "Turtle, hurry and find your six brothers."

Turtle swam to find them. It took her a whole day to find the first. It took another day to find the next. After six days, turtle had found her six brothers. "Come," she said, "Great Spirit wants us."

Great Spirit called down. "Turtles! Form a line, all of you—head to tail, north to south. Umm—you three on the south, please move a little to the east. Hmmm. Yes, that's just right. What a beautiful land you turtles will make! Now listen! It is a great honor to carry this beautiful land on your backs. So you must not move!"

The turtles stayed very still. Great Spirit took some straw from his supply in the sky. He spread it out on the turtles' backs. Then he took some soil and patted it down on top of the straw.

Great Spirit cleaned his hands on a fluffy white cloud. Then he went to work, shaping mountains and valleys and lakes and rivers. When he was finished he looked at the beautiful land he had made. Great Spirit was very pleased. But soon trouble came. The giant turtles grew restless. They wanted to stretch their legs.

"I want to swim east," said one. "This beast goes east."

"West is best. I'll swim toward the setting sun," said another.

The turtles began to argue. They could not agree which way to move. One day, four of the turtles began to swim east. The others began to swim west. The Earth shook! It cracked with a loud noise. But after a minute, the shaking stopped. The turtles had to stop moving because the land on their backs was so heavy. They had only been able to swim a little way from each other. When they saw that they could not swim away, they stopped arguing and made up.

Every once in a while, though, the turtles argue again. Each time they do, the Earth shakes.

HELP: Hands-on Earthquake Learning Package. (1983). California Edition. Environmental Volunteers, Inc.

Draw and Write

Name _____

1. Draw a picture of the earthquake experiment.

2. Use the words in the word bank to write about what happened.

Word Bank	building	fall	box
	move	earthquake	Earth

Turtle Dot-to-Dot

Name _____

I heard a legend from the San Gabrielino Indians.

The Indians thought that big turtles carried the land on their backs. They thought that an earthquake happened when the turtles moved in different directions.

1. Connect the dots.

2. Color the turtle carrying land on its back.

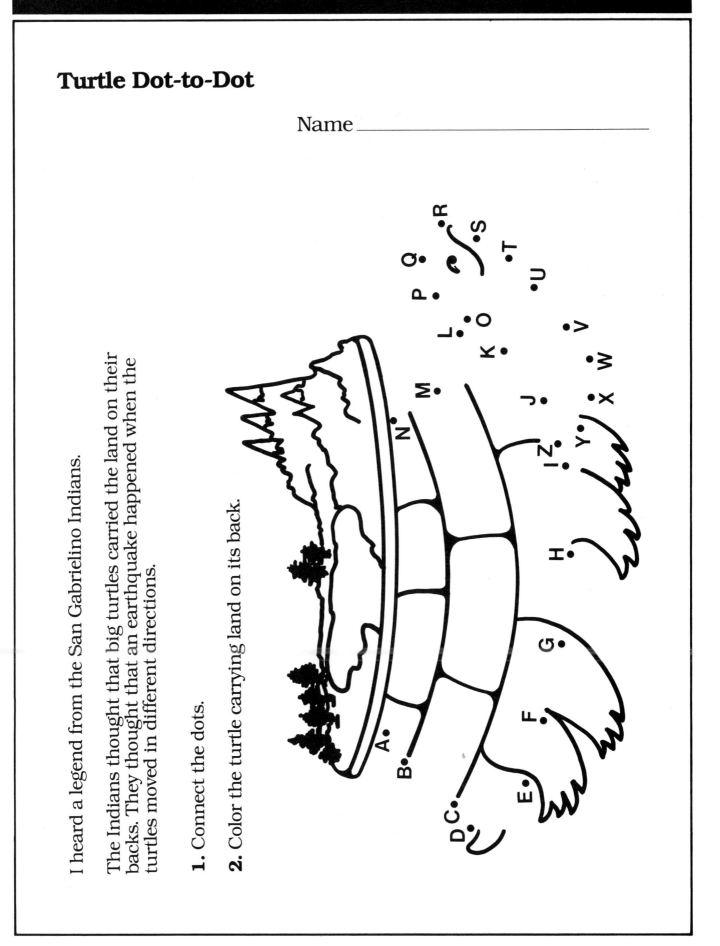

World Map

Miles

0   1000   2000   3000

Kilometers

0   2000   4000   6000

World Map with Legend Sites

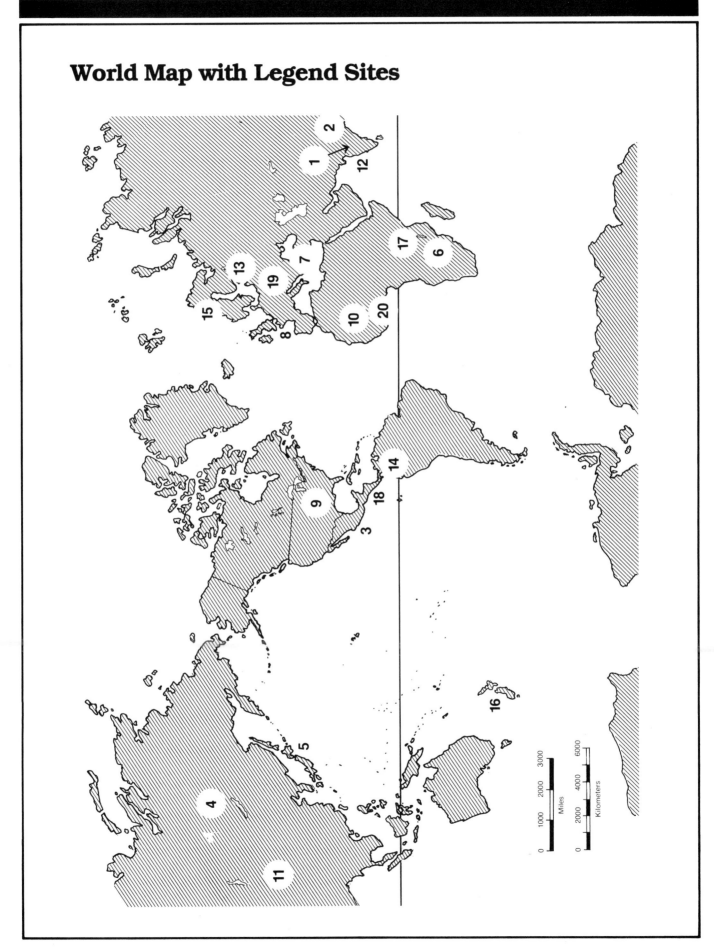

World Map with Epicenters

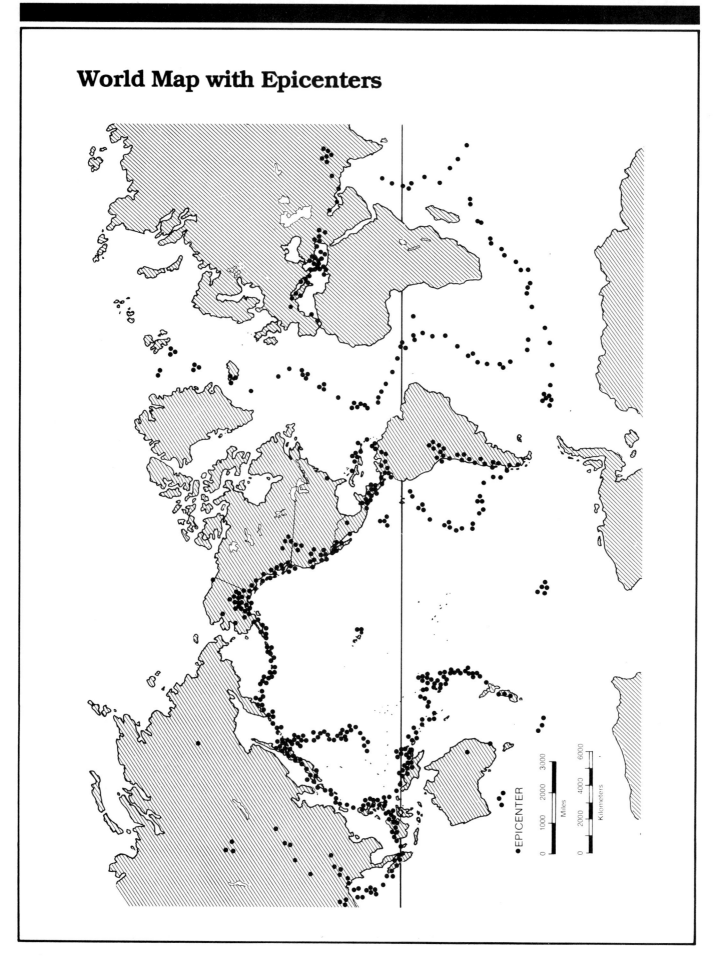

● EPICENTER

Miles

Kilometers

Elastic Rebound

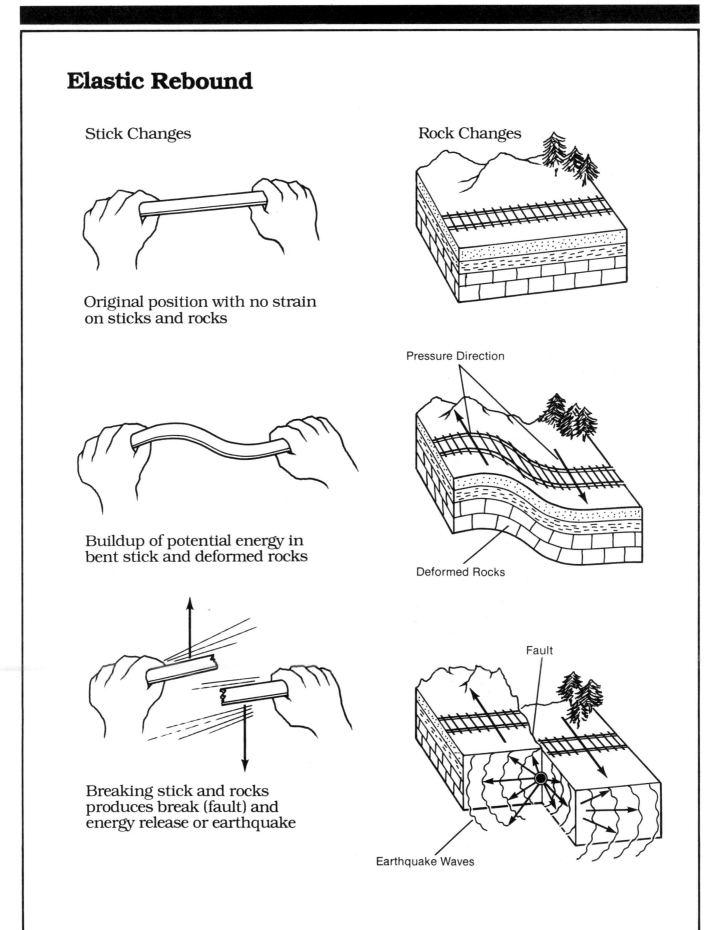

Stick Changes

Original position with no strain on sticks and rocks

Buildup of potential energy in bent stick and deformed rocks

Breaking stick and rocks produces break (fault) and energy release or earthquake

Rock Changes

Pressure Direction

Deformed Rocks

Fault

Earthquake Waves

Dresser Drawers

Smooth drawer surfaces
slide easily

However . . .

A great force is needed to move
a sticky drawer

A sticky drawer opens with a
jerky movement

Earthquake Terms

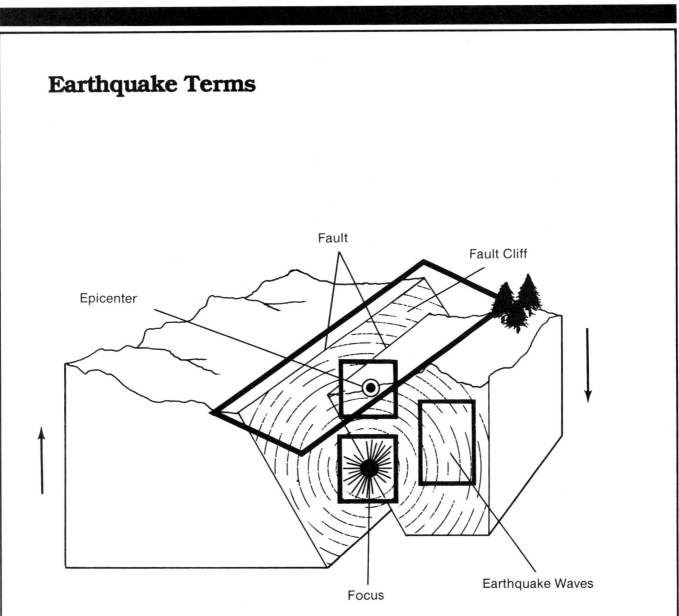

Fault

Fault Cliff

Epicenter

Focus

Earthquake Waves

Definitions:

Focus

The focus is the place where an earthquake starts.

Epicenter

The epicenter is the point on the Earth's surface directly above the focus.

Fault

A fault is a break in the Earth's rocky surface along which the two sides have been displaced relative to each other.

Earthquake Waves

Earthquake waves are waves caused by the release of energy in the Earth's crustal rocks.

Earthquake Terms Worksheet

Name _____

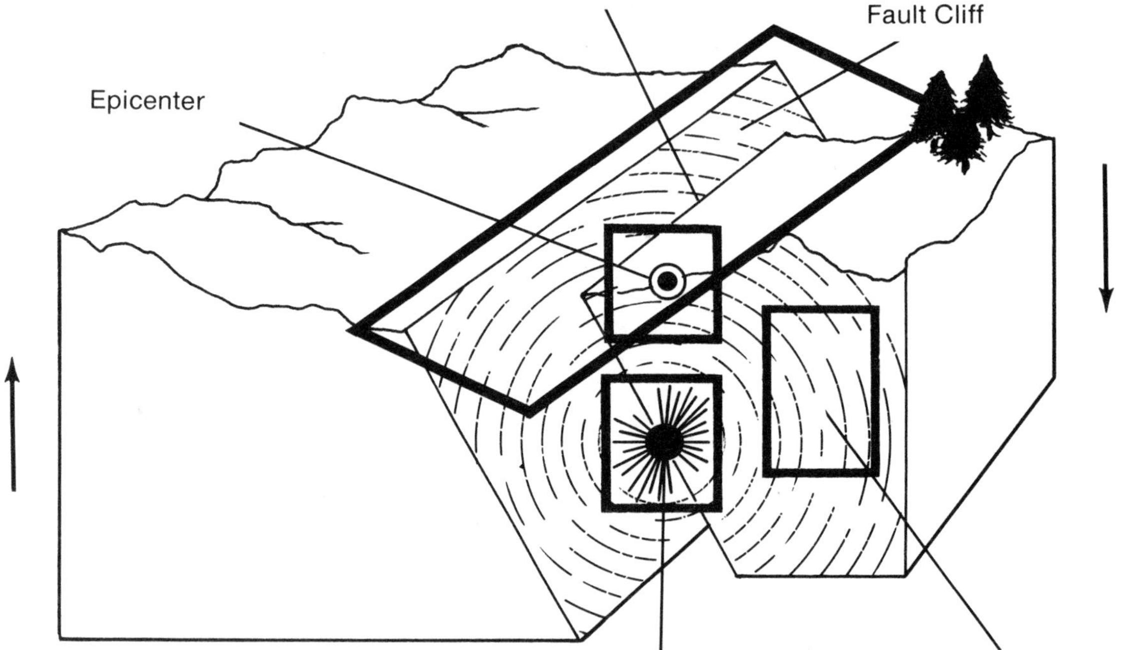

Definitions:

Focus _____

_____

Epicenter _____

_____

Fault _____

_____

Earthquake Waves _____

_____

U.S. Map with Epicenters

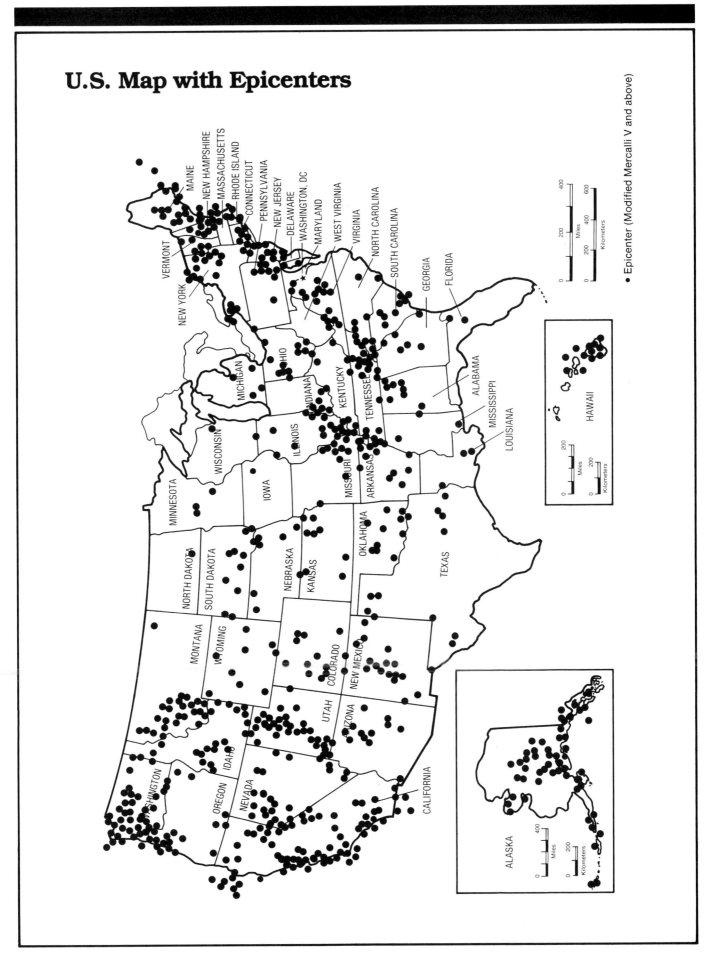

Why and Where
Earthquakes Occur

EARTHQUAKE CURRICULUM, K-6
SCOPE AND SEQUENCE CHART

Unit II: Why and Where Earthquakes Occur

Level	Concept	Laboratory	Mathematics	Language Arts	Social Studies	Art
K-2	The Earth is made up of layers. Earth's outer layer is broken into pieces called plates. The movement of Earth plates is the cause of most earthquakes.	Egg analogy of the Earth layers Earth layer simulation game		Vocabulary development of earthquake words Creative writing	Map puzzle of Earth plates	Color, cut, and paste Earth plates Shape recognition of Earth plate puzzle
3-4	The Earth has a layered structure. Earth's outer layer, the lithosphere, is broken into pieces called plates. Convection currents in the mantle might be the cause of plate motion which results in earthquakes.	Egg analogy of Earth layers Hand movement simulation of Earth layer motion Convection current demonstration	Scale measurements Bar graph of Earth layers	Written description of Earth's interior Vocabulary development of earthquake words	Earth size and distances Map study of epicenter and plate locations	Color in Earth layer diagram Three dimensional model of Earth layers
5-6	The Earth has a layered structure and an outer layer broken into pieces called plates. Three basic movements take place at the edges of the plates. Plate movements create special surface features near the edges of the plates. Convection currents in the mantle may be the cause of plate movements.	Models of Earth plate motions Convection current demonstration	Scale model of Earth layers Metric measurement	Vocabulary development of earthquake words	Map study of epicenter and plate locations Geologic features of the Earth's surface	Model of Earth layers Epicenters map coloring

Why and Where Earthquakes Occur

Although our Earth feels solid as we walk along its surface, it is really only partly so. The Earth is divided into three main layers that can be visualized by using a hard-boiled egg as a model. There is a hard outer surface, a softer middle layer, and a central core. The outermost layer of the Earth is broken into irregular pieces, called *plates*, which make the Earth resemble a spherical jigsaw puzzle. These plates are in very slow but constant motion. Plates move in three different ways—colliding with each other, spreading apart, or sliding past one another. Earthquakes can release the energy stored in rocks by any one or a combination of these three kinds of movement. Today many scientists believe that the plates float on currents created in hot plastic-like material beneath the plates.

Why and Where Earthquakes Occur

In Unit I we defined earthquakes in a general way, particularly as they affect human beings. To really understand why earthquakes occur, however, we need to know something about the makeup of our Earth. Two concepts are basic to all of the lessons in this unit: that the planet we live on is composed of layers, and that its outermost layer and surface are broken into irregular pieces called *plates*.

The Layers of the Earth

The simplest way of describing the Earth's layers is to compare the globe to a hard-boiled egg. It has a *crust* something like the shell, a middle layer, or *mantle*, something like the white, and a *core* that is something like the yolk. The crust and the upper portion of the mantle are often referred to together as the *lithosphere*, or rock sphere. Scientists further divide the core into the *inner core* and the *outer core*.

Crust and Lithosphere
The Earth's crust varies in thickness from about 65 km on the continents to only about 10 km on the ocean floors. Even at its thickest, the crust is not nearly as thick in relation to the whole bulk of the Earth as the shell of an egg is to the egg. This becomes obvious when we compare 65 km to the radius of the Earth, 6,370 km.

The lithosphere is the outer solid portion of Earth that includes the crust and the uppermost part of the mantle. The lithosphere has an average depth of 100 km.

Lower Mantle and Core
Directly below the lithosphere is the *asthenosphere*, a region of the mantle with a plastic, semisolid consistency, which reaches to about 200 km below the surface. The mantle continues to a depth of 2,900 km.

The liquid outer core, which might be compared to the outer two-thirds of an egg's yolk, reaches from 2,900 km

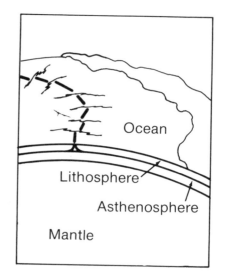

to a depth of about 5,100 km. The solid, metallic inner core goes the rest of the way to the center of the Earth. Both are composed primarily of iron and nickel.

The oldest rocks of the crust have been dated by radioactive decay at about 3.8 billion years old. We do not know when the lithosphere began to form, but we assume that it broke into plates at this time.

The Earth's Plates

Most earthquakes are caused by large-scale movements of the Earth's lithospheric plates, and occur at the boundaries between the plates. Experts recognize seven to twelve major plates and a number of smaller ones. The plates take their names from continents (the North American plate); from oceans (the Pacific plate); and from geographic areas (the Arabian plate).

Slow and Steady Motion
The plates are in very slow but constant motion, so that seen from above, the Earth's surface might look like a slowly moving spherical jigsaw puzzle. The plates move at rates of 2 to 15 cm, or several inches, in a year: about as fast as our fingernails grow. On a human scale, this is a rate of movement that only the most sophisticated instruments can detect. But on the scale of geological time, it's a dizzying speed. At this rate, those almost-four-billion-year-old rocks could have traveled all the way around the Earth eleven times.

Three Kinds of Plate Movements
The movement of the plates is generally one of three kinds—spreading, colliding, or sliding. When plates are spreading, or separating from each other, we call their movement *divergent*. When they are colliding, or pushing each other, we call the movement *convergent*. Movement in which plates slide past each other is called *lateral* (or transform) plate movement. Earthquakes can accompany each of the three types of movement.

Types of Plate Movements

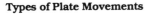

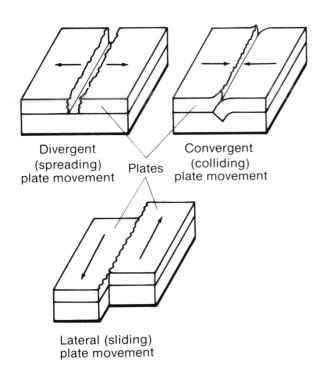

Divergent
(spreading)
plate movement

Plates

Convergent
(colliding)
plate movement

Lateral (sliding)
plate movement

Plate Tectonics

Continental Drift: 1910 to 1960

The theory of plate tectonics originated early in this century, although it did not gain general acceptance until the late 60s. The German meteorologist, geophysicist, and explorer Alfred L. Wegener is now given credit for the first step in understanding the movement of the lithosphere. In the period 1910–1912 he formulated the theory called *continental drift*, and collected evidence from the rocks, fossils, and climate of various continents to show that they had once been joined together. Wegener had little data on the oceanic crust, so he thought that the continents merely moved through that crust.

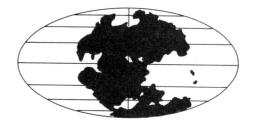

Earth land masses about 200,000,000 years ago.

Plate Tectonics: 1960 to the Present

In the early 1960s, Fred Vine and Drummond Matthews showed that the ocean floor was spreading apart at the mid-ocean ridges. They and others soon realized that the continents were also moving. By 1968 a new explanation for the dynamics of the Earth's surface had been born, and christened *plate tectonics*.

Earth land masses about 50,000,000 years into the future.

Convection Currents

The force that drives the plates, however, is still something of a mystery. Wegener thought that centrifugal force, caused by the rotation of the Earth, was the cause of continental drift. The weight of modern scientific opinion favors convection currents—systems of heat exchange that form in the Earth's mantle.

Beneath the lithosphere the mantle is semi-molten to a depth of about 260 km. Its plastic-like material rises in response to heat and sinks when the temperature drops. You can see this kind of movement if you boil water in a clear glass pot.

This convective movement acts as a drag on the underside of the lithospheric plates, causing them to separate where mantle material is rising and collide where it sinks. As the plates are dragged along over the mantle, like potato chips riding on honey, the leading edges of some plates are destroyed, while others pick up new material. Sometimes the edge of one plate slides under another, in the process we call *subduction*.

Some scientists explain the motion of plates as a downhill sliding. They are high at the mid-ocean ridges, and extend deep into the mantle at their leading edges. As a subducting plate sinks, it fractures from the stress, and causes deep earthquakes. Eventually, because of the high temperature of the mantle, the subducting plate melts. Then this molten plate material rises into the crust, where it feeds volcanoes. The molten crust and the sediments which are carried with it yield rich deposits.

Somehow, these various processes maintain a kind of balance, so that the size of the lithosphere stays about the same. Remember to emphasize, with your students, the great sweep of geological time in which tectonic processes occur. Discovering the dynamic nature of this seemingly solid Earth should be exciting, but not frightening.

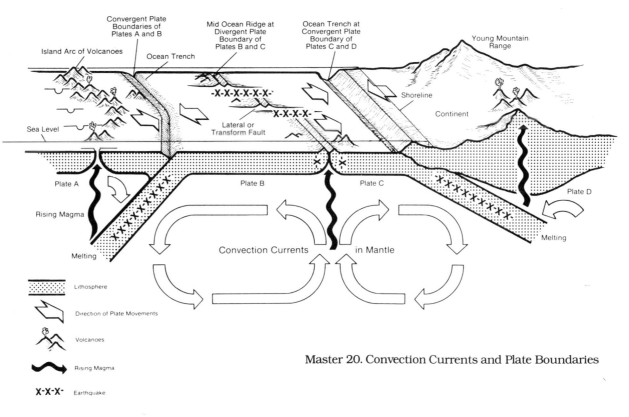

Master 20. Convection Currents and Plate Boundaries

Inside Planet Earth

Content Concepts

1. The Earth is made up of layers.

2. Its outer layer is broken into pieces called *plates*.

3. The movement of the Earth's plates is the cause of most earthquakes.

Vocabulary

layer
model
core
mantle
crust
plate

Objectives

Students will
—name and identify layers of the Earth.
—observe a model of the Earth's plates.
—create a model of the Earth's layers with their bodies.
—construct a representation of the Earth's plates with jigsaw puzzle pieces.

Activity One: Earth from the Inside Out

Materials for the teacher
• Transparency made from Master 12, Layers of the Earth
• Overhead projector
• Hard-boiled egg with the Earth's plates outlined in permanent marker (Crude markings will do.)
• Kitchen knife

Materials for each student
• A color-coded sign saying Core (red), Mantle (yellow), or Crust (blue), perhaps on a string to hang around the neck
• Crayons or markers
• Worksheet made from Master 12, Layers of the Earth
• Scissors
• Paste

Learning Links

Language Arts: Vocabulary building, following directions

Social Studies: Locating plates on a world map and identifying major global features (continents and oceans)

Art: Coloring, cutting, pasting, shape recognition

Procedure

1. Show the transparency on the overhead projector, pointing out the three basic layers of the Earth—core, mantle, and crust—and describing each.

2. Show students the egg and point out the marks that indicate the plates.

Explain: The Earth's top layer is broken into pieces called *plates.* The plates are always moving, but usually very slowly—about as fast as your fingernails grow. Sometimes, when the plates move away from each other, bump into each other, or grind past each other, we experience earthquakes. Then we feel shaking, and sometimes we hear rumbling.

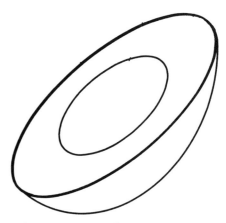

A cross section of a hard boiled egg suggests the layered structure of the Earth.

3. With a sharp knife, slice the egg, shell and all, and show students the layers inside. Explain that the crust is something like the shell, the white is something like the mantle, and the yolk is something like the core.

4. Invite students to use their bodies to represent the layers of the Earth.

core

The core, the deepest layer of the Earth, is like a large, hot iron ball. It helps to heat the Earth from inside like a furnace.

man • tle

The mantle is the layer between the core and the crust. It is mostly solid. Just below its top is a semisolid layer with a consistency something like modeling clay or gelatin dessert.

crust

The crust is the top layer of the Earth, hard and very thin compared to the other layers.

Teacher Take Note: In later grades students will also learn about the *lithosphere,* the layer to which the plates belong. For now the three basic layers are enough.

a. Select a small group of children (perhaps three or four) to represent the core, and give them red signs which say Core. Ask them to sit in the center of the room.

b. Select a larger group (as many as fifteen students) to represent the mantle. Give them yellow Mantle signs and ask them to surround the core group.

c. Give blue Crust signs to about six more students.

d. Instruct the core students to stand almost still, but show that they are very hot, perhaps by mopping their brows and fanning themselves.

e. Ask the mantle students to form small groups of three or so, and stand around the core. Each group should move together in slow circular motions, as slowly as if they were moving through toothpaste.

f. Direct the crust students to form a circle, or layer, one student deep around the mantle students.

g. Tell the mantle students that when you call out "Earthquake," they are to bump into the crust students, causing them to move and breaking their circle. This transfer of energy from mantle students to crust students simulates roughly what happens during an earthquake.

5. Distribute copies of Master 12. Direct students to color the Earth's layers in different colors: red for the core, yellow for the mantle, and blue for the crust. Readers can cut out the labels and paste them in the correct boxes.

Activity Two: Giant Jigsaw Puzzle

Materials for the teacher
- Egg model from Activity One
- Transparency made from Master 13, Earth Plates
- Wall map of the world or transparency of Master 5, World Map
- Transparency made from Master 14a and 14b, Earth Plate Puzzle Pieces (2 sheets)
- Overhead projector

Materials for each student
• Handouts made from Masters 13, 14a, and 14b
• Crayons
• Scissors
• Paste
Optional: Handouts made from Master 15, Earth Layers Worksheet, and Master 16, Earthquake Words

Procedure

1. Review the previous lesson. Repeat the egg demonstration to establish the relationship of the crust to the shell and the existence of the plates.

2. Recall the turtle story in Unit 1, and explain that the theory of plate movement gained general acceptance among scientists only about 20 years ago. Also remind students of the activity in which they represented the layers of the Earth. Ask:

What causes most earthquakes? (The Earth plates move.)

When one part of the crust moves, what happens to the other parts of the crust? (They move too.)

3. Display Master 13, Earth Plates, on the overhead, and compare it to the world map. Explain that the Earth's crust can be divided into major plates which fit together like the pieces of a gigantic jigsaw puzzle. Help students observe that some of the plate boundaries roughly follow continental boundaries.

4. Project Master 14a and 14b, one sheet at a time, and hand out worksheets made from those masters and Master 13.

5. Direct students to color all the shaded areas on the Master 14 pages brown. These represent the Earth's major land masses. Have them leave the remaining areas white. These represent oceans and seas.

6. Ask students to count the puzzle pieces so that they perceive the boundaries and can point to each piece. (This is important to be sure that they are interpreting positive and negative space correctly.) Point out that one plate has no land on it, and another has very little land.

7. Direct students to cut out the puzzle pieces and paste them on the worksheet made from Master 13, the Earth plate outlines. Be sure they understand that their diagram represents a flattened view of the Earth and its plates.

Extensions

1. Dictate or write a story about people who live on a planet that has different layers, differently shaped plates, and different plate movements than our Earth.

2. Rewrite the turtle story from Unit One. How would you explain an earthquake if you were a modern Gabrielino who had studied about the layers of the Earth and its plates?

3. On a paper plate, draw a diagram of the layers of the Earth. Label each layer, indicating its depth and relative temperature. (In general, temperatures increase from the outside of the Earth to its center.)

4. Follow the directions on a worksheet made from Master 15 to identify the layers of the Earth.

5. Follow the directions on Master 16, Earthquake Words.

Some of the smaller plate regions are not cut apart into puzzle pieces on Masters 14a and 14b as they would be too small for the children to handle comfortably.

Plates Going Places

Vocabulary

crust
lithosphere
mantle
outer core
inner core
plates
convection current
diameter
magma
divergent plate boundary
lateral (transform) plate
    boundary
convergent plate boundary

Learning Links

Language Arts: Participating in class discussions, writing paragraphs, following directions

Social Studies: Locating plate boundaries, locating various geographic features

Math: Interpreting a graph of the thickness of Earth's layers, observing the proportions of the layers to each other

Art: Drawing the interior of the Earth, constructing a model of the Earth's interior

Content Concepts

1. The Earth has a layered structure.

2. Its outer layer, the lithosphere, is broken into pieces called *plates.*

3. Convection currents in the mantle might be the cause of plate motion which results in earthquakes.

Objectives

Students will
—describe the structure of the interior of the Earth.
—name and identify the layers of the Earth.
—interpret a graph of the approximate thickness of the Earth's layers.
—observe a model demonstrating the layers of the Earth and its plates.
—relate earthquake epicenters to plate boundaries.
—identify 12 major plates of the Earth.
—demonstrate the motions of plates.
—observe a convection current.

Activity One: What's Inside

Materials for the teacher
- A globe of the Earth
- Transparency made from Master 17, A Pizza the Earth
- Transparency made from Master 18, Graph of the Earth's Layers, colored according to the directions in 3 and 4 below
- Overhead projector

Materials for each student
- Worksheet made from Master 17
- Worksheet made from Master 18, Graph of the Earth's Layers
- Crayons or colored pencils
- Metric ruler

Procedure

1. Show the students the globe. Define the term *diameter*, then tell them that the Earth's diameter is 12,760 km, or 7,660 miles. Put this distance in context by comparing it to a distance students are familiar with, such as the distance from their town or city to a neighboring community.

2. Explore students' ideas about the inside of the Earth. Is it the same all the way to the center? Distribute art supplies and ask them to draw what they think the inside of the Earth is like, then write a paragraph describing the drawing. (This activity will help you to know what background they are bringing to the topic.)

3. Project the transparency of the Earth's layers, Master 17, and distribute the matching worksheet.

a. Explain that the drawing is a model of the layers inside the Earth. Briefly describe each layer, and have students label the inner core, outer core, mantle, lithosphere, and crust as you speak.

con • vec • tion
cur • rent

A convection current is a circular movement in a fluid in which hot material rises and cold material sinks.

lith • o • sphere

The lithosphere is the solid outer region of the Earth in which earthquakes begin. It contains the crust and the uppermost portion of the mantle.

out • er   core

The outer core is the liquid portion of the Earth's core.

in • ner   core

The inner core is the solid central portion of the Earth.

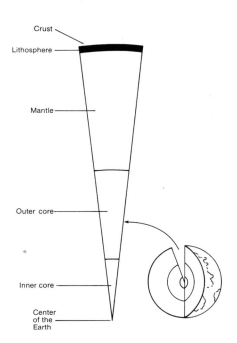

Master 17. A Pizza the Earth answers

b. Ask students to color each of the Earth's layers a different color. Color the area from the beginning of the lithosphere out to the surface yellow, then go over the outermost section with blue to indicate the crust. (The overlapping colors, which should produce green for the crust, will help students to understand that the crust is part of the lithosphere.)

4. Distribute Master 18, Graph of the Earth's Layers. Ask students to color the bars which represent the approximate thickness of the various layers, coloring each bar the same color they used for that layer on their worksheets (Master 17). Use the transparency of Master 18 to discuss the proportions of the layers with your students.

5. (Optional) During another class period or as homework, invite students to make a three-dimensional model showing the layers of the Earth. Tell them they must label the layers and make them in correct proportion to one another. They may choose any material and manner of construction they like. You may want to display some of these models in a school display case.

Activity Two: We're All Cracked Up

Materials for the teacher
- Several hard-boiled eggs
- Small kitchen knife
- Narrow permanent marker
- Free-flowing broad permanent marker

Procedure

Teacher Take Note: It may take several tries to cut the egg neatly. A very sharp knife will help.

1. Before class, cut a hard-boiled egg in half with its shell on. On one half, make a dot of color in the center of the yolk with a permanent marker to represent the inner core. Color the outside of the shell with the broad marker to represent the crust.

Rap another hard-boiled egg on any hard surface to produce a pattern of large cracks. When you have a design you like, outline the edges of the cracks with the narrow permanent marker. (This may also take several attempts. You do like egg salad, don't you?)

2. Use the marked half of the cut egg as a model to review the layers of the Earth with your students. Ask the following questions.

Which layer of the Earth does the shell represent? (The lithosphere. The color on the outside represents the crust, which is less than half as thick as the lithosphere itself.)

Which layer does the white represent? (the mantle)

Which two layers does the yolk represent? (the outer core and inner core)

3. Hold up a whole cooked egg and ask students what would happen to the shell if you rapped it on your desk. (It would develop cracks.)

4. Show them the cracked egg you prepared in advance and point out that the shell is now divided into adjoining sections. The lithosphere is similarly divided into sections, which we call *plates*. The plates of the Earth include a portion of the upper mantle as well as the crust. We use the term *lithosphere* to describe the part of the Earth to which the plates belong, from the surface down to a depth of about 100 km.

5. Explain that unlike the sections of eggshell, the plates of the Earth are in motion. They move very slowly (at a rate of only a few centimeters a year), over a portion of the mantle that has plastic properties, rather like the silicone putty we used in Unit I. This movement can cause earthquakes.

Activity Three: Plates of the Earth

Materials for the teacher
- Transparency of Master 19, Plate Boundaries Map
- Overhead projector

Materials for each student
- Handout made from Master 7, World Map with Epicenters
- Handout made from Master 19
- Crayons or colored pencils

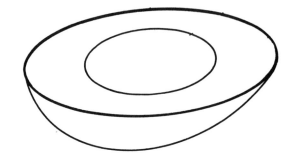

Sliced, hard-cooked egg displays layers something like the Earth's. (So does an avocado, if you don't like cooking.)

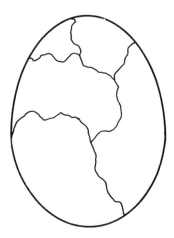

Procedure

1. Distribute copies of the epicenter map and the plate boundaries map.

2. Ask students what relationship they see between the locations of earthquakes and the plate boundaries. They should be able to see a correlation.

3. Point out the arrows on the plate boundaries map, Master 19, which indicate the direction in which each plate is moving. Ask them to color the arrows red.

4. Explain that each plate has a name, and point each one out as you read its name aloud. Instruct students to put their red pencils or crayons aside and use different colors to color all of the plates—lightly, so the names and arrows can still be seen.

5. Either in a class discussion or on a worksheet followed by a class discussion, cover these points:

How many plates are there on the map? (Twelve. Explain that some experts identify only seven, and others count as many as twenty.)

Locate India. Where do you see a plate boundary in India? (on the northern border) What geographic feature do you find there? (mountains)

Locate the Atlantic Ocean. Are there any plate boundaries in that ocean? (Yes. Plate boundaries divide the ocean from north to south.)

Which large island in the Atlantic Ocean has a plate boundary going through it? (Iceland)

6. Project the transparency of the plate boundaries map.

7. Again point out the arrows which indicate plate movement, and explain that this movement is of three kinds: divergent, lateral (or transform), and convergent. Demonstrate hand motions to simulate each kind of movement, and practice them with the class as you give examples of each.

a. Divergent—Begin with fingernails pressing against each other and slowly pull hands apart. Explain that this kind of plate movement is happening on the floor of the Atlantic and Pacific Oceans. As plates move apart, melted rock, or *magma* rises from the upper mantle to fill the spaces. Examples: South American plate and African plate; North American plate and Eurasian plate

b. Lateral—Place hands side by side and slide them slowly past each other. Explain that this kind of activity is occurring right now along the San Andreas fault in California. Example: North American plate and Pacific plate

c. Convergent—Start with hands facing each other and six inches apart. Bring them together so that one hand is forced under the other. The top hand should ride up and make a fist. Explain that converging plates form high mountains such as the Himalayas.

As plates move together, one of the plates is pushed down under the other: Examples: Australian-Indian plate and Eurasian plate, Nazca plate and South American plate

Activity Four: Hot Stuff Rises and Cold Stuff Sinks

Materials for the teacher
- Clear heatproof glass baking dish, 23 cm x 13 cm x 7 cm
- Immersion heater (plug-in coil used to heat small quantities of water)
- Sandwich-size plastic bag with twist tie
- Tape
- 2 eyedroppers
- Red food coloring
- Blue food coloring
- A handful of solid paper circles from a hole puncher
- Ice cubes
- Cool water
- Transparency made from Master 20, Convection Currents
- Overhead projector

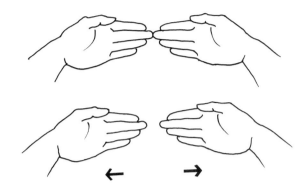

a. Divergent: Begin with fingertips together and slowly pull hands apart.

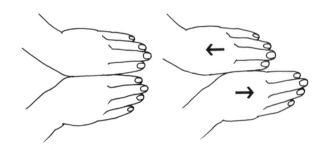

b. Lateral: Begin with hands side by side. Slide one forward and the other back, so they pass by each other.

c. Convergent: Begin with knuckles facing each other. Bring hands together, letting one slide under the other.

Procedure

1. Review the concept that Earth's lithosphere is broken into pieces called *plates.* Scientists believe that the plates move because of movement inside the mantle, the way groceries move on the conveyor belts in supermarket checkout lines. This demonstration illustrates what may take place.

2. Fill the glass baking dish almost completely full of cool water.

3. Put about six ice cubes in the plastic bag and close it with the twist tie.

4. Place the bag in the water at one end of the dish and tape it to the side so it can't float away.

5. Place the immersion heater in the water at the other end of the dish and plug it in. *Warn students to stay away from the heat source.*

6. Wait about one minute for the water to heat. Then use an eyedropper to put several drops of red food coloring on the bottom of the dish near the heater. Ask students to observe what happens. (Some of the coloring will rise to the top and float toward the other end of the dish.)

Teacher Take Note: An immersion heater is safer than most other heat sources. You can buy one for $3-4 at most hardware stores. It is also a handy way to heat a cup of water for tea, coffee, or broth.

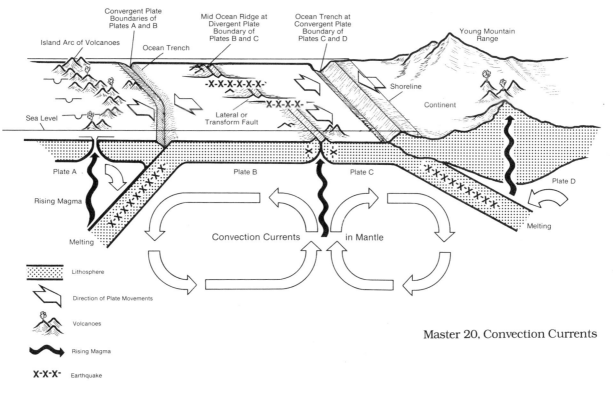

Master 20, Convection Currents

7. Now use the second dropper to put a few drops of blue coloring into the water just under the surface, near the ice. Ask students to describe what they see. (The coloring will sink and move along the bottom of the water toward the other end of the dish.)

8. Put a few of the paper circles on top of the water in the warm end. Students will see them moving around on the surface of the water. Explain that the Earth's plates may move on the semi-solid layer of the mantle in a similar way, because of temperature changes in the mantle. The systems of heat exchange that cause their movement are called *convection currents*. Hot material rises, while cold material sinks.

9. Project the transparency of Master 20, Convection Currents and Plate Movements, and point out that where two convection currents are rising together, the plates are forced apart. Where two currents are sinking together, the plates are forced together. Scientists hypothesize that these movements are the cause of many earthquakes.

10. If necessary, repeat the demonstration until all the students have had a chance to observe it at close range.

Extensions

1. Read Jules Verne's *Journey to the Center of the Earth* to students as a class activity, or make it an extra reading assignment.

2. Show pictures of Icelandic rifts, the San Andreas fault, the Himalayan mountains, and other physical features of the sort that occur at plate boundaries.

3. Show the class a film or filmstrip on plate tectonics. (Because most of them were designed for older students, you may want to show just portions, or use the images and provide your own narration.)

Be sure to add the colored drops to the water just below the surface as drops on the surface will diffuse too quickly and not give the best effect.

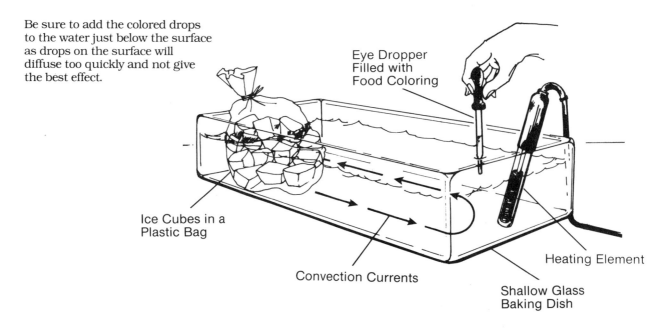

Eye Dropper Filled with Food Coloring

Ice Cubes in a Plastic Bag

Convection Currents

Heating Element

Shallow Glass Baking Dish

Layers, Plates, and Quakes

Content Concepts

1. The Earth has a layered structure.

2. The Earth's outer layer is broken into pieces called plates.

3. Three basic kinds of movement take place at the edges of the plates.

4. Plate movements create special surface features near the edges of the plates.

5. Convection currents in the mantle may be the cause of plate movements.

Vocabulary

crust
lithosphere
mantle
outer core
inner core
plate
lateral (transform) plate
    boundary
convergent plate boundary
divergent plate boundary
volcano
magma

Objectives

Students will
—make a model of the layers of the Earth.
—be able to describe the composition of the layers and their
    interrelationships.
—model and describe activity at the three major types of plate
    boundaries.
—observe a demonstration of convection currents and relate
    the process to plate movement.

Learning Links

Language Arts: Discussion, note taking, vocabulary building, following directions

Math: Using a scale to build Earth wedge model

Art: Drawing, cutting, and taping on paper models; building convection model

Activity One:
Crust to Core: A Pizza the Earth

Materials for the teacher
- Transparency made from Master 17, A Pizza the Earth
- Overhead projector
- Transparency markers

Materials for each student
- 3 sheets of unlined paper, standard size
- No. 2 pencil
- Meter stick
- Tape
- Copies of Master 18, Graph of the Earth's Layers
- Copies of Master 17 (optional)

Procedure

1. Elicit from class what they think the Earth is like below the surface. Accept various opinions. Depending on answers, class may need to use all or part of the first activity from grades 3-4 in this unit.

2. Display the transparency of layers of the Earth. Explain that the Earth is layered and that we have learned about these layers largely from the study of earthquake waves. Define *crust, lithosphere, mantle, outer core,* and *inner core* (see the lower-grade lessons in this unit), and ask students to write definitions of the layers in their notebooks for future reference. (Or give the students copies of Master 17, A Pizza the Earth, and have them add the definitions there.)

3. Tell the class that they are going to create a scale model of a slice of the Earth, from its surface to the center, using the following procedure:

a. Attach three pieces of unlined paper by taping together the shorter sides to make a strip about 80 cm long.

b. Turn paper over to the untaped side.

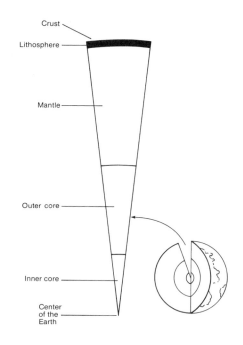

Master 17. A Pizza the Earth

"This Pizza the Earth sure has a thin crust!"

mag • ma

Magma is liquid rock beneath the Earth's surface. When it erupts it is called *lava*.

vol • can • o

A volcano is a mountain of erupted, hardened lava at the surface of the lithosphere.

c. Draw, with the aid of a meter stick, a triangle 10 cm wide on top and 64 cm on its other two sides. (This is a scale of about one millimeter for each kilometer of the Earth's radius.) Label the 10-cm side Earth's Surface, and the opposite end (the point of the wedge) Center of the Earth.

d. Compute the scaled distance from the Earth's surface to the bottom of each of the layers, using the data from Master 18, Graph of the Earth's layers. (Students will have to know the scale—1 millimeter to 1 kilometer—and the definitions of the layers to be able to perform this task correctly. Be prepared to offer help as needed.)

e. Label the layers.

4. When the wedge models of Earth are completed, ask students to answer the following questions:

Which of Earth's layers is the thickest, and accounts for most of its volume? (the mantle)

On which layer or layers are the plates? (lithosphere, or crust and upper mantle)

In which layer or layers can faulting occur to create an earthquake? (again, lithosphere or crust and upper mantle)

How does the part of the earth we live on—the crust or lithosphere—compare in thickness to the Earth's interior? (It's the thinnest part.)

Activity Two: Busy Boundaries

Materials for the teacher
- Overhead projector
- Transparency made from Master 7, World Map with Epicenters
- Transparency made from Master 19, Plate Boundaries Map
- Transparency marker

Materials for each student
- Copies of Masters 7 and 19
- No. 2 pencil

Procedure

1. Project transparency of world epicenter map and provide students with copies.

2. Conduct a discussion about where earthquakes occur, and develop the concept that most epicenters are located in certain belts or zones. Have students shade their epicenter maps lightly in pencil to indicate the regions with many epicenters. Be sure they highlight the "ring of fire" around the Pacific Ocean, the Mid-Atlantic ridge, the region between northern Africa and southern Europe, and the area where northern India meets the rest of Asia.

3. Distribute copies of the plate boundaries map. On the projector, place a transparency of this map over the epicenter map transparency, which you have shaded as in step 2 above.

4. Review the concept of lithospheric plates, sections of lithosphere that can move sideways, and point out on the transparencies that most earthquakes occur in regions of special Earth surface features which correspond to the bound-

Master 19, Plate Boundaries Map

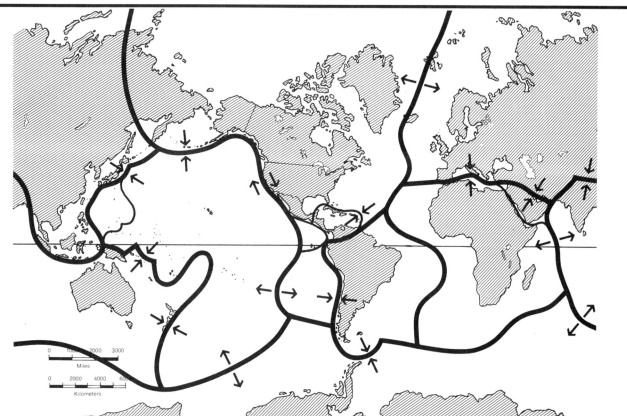

aries of the plates. (Be sure to point out, however, that some earthquake epicenters are found within the plates as well.) End with a brief description of the concept of plate tectonics (see unit background) and have students take a few notes.

5. Ask students why they think most earthquakes are found at plate boundaries. Accept various answers for now, but build toward the understanding that plate movement appears to account for most earthquakes.

Activity Three: Slide, Collide, and Separate

Materials for the teacher
- Overhead projector
- Transparency made from Master 19, Plate Boundaries Map

Materials for each student
- Copy of Master 19
- 10 sheets of lined notebook paper or other 8½" x 11" sheets
- One sheet of colored construction paper
- Scissors
- Transparent tape
- Metric ruler

Procedure

1. Use the transparency and student copies of Master 19 to explain that different types of interactions occur among lithospheric plates at their boundaries. You may want to use the hand movements from Level 2, Activity Three of this unit to demonstrate.

a. Lateral boundaries exist where two plates slide and grind past each other as they move in parallel or opposite directions.

b. Convergent boundaries exist where two plates collide and destroy lithosphere by compacting, or shortening, and melting. There are two major types of convergence:

When two ocean boundaries or an ocean boundary and a continental boundary collide, an ocean plate edge sinks and melting occurs. Plate boundaries of this type are associated with ocean trenches and island arc volcanoes. The melting forms magma, which rises, creating the volcanoes of the island arcs.

When two plates that have continental areas at their convergent boundaries collide, the lithosphere crumples up and new young mountain ranges form. This is happening today where India is colliding with Asia, forming the Himalaya Mountains.

c. Divergent boundaries exist where two plates diverge or separate, as at mid-ocean ridges. Divergence results in formation of new lithosphere and crust, because separation allows liquid rock, or magma, to rise from the mantle below, forming volcanoes and new rock.

2. Tell the class that they are going to make some simple models of two major types of plate boundaries. If the class has never done hand motions to model the activity at plate boundaries, do Activity Three from the Grades 3-4 section of this unit first.

3. Ask students to get out their notebook paper and make two stacks of five sheets each. Then give them the following directions:

a. Using large letters, label the top sheet of one stack Plate A and the top sheet of the other Plate B. From now on, we will refer to the stacks of paper as "plates."

b. With scissors, cut 1-cm slashes at 2-cm intervals, fringing the long side of each plate. These slashes will represent the broken-up, crushed rock at the plate boundary.

c. Hold the plates together, one in each hand, in front of you. Push one plate forward and pull the other back towards your body.

What did you feel? (sliding with frequent hitches as the slashed edges engage)

What do you think this model represents? (A lateral plate boundary. The sliding motion represents fault creep, and the jerky motion represents the buildup and release of energy in an earthquake. The San Andreas lateral boundary in California exhibits this kind of motion. Plates slide, but locking of sections occasionally results in earthquakes.)

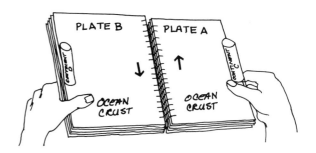

Lateral boundary: Edges slide, but sometimes catch and jerk.

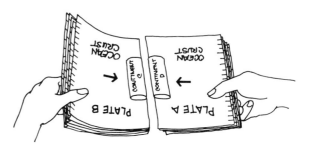

Convergent boundary with continents: Plate edges hump up, and may form mountains over time.

Convergent boundary with oceanic crust: One plate edge is forced under the other. This process may account for the formation of oceanic trenches.

4. Tell students that next they will use their Plates A and B to model another type of plate boundary. Give these directions:

a. Label the top of each plate Ocean Crust.

b. Cut the sheet of colored construction paper in half lengthwise and make a loop out of each section. Tape the loops closed, and press down on each one gently to flatten it.

c. Label one loop Continent C and the other Continent D, or make up names and write them on the loops. These loops will represent continents or continental crust.

d. Tape the middle of each loop to the short side of one of the plates, with the closed side facing out.

e. Hold a plate-continent combination in each hand with the continent edges facing each other. Push the two plates together and observe what happens to the continents riding on the plates.

What do you see? (The plates will hump up and the edges of the continents will rise.)

What might this represent? (The demonstration represents the convergence of two plates, the shortening or folding of the crust, and the formation of mountains.)

f. Turn the plates around so their plain short edges (without continents) face each other, then push those edges together.

What happened? (One of the plates slid under the other.)

What might this represent? (It represents two plates of oceanic crust converging. The depression which results represents an oceanic trench.)

5. Help students to summarize their observations, and answer any questions they may have.

Extensions

1. Research how scientists have discovered about the various layers of the Earth through the study of earthquake waves.

2. To the wedge model on Master 17 add the hydrosphere (average thickness of the oceans, about 3.8 km) and the atmosphere (about 960 km thick).

Activity Four: The History of Geography

Materials for the teacher
- Transparency made from Master 20, Convection Currents and Plate Cross Section
- Transparency made from Master 21, Formation and Break-up of Pangaea
- Overhead projector
- Materials and directions from Unit II, Level 2, Activity Four
- World map or globe

Procedure

1. Ask students what they think might cause the plates of the Earth to move. Accept various suggestions, then explain that the mechanism of plate movement is one of the major unsolved mysteries in Earth studies. The most widely accepted explanation is that convection currents in the Earth's mantle drive the plates. If students are not clear on the definition of *mantle*, review the definitions in Level 1.

2. Briefly describe convection currents and project Master 20, Convection Currents and Plate Cross Section. Give several common examples of convection, such as hot air rising and cold air falling, in the classroom, or warm water rising to the top and cool water sinking to the bottom, in a lake or pool.

3. Discuss possible energy sources for convection and the movement of plates. (Many Earth scientists believe that heat energy is produced within the interior of the Earth, perhaps by the decay of radioactive materials like uranium and radium within the core and mantle.)

4. Refer to a globe, a world map, or a transparency of a world map, and show how Africa and South America could fit together, almost like parts of a jigsaw puzzle. Students may see a similar fit among Europe, North America, and Greenland. Query class for a reason for this fit, and lead up to a brief discussion of Pangaea, the supercontinent of 200,000,000 years ago.

5. Using the transparency of the breakup of Pangaea (Master 21), very briefly show how we think the supercontinent changed to become the continents of today. Be sure to emphasize that the continents move only as parts of plates, not by themselves.

6. Indicate to the class that they are going to observe a model showing how convection currents could move the plates and the continents that ride on them. This model may explain the breakup of the supercontinent Pangaea over the last 200,000,000 years.

7. Do Activity Four, "Hot Stuff Rises and Cold Stuff Sinks," from Level 2 of this unit.

8. Again direct students' attention to the transparency of Master 20, Convection Currents and Plate Cross Section. Point out and briefly discuss what happens where convection currents rise and sink.

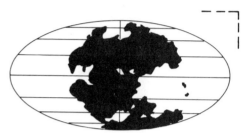

200,000,000 years ago

65,000,000 years ago

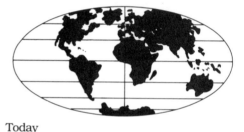

Today

50,000,000 years from now

Master 21, Formation and Breakup of Pangaea

Unit II. Why and Where Earthquakes Occur

Materials List

Grades K-2
hardboiled egg
permanent marker
paper
crayons
markers
scissors
paste
overhead projector
kitchen knife

Grades 3-4
globe
crayons
colored pencils
glass baking dish
immersion heater
plastic bag with twist tie
tape
eyedroppers
red food coloring
blue food coloring
ice cubes
hardboiled eggs
small kitchen knife
overhead projector
narrow permanent marker
broad permanent marker
paper circles from hole puncher

Grades 5-6
unlined paper
pencils
metric stick
watch with second hand
colored pencils or crayons
lined paper
colored construction paper
scissors
transparent tape
metric ruler
glass baking dish
plastic bag with twist tie
immersion heater
tape
blue food coloring
red food coloring
eyedroppers
paper hole punches
ice cubes
globe
overhead projector
transparency markers

Instructional Resources (Books, maps, pamphlets, slides)

Branley, F. M. (1974). *Shakes, Quakes, and Shifts: Earth Tectonics.* New York: Thomas Y. Crowell.

Cazeau, C. J. (1977, February). Earthquake. *Instructor*, 86, pp. 76-82.

Earthquakes and Volcanoes. (1982). Washington, DC: National Geographic Society. (Multimedia curriculum package).

Fodor, R. V. (1978). *Earth in Motion: The Concept of Plate Tectonics.* New York: William Morrow and Co.

Fradin, D. B. (1982). *Disaster! Earthquakes.* Chicago: Children's Press.

Lauber, P. (1972). *Earthquakes.* New York: Random House, Inc.

Leifer, I. (1978). Global Jigsaw Puzzle: *The Story of Continental Drift.* New York: Atheneum Publishers.

Markle, S. (1987, March). Hands-on Science: Earthquake! *Instructor*, 96, pp. 7, 97-99

Miklowitz, G. D. (1977). *Earthquake!* New York: Julian Messner.

National Oceanic and Atmospheric Administration. (1981). *Catalog of Significant Earthquakes*. Boulder, Colorado: National Geophysical Data Center.

Reuter, M. (1977). *Earthquakes: Our Restless Planet*. Milwaukee, Wisconsin: Raintree Publishers, Ltd.

Story of the Earth, The. North American Edition. Geological Museum. pp. 11-14, 17, 30-31.

Walker, B., and others. (1982). *Planet Earth Earthquake*. Alexandria, Virginia: Time-Life Books.

Weiss, M. E. (1975). *The Story of Continental Drift*. New York: Parents Magazine Press.

Maps

National Oceanic and Atmospheric Administration. (1980). *Significant Earthquakes 1900-1979*. Boulder, Colorado: National Geophysical Data Center.

Tarr, A. C. (1974). *World Seismicity Map*. Prepared by the USGS from earthquake data of the National Oceanographic and Atmospheric Administration. Reston, Virginia: United States Geological Society.

References

Bolt, B. A. (1988). *Earthquakes*. San Francisco: W. H. Freeman and Co.

Brownlee, S. (1986, July). Waiting for the big one. *Discover*, 7, pp. 52-71.

Earthquake Country: A Teachers Workshop. (1978, February 25-26). Far Western Section of National Association of Geology Teachers and California Science Teachers Association.

Glenn, W.H. (1983, January). The Jigsaw Earth: Putting the Pieces Together. *The Science Teacher*, 50, pp. 31-37.

Glenn, W.H. (1983, February). Drifting: Continents on the Move. *The Science Teacher*, 50, pp. 20-26.

Hallam, A. (1973). *A Revolution in the Earth Sciences From Continental Drift to Plate Technics*. New York: Oxford University Press.

HELP: Hands-on Learning Package. (1983). Palo Alto, California: Environmental Volunteers, Inc.

Mathews, S. W. (1973, January). This Changing Earth. *National Geographic*, 143, pp. 1-37.

Muir, R. (1987). *Earthquakes and Volcanoes: Causes, Effects, and Predictions*. New York: Weidenfeld and Nicolson.

National Oceanic and Atmospheric Administration. (1976). *Catalog of Earthquake Photographs—Key to Geophysical Records*, Documentation No. 7. Boulder, Colorado: National Geophysical Data Center.

Tarbuck, E. J., and F. K. Lutgens. (1987). *The Earth: An Introduction to Physical Geology*, 2nd ed. Columbus: Merrill Publishing Co.

Wilson, J. T. (1972). *Continents Adrift: Readings from Scientific American*. San Francisco: W. H. Freeman and Co.

Layers of the Earth

Name _____

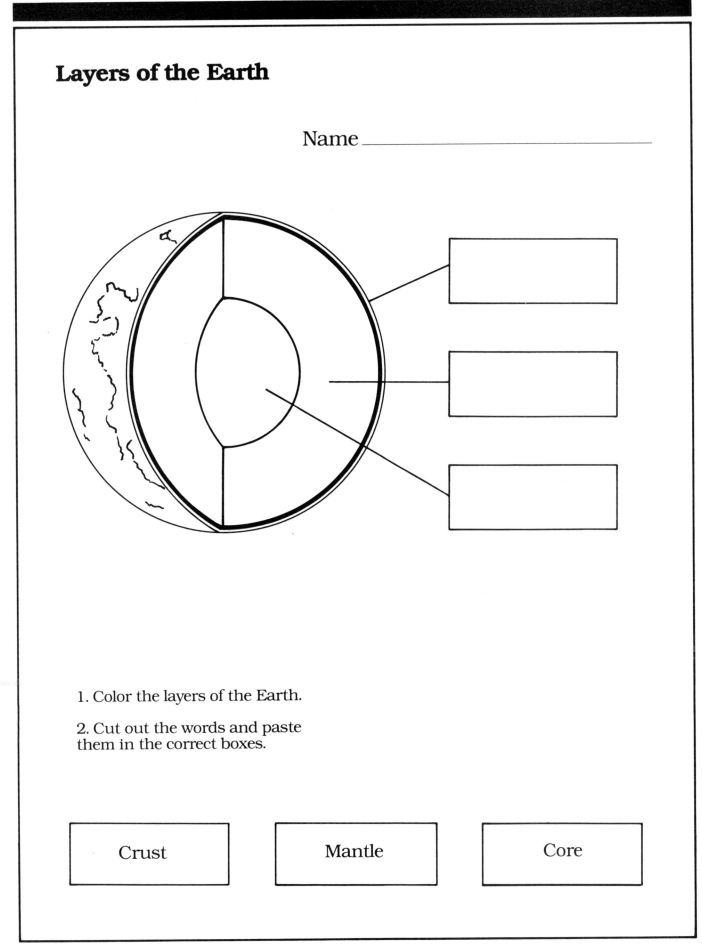

1. Color the layers of the Earth.

2. Cut out the words and paste them in the correct boxes.

Crust	Mantle	Core

Earth Plates

Name _____

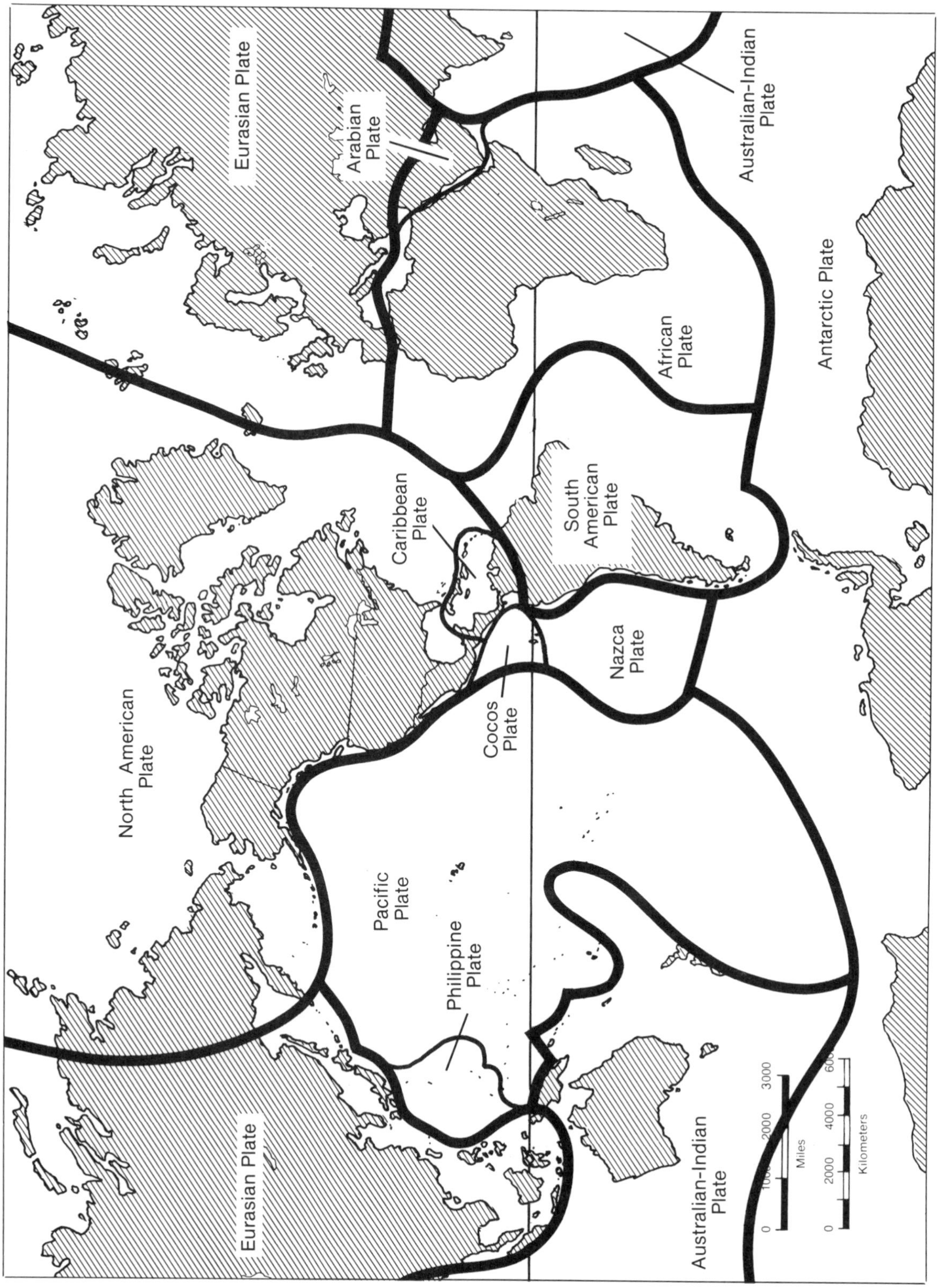

Eurasian Plate

Arabian Plate

Australian-Indian Plate

Antarctic Plate

African Plate

South American Plate

Caribbean Plate

Nazca Plate

Cocos Plate

North American Plate

Pacific Plate

Philippine Plate

Eurasian Plate

Australian-Indian Plate

Miles

3000

2000

1000

0

Kilometers

6000

4000

2000

0

Earth Plate Puzzle Pieces

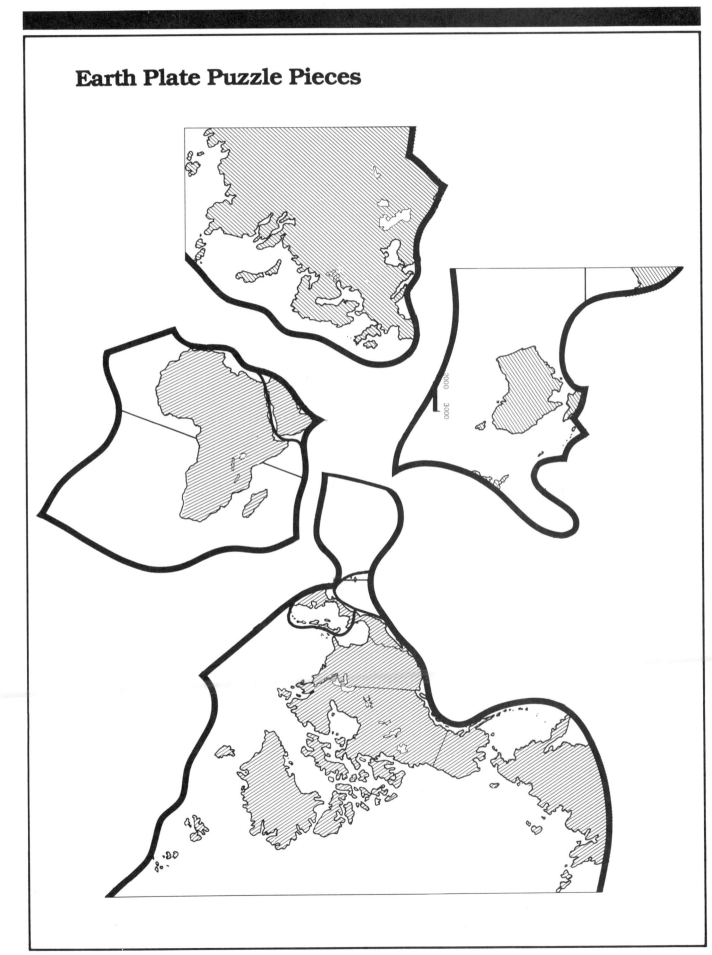

Earth Plate Puzzle Pieces

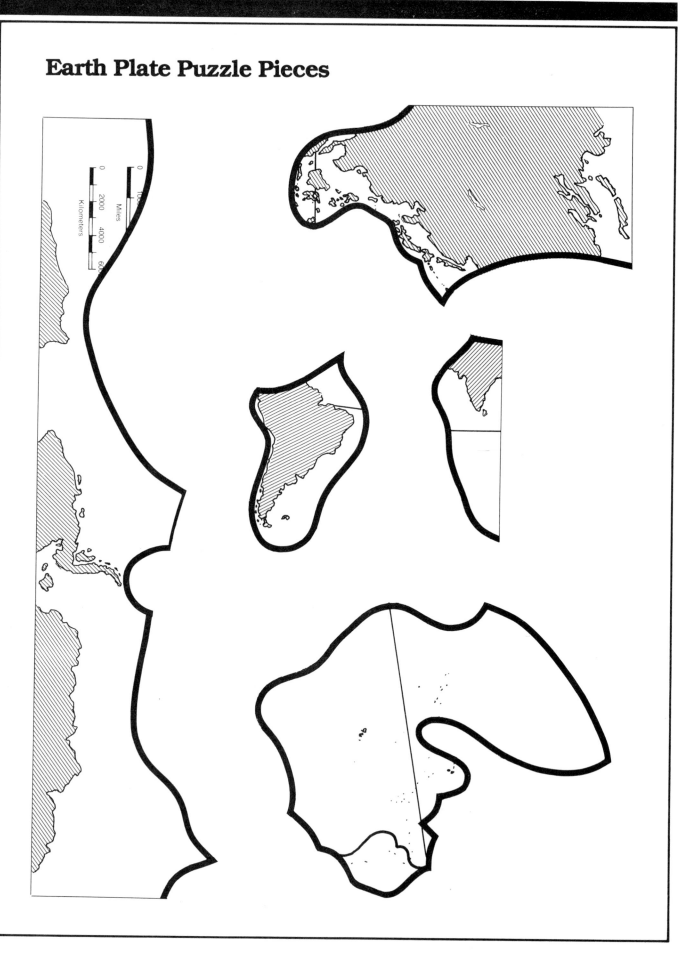

Earth Layers Worksheet

Name _____

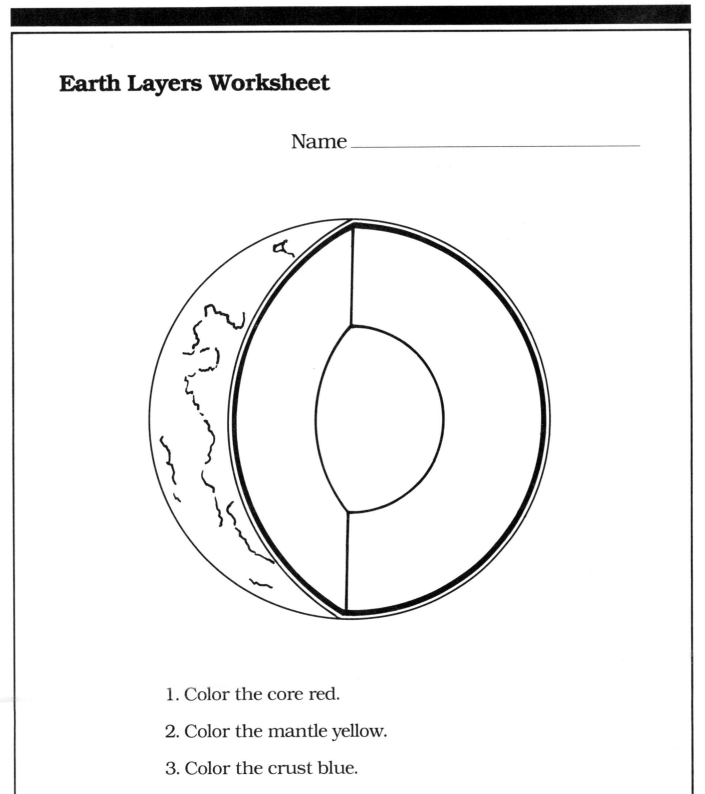

1. Color the core red.

2. Color the mantle yellow.

3. Color the crust blue.

4. Put a brown line around the very hot layer.

Earthquake Words

Name _____

1. Find these earthquake words and circle them.

sudden	earthquake	plates	mantle	core
crust	movement		layers	

D G T U I O E X C A C T N S T B I P L M T F Q W Z C

N C O R E F Y Q X R B K J D Y T Q X U L A Y E R S B

E A R T H Q U A K E C O L S Y I M A N T L E G L P X

D T S U D D E N K O Q Z E W C R U S T M O T H E R

R M O V E M E N T U P W O U H R C P L A T E S Y E

2. Write a sentence to tell about the Earth's parts.

_____

- -
_____
_____
- -
_____
_____
- -
_____
_____
- -
_____

A Pizza the Earth

Name _____

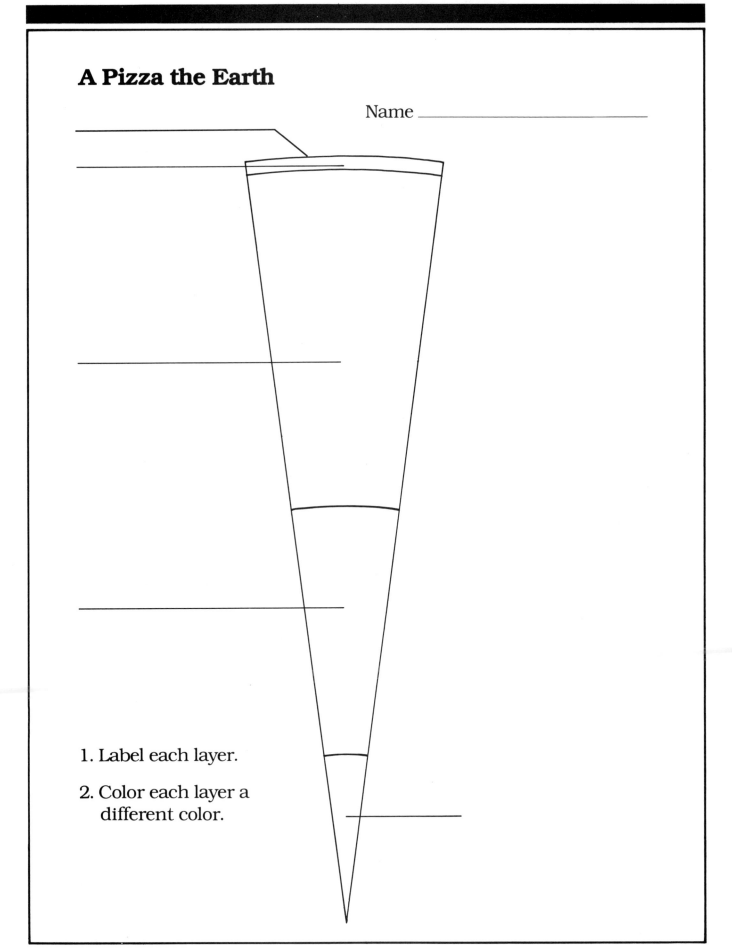

1. Label each layer.

2. Color each layer a
   different color.

Graph of the Earth's Layers

Name _____

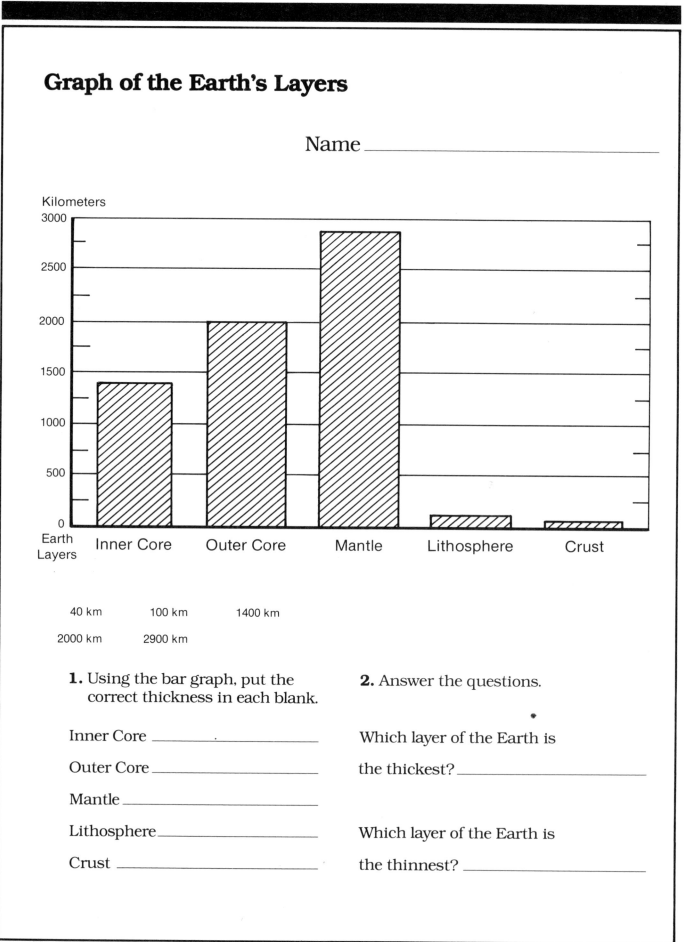

40 km   100 km   1400 km

2000 km   2900 km

1. Using the bar graph, put the correct thickness in each blank.

Inner Core _____

Outer Core _____

Mantle _____

Lithosphere _____

Crust _____

2. Answer the questions.

Which layer of the Earth is

the thickest? _____

Which layer of the Earth is

the thinnest? _____

Plate Boundaries Map

Name _____

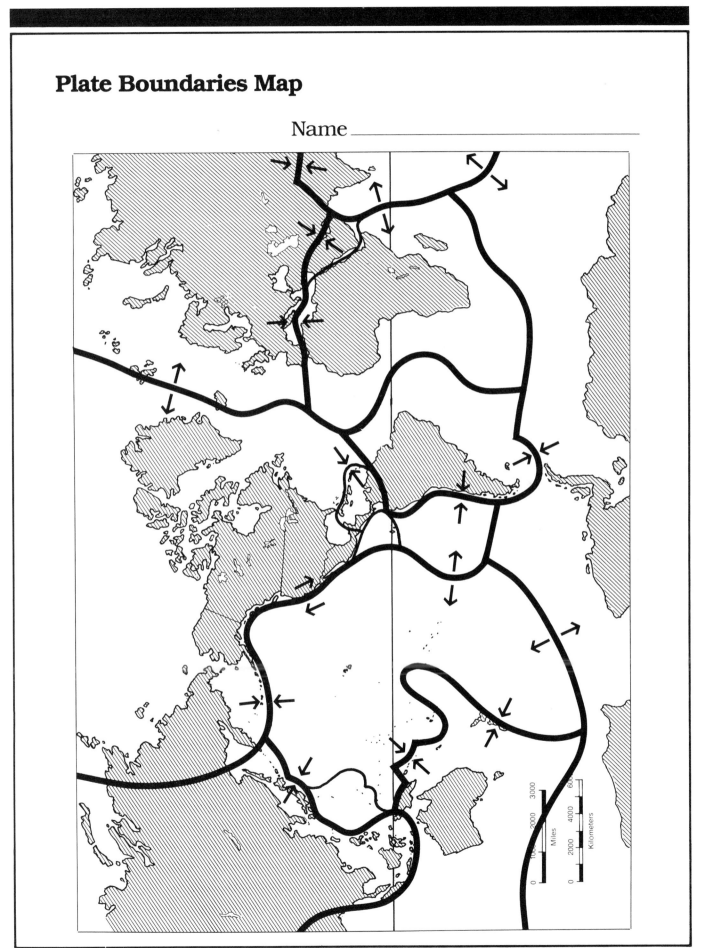

Convection Currents and Plate Cross Section

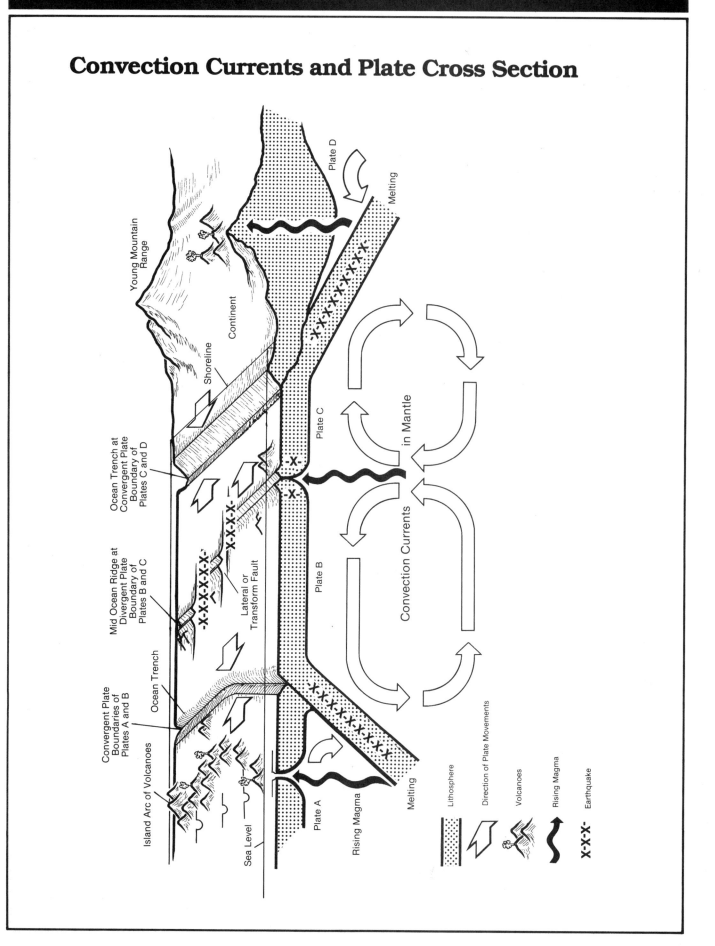

Formation and Breakup of Pangaea

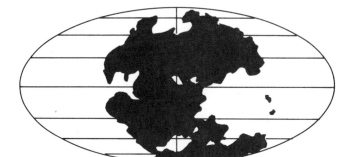

Earth's land masses about 200,000,000 years ago when there was one large land mass—Pangaea, or supercontinent.

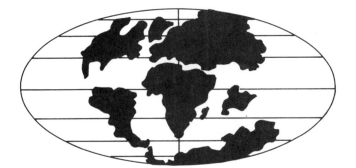

Earth's land masses about 65,000,000 years ago when the supercontinent broke up into smaller continents.

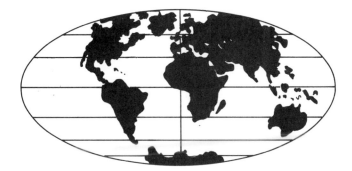

Earth's land masses today where India has collided with Eurasia. Eurasia continues to separate as the Atlantic Ocean widens.

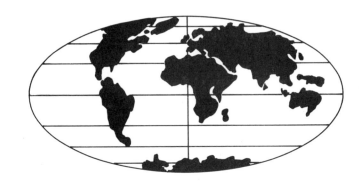

Earth's land masses about 50,000,000 years into the future.

Physical Results of Earthquakes

EARTHQUAKE CURRICULUM, K-6
SCOPE AND SEQUENCE CHART

Unit III: Physical Results of Earthquakes

Level	Concept	Laboratory	Mathematics	Language Arts	Social Studies	Art
K-2	Earthquakes cause changes in the Earth's surface.	Hand movement simulation of Earth plate motion Fault movement game Shoe box simulation of earthquake results	Math facts practice	Vocabulary development of earthquake words Vowel sounds	Features of a community Map making	Illustration of a community Model construction
3-4	Small-scale topographic changes are associated with plate movements. Earthquake activity causes small scale topographic changes.	Paper simulations of rock layers and models of faults Sand simulation of liquefaction Landslide simulation Cake simulations of fissures	Planes and angles recognition Measurement practice	Write-up of landslide activities Vocabulary development of earthquake words	Effects of faults, landslides, and fissures Geographic features locations	Fault model construction Slope model
5-6	Tectonic movements, including earthquakes, are among the major forces which create Earth's landscape. Mountains, plains, and plateaus are the major features of the continents. Many of the Earth's most significant landscape features are under the oceans.	Paper simulation of rock layer movement Mountain building simulation Ocean turbidity current simulation		Vocabulary development of earthquake words	Map study of plate boundaries	Shoreline model making

Physical Results of Earthquakes

Over billions of years, Earth motions and earthquakes have played a major part in shaping the physical features of our Earth, both on land and under water. Over time, small-scale changes make foothills and minor cracks; large-scale changes produce towering mountains and deep valleys. As the plates of the Earth's surface move, warping slowly up, down, and sideways in relation to each other, we may feel these movements as earthquakes. The waves of energy they release not only shake the Earth, but also alter the nature of many soils, giving them an unstable liquid-like consistency. Then structures sink, tip, and topple, and hillsides crumble.

Physical Results of Earthquakes

If there were no plate motions, our planet would not look like home. There would be no mountains, no valleys, and no plateaus. Without the uplifting of land caused by *tectonic* (mountain building) processes, most land above sea level would be a boringly flat surface, whittled down by the processes of erosion.

Earth-Shaking: Earth-Shaping

Earthquakes and other tectonic events have been occurring for as long as the Earth has existed. The changes in the landscape associated with these events range from small cracks in the soil to the raising *(uplifting)* or lowering *(downdropping)* of huge chunks (or *blocks*) of the lithosphere.

No large mountain or deep valley has been formed as the result of a single earth-shaking event. The raising and lowering of sections of the Earth generally happens gradually, in small increments. Over thousands and millions of years these increments may add up to significant changes, such as fault block mountains and deep graben valleys.

Faults and Folds

As a result of plate motions, the accumulated stress and strain within the rocks of the lithosphere may cause great warps or folds in rock layers. Where rock is strained beyond its limit, it will fracture, and the rock mass on either side will move abruptly.

Up, Down, or Sideways
A fault is a fracture within the Earth's crust along which significant movement has occurred. Faults are often classified according to the direction of movement and whether movement is predominantly horizontal or vertical.

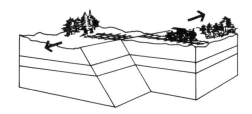
Horizontal Fault Movement

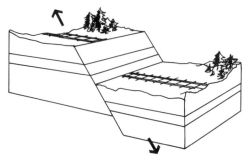
Vertical Fault Movement

Displacement of rock along a fault can occur as a result of vertical or horizontal fault movement. Vertical fault movement changes the elevation of a rock mass on one side of the fault relative to the rock mass on the opposite side. Rock masses on one side of the fault can also shift horizontally in relation to the opposite side. Fault movement is always stated in relative terms.

Vertical fault movement may result in cliffs along the fault line. Horizontal or lateral fault movement may cause roads and river banks to change their position. In the lessons that follow, students will use hand movements and paper models to illustrate these fault movements.

Folding Rock Layers

Folding is another way that rock layers respond to stress. They may crumple sideways, without fracturing, like wrinkles in a rug. We can see small folds in hand specimens of sedimentary rock; larger examples of folded rock layers can be seen in mountainsides and road cuts. Some mountain chains, such as the Alps or the Folded Appalachians, show primarily folded structures.

Soil Liquefaction

Although deep-down earthquake action takes place in the rocky lithosphere, much of the dollar damage that occurs in earthquakes results from the *liquefaction* of soil. When earthquake vibrations pass through soil which has a high liquid water content, the soil loses the properties of a solid and takes on those of a semi-liquid, like quicksand or pudding. The foundations of heavy buildings suddenly lose the support of the soil, and they may topple, or settle deeper into the Earth.

You have experienced liquefaction on a small scale if you have ever walked along the beach and seen water rise to the top of the sand at your every step. When liquefaction happens on a large scale, however, as it did at Niigata, Japan, in 1964, it spells disaster.

Why Land Slides

Earthquakes may trigger many landslides, particularly during the rainy season. The potential for landsliding is highest in soft sediments on steep slopes; where seasonal rainfall is high; where vegetation is shallow, rotted, or sparse; where erosion is high; and where ground shaking is intense.

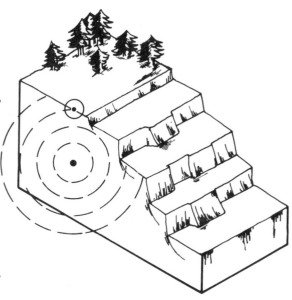

Underwater Earthquakes

It is difficult to adjust our focus wide enough, in both space and time, to recognize the geological events and structures that surround us on dry land. It is even more difficult to think about those events and structures when they occur underwater, where we cannot see them. Yet water covers about 70 percent of our planet, and the same tectonic forces are at work on the floors of the oceans as on the continents.

Although the same processes are at work, we need a new vocabulary to understand them. Mountain ranges in the ocean are called *mid-ocean ridges*; plains are called *abyssal plains*. Landslides occur as well, but we call them *turbidity currents*. The fourth activity for grades 5 and 6 gives students a chance to model this underwater event.

A Word to the Wise

If you can communicate the scope and magnitude of tectonic events to your students, and make them aware that earthquakes are something more than disasters on a human scale, you will have done a great deal. Enjoy these activities with them.

Earthquakes Shape Our Earth

Content Concept

Earthquakes cause changes in the Earth's surface.

Vocabulary

fault
rural

Objectives

Students will
—demonstrate three faulting actions.
—describe a rural community.
—draw a model of such a community.
—demonstrate the effects of earthquakes on the model community.

Learning Links

Language Arts: Discussing features of a rural community, describing results of earthquake simulations, matching vowel sound of *fault*

Social Studies: Extending the concept of community, completing a map

Art: Drawing a diagram of a community, constructing a model

Activity One: Earth Movers

Materials for the teacher
● Overhead projector
● World map or transparency of Master 13, Earth Plates
● Transparency of Master 22, Faulting Actions

Procedure

1. Review with the students the concepts that the Earth's surface is made up of plates, and that those plates have been shifting and moving over millions of years. Direct their attention to the map.

2. Explain that earthquake movement does not occur just at the edges of the plates, but also within the continents. Movements may happen at cracks in the Earth called *faults*. These movements are of two main kinds—up and down, and sideways.

3. Display Master 22 and point out the directions of the two movements. Demonstrate the types of faults with hand movements, and ask students to perform the movements along with you.

Up and down movements

(Down movement (Normal faulting). Make your hands into fists and press the flat edges of the fingers together. Release the pressure and let one hand drop about 4 cm. The straight fingers and knuckles of the other hand will resemble a fault cliff.

Up movement (Reverse faulting). Press knuckles and fingers tightly together as before. Without releasing the pressure, let one hand slide *up* about 4 cm. Again, the result will look like a cliff, but students should be able to see the difference in the two processes.

Sideways movement (Lateral, or transform faulting). Press the sides of the hands together. As you release the pressure, slide your two hands past each other in a jerky motion. You will feel the vibrations and see the horizontal displacement of the two sides which occurs in this type of faulting.

fault

A fault is a crack in rock or soil where movement has taken place.

ru • ral

A rural community is a farming community where people do not live close together as they do in cities.

Master 22, Fault Movements

Horizontal Fault Movement

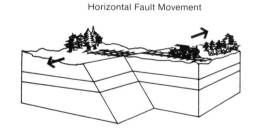

Illustrate lateral sideways movement by sliding one hand next to the other.

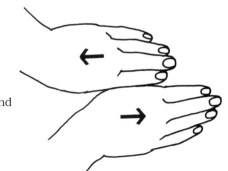

Vertical Fault Movement

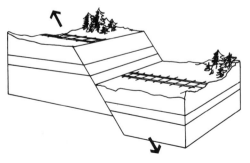

Illustrate up and down plate movement by raising and lowering fists in relation to each other.

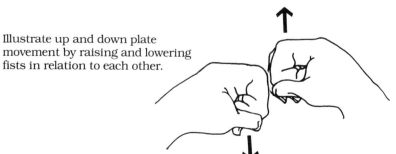

4. Divide the class into teams for a fault movement game. Teams take turns sending a member to demonstrate one of the fault movements to the other team. When a member of the other team identifies the movement and tells what it causes on the Earth's surface, the team scores a point. Play continues until every child has had a chance to demonstrate at least one of the movements.

Activity Two: Model Communities

Materials for the teacher
- Overhead projector
- Transparency made from Master 23, Rural Community after an Earthquake

Master 23, Rural Community After an Earthquake

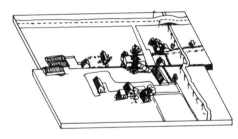

Materials for each pair of students
- Two empty shoe boxes or two ½-gal. milk cartons
- Pencils and felt markers or crayons
- Drawing paper
- Masking tape
- Copies of Master 24, Fault Model, and Master 25, Fault Worksheet
- Scissors

Procedure

1. Review faulting actions with students. Project Master 23, and ask students what they see. Discuss the effects of the earthquake on the rural community pictured.

2. Tell the class that they are going to draw a similar community. Ask them to name some physical features of a rural community, and list them on the overhead or on the blackboard. (Do not include people or animals.) Your list may look something like this:

long fences	stores
crops planted in rows	bridges
roads	trees
houses	utility poles and wires

3. Distribute sheets of paper, and ask students to work in pairs to plan their model communities. Ask them to fill the whole paper, and include some of the features they listed above. Encourage them to completely cover the paper with their drawing, placing houses or barns in the center of the page, and running fences and roads across it.

4. When planning is complete, distribute shoe boxes or milk cartons and masking tape. Have students tape the boxes together, then turn them upside down and tape their drawings on the bottoms of the joined boxes. Tell them that the place where the two boxes are joined represents a fault, and let them use their pencils to tear the paper in half along that line.

5. Direct students to turn the boxes over again and remove the masking tape that holds them together, without removing the pictures. Now they can use the boxes to simulate the two faulting actions that they have demonstrated with their hands: up and down faulting, and sideways faulting. Remind them that earthquakes result from a release of energy, and ask them to place pressure on the fault and release it rapidly each time they want to bring the boxes into a new position.

6. Ask students to observe and describe the changes to their community after each simulation.

7. Distribute student copies of Master 24, Fault Model, and Master 25, Fault Worksheet. Go over the fault worksheet with your students, then give them class time to work. Discuss the results.

Teacher Take Note: Shoeboxes are available in quantity from most shoe stores. A phone call should easily locate a supply. If you wish, you may use a large box from boots to design a demonstration model.

After children have lightly taped shoeboxes together, they can turn them over and firmly tape their rural community drawing to the bottom.

Extension

Use worksheets made from Master 26, Earthquake Math Facts, for practice in doing math facts and spelling *earthquake.*

Landscape on the Loose

Content Concepts

1. Small-scale topographic changes are associated with plate movements.

2. Earthquake activity causes small-scale topographic changes.

Vocabulary

normal fault
reverse fault
lateral (or transform) fault
Appalachian mountains
fault plane
fold
groundwater
landscape
steepness
landslide
liquefaction
fissure

Objectives

Students will

—understand that many landscape features are a result of earthquake activity.

—construct models of three types of faults, and be able to name and identify them.

—demonstrate the formation of folded rock.

—demonstrate liquefaction, and describe how it happens.

—demonstrate a landslide and describe some factors that influence the results of landslides triggered by earthquakes.

—observe the formation of fissures.

Learning Links

Language Arts: Labeling types of faults, following oral instructions, writing paragraphs

Social Studies: Locating geographic features, discussing how faults, landslides, and fissures affect people's lives and property

Math: Measuring materials for liquefaction demonstration

Art: Making fault models, constructing landslide models

Activity One: Up, Down, and Sideways

Materials for the teacher
• Overhead projector
• U.S. map or transparency made from Master 28a, Landscape Regions of the U.S.
• Master 28c, Landscape Regions Key

Materials for each student
- Worksheet made from Master 27, Fault Planes
- Scissors
- Colored pencils or crayons
- Unlined paper
- Paper clip

Optional: Light cardboard or heavy construction paper and glue stick

Procedure

1. Distribute worksheets with fault diagrams. Tell students that they are going to make models to illustrate the three basic types of faults, beginning with Diagram A on the worksheet.

2. Explain that horizontal spaces A–D represent different rock layers below the surface, as we might see them exposed on the side of a cliff. Instruct students to color each layer a different color.

3. Instruct students to cut out the diagram along the bold outside lines, and then cut carefully along the diagonal dashed line labeled Fault Plane. Have them hold one piece in each hand, with the cut edges together, so that the pieces form a perfect rectangle.

4. Now ask students to move the right-hand side of the model down until the two Xs are side by side. Explain that they have just demonstrated a normal, or gravity fault. Ask:

What is the position of Rock Layer D on the top left of the model? (pointing away from the fault plane)

What do you see on the left-hand side of the fault plane? (Rock layer D now forms a steep cliff.)

Teacher Take Note: To make these models more durable, you may want to either print the worksheets on heavy paper or have students glue them to a piece of light cardboard before coloring and cutting.

Master 27, Fault Planes

Diagram A

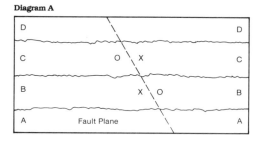

Diagram B

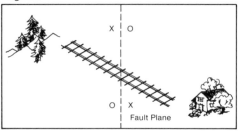

fault   plane

A fault plane is a surface along which faulting movement has occurred.

fis • sure

A fissure is an open crack in the ground.

liq • ue • fac • tion

Liquefaction is the process in which soil or sand suddenly loses the properties of solid material and instead behaves like a liquid.

5. Ask students to return the model to its original position, and then to move the right side up until the two Os are side by side. Explain that this demonstrates a reverse, or thrust fault. Ask:

What is the position of Rock Layer D on the top right of the model? (pointing toward the fault plane)

What do you think will happen to the rock and soil hanging over the fault plane, above Rock Layer D on the left-hand side? (The rock and soil will eventually collapse because of the pull of gravity.)

6. Now ask students to look at Diagram B on the worksheet. Explain that this is the view they would have from an airplane flying over the Earth's surface. Give the following directions:

a. Cut out the diagram along the outside bold lines, then cut carefully along the dashed line in the center labeled Fault Plane.

b. Put the model flat on your table or desk. Hold it together, with one side in each hand, so the two sides form a perfect rectangle. Keeping the left side still, move the right side until the two Xs are aligned along the edge of the fault plane. Now reverse the procedure, lining up the two Os. Ask these questions:

What kind of movement occurred along the fault? (sideways, as in a lateral or transform fault)

Do you know of a place where this kind of movement occurs, causing earthquakes? (the San Andreas Fault)

If you saw pictures of an area where an earthquake had just occurred, how would you recognize lateral faulting? (Fences, roads, crop rows, orchards, and railroad tracks would all be offset. Sometimes streams are offset also, and flow at right angles along the fault plane.)

7. Explain that sometimes, when rock layers are exposed to pressure, they do not break or fault, but fold instead. Give these directions for a simple model of folding activity.

a. Have students cut a narrow strip (about 7 cm) from a standard sheet of paper.

b. Place it on top of a hardcover book, along the front edge. Hold it in place at the center with a paper clip.

c. Slowly push the paper from both sides toward the center. Notice the hills and valleys that form as it folds.

8. Point out the Appalachian Mountains on a United States map or Master 28a, and explain that parts of the Appalachians and other U.S. mountains were formed by the folding of rock layers.

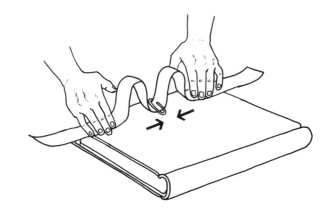

Push the paper slowly from both sides toward the middle.

Activity Two: Liquefaction Lab

Materials for each small group
- Newspapers to cover work surfaces
- About 300 mL (1 1/4 cup) of medium- to fine-grained sand
- About 100 mL (1/3-1/2 cup) of water
- 1-lb size plastic margarine tub
- Measuring cup or beaker marked in metric units

Teacher Take Note: Since sands vary greatly in their absorbency, you'll want to experiment with these proportions before you present the activity to your students.

Liquefaction of soil can cause buildings to slump, and sometimes to collapse entirely.

Procedure

Introduce the activity by telling students that liquefaction accounts for considerable damage to property. Define the term. Tell students that they have experienced it if they have ever felt a foot sink into a patch of extremely muddy ground. Give these instructions for the simulation:

a. Place about three fourths of the sand in the bottom of your bowl. Spread it out to form a flat, even surface. This represents soil in an earthquake zone.

b. Slowly sprinkle about half the water over the surface of the sand. This will represent precipitation.

c. Wait about a minute for the mixture to settle. Carefully add more sand if there is any standing water. The surface of the sand should be firm to the touch.

d. Sprinkle a small amount of sand over the top to form a dry surface layer. Press gently with three fingers to test for firmness, and add more sand if necessary.

e. Slide the bottom of the bowl rapidly back and forth on your desk until you see water coming up to the surface. (Explain that the shaking simulates earthquake waves traveling through the ground.) Now press your fingers into the sand.

What happened? (They should sink easily, because the waves of energy you produced have caused water to move up and liquefy the sand.)

What would happen to buildings on top of the soil that was liquefied? (They would topple over or sink into the soil.)

Activity Three: A Slippery Slope

Materials for each small group
- Newspapers to cover work surface
- Large tray (Ask your grocer for a supply of large plastic foam meat trays.)
- Local soils of various textures, or potting soil
- Builders sand
- Fine gravel
- Aluminum foil
- Water

Procedure

1. Tell your students that they are going to make a model of a landslide, following these steps:

a. Cover your work surface with several layers of newspapers. In the meat tray, build a hill from moistened sand or soil. It may be any height or shape you choose. You may want to make one side steeper than the other.

b. Wrap a sheet of foil around your hill to simulate the slippery layer of rock or soil that allows outer layers to slide off during an earthquake.

c. Completely cover the foil with another layer of sand, soil, or gravel.

d. Predict the effect of an earthquake on your own model and those of your classmates.

Which hills will receive the most severe damage?

Which will receive the least?

Which parts of each hill will be most affected by an earthquake?

e. Hold the tray on which your hill rests with both hands, and slide it back and forth sharply on your desk or work surface to simulate an earthquake.

2. After all the groups have produced their landslides, observed other groups' results, and finished cleanup, conduct a class discussion including these questions:

How did the shape of the hill affect the landslide? (In most cases, the steeper the slope, the more easily the material will slide down.)

How did the type of material above the foil affect the landslide? (Various answers are possible.)

What would have happened if you had used less water in your soil mixture? What if you had used more? (Landslides are more likely when the surface is waterlogged.)

How should the potential of a site for landslides caused by earthquakes affect decisions on locating homes and other structures on or under it? (Such a site would make a poor choice unless it can be reinforced in some way.)

What are some events other than earthquakes that can cause landslides? (heavy rains, freezing and thawing of the ground, erosion)

3. Have each small group write a report describing how they made their hill, what they observed during the landslide, and how their simulation compared to others in the class.

Teacher Take Note: There is bound to be some mess with this procedure, but you can keep it to a minimum by limiting the amount of soil, water, and time that you provide. Do some hill building of your own before class, to get the feel of the activity.

Extensions

Show pictures of famous landslides caused by earthquakes, such as those that happened at Hebgen Lake in Montana, and in Alaska during the 1964 earthquake. Invite students to research and present reports on these or other landslide events.

Activity Four: Earthquake Cake

Materials for the teacher
- Inexpensive packaged cake mix
- Eggs, water, other ingredients in package directions
- Aluminum foil cake pan

Procedure

1. Prepare the cake at home according to package directions; cool, cover, and bring to school.

2. Conduct a class discussion about fissures. Explain that during earthquakes, the surface of the Earth sometimes develops cracks which scientists call *fissures*. These cracks develop near the epicenter of an earthquake. The energy released by the earthquake travels through the lithosphere to the surface in waves. As the energy travels through the ground, the ground moves, and sometimes cracks.

3. Pick up the cake pan and bend the bottom back and forth several times to simulate earthquake waves. You may want to call the spot where you place your thumbs the *focus* of the cake-quake. (See Unit I, vocabulary for grades 5 and 6.)

4. Let students observe the result and tell you what they see. Point out that the cracks will not close, but will stay open unless disturbed. Ask the class:

> Would earthquake fissures stay open like this, or would they close again immediately? (There is a common misconception that earthquake fissures open and close, swallowing people, animals, and buildings. There is no scientific record of any earthquake fissure ever doing this.)

> When would an earthquake fissure close? (It would stay open until weathering and erosion gradually filled it in.)

5. Share samples of cake, and tell students that they will be learning how to deal with actual earthquake hazards in future classes.

Building Up and Breaking Down

Content Concepts

1. The major landscape features we see on the continents are mountains, plains, and plateaus.

2. Tectonic movements, including earthquakes, are among the forces which create Earth's landscapes.

3. Many of the Earth's most significant landscape features are under the oceans.

Vocabulary

mountain
plain
plateau
continental slope
abyssal plain
underwater delta
turbidity current

Objectives

Students will

—describe three major landscape features: mountains, plains, and plateaus.

—identify mountains, plains, and plateaus on a landscape map.

—construct models of various types of mountains and relate those models to specific places in the United States.

—identify, from observing illustrations of the Earth's surface features, which of them were created by earthquakes.

—identify abyssal plains and underwater deltas, and model their formation.

Learning Links

Social Studies: Identifying landscape regions of the United States and identifying ocean bottom features

Art: Constructing model of ocean floor activity and shoreline

moun • tain

A mountain is a portion of the landscape that is usually higher than surrounding areas and has steep slopes with faulted, folded, or tilted rocks.

plain

A plain is an area of horizontal rocks that is generally lower than surrounding regions.

plat • eau

A plateau is an area of horizontal rocks that is higher than surrounding areas and usually has some areas of steep slopes.

Activity One: Mountain, Plain, and Plateau

Materials for the teacher
- Transparency made from Master 28a, Landscape Regions
- Master 28b and 28c for reference
- Overhead projector
- A variety of scenic photographs showing major Earth features—mountains, plains, plateaus, and oceans

Materials for each student
- Crayons or colored pencils
- Class notebook
- Handout made from Master 28a, Landscape Regions Worksheet
- Handout made from Master 1, U.S. Map without Labels

Procedure

1. Explain that landscape features related to earthquakes range from major features like mountains, plains, and plateaus to smaller features like cliffs and valleys, and very small features like crushed and scratched rock along faults. This unit deals with the major features.

2. Have class members suggest some examples of mountains, plains, and plateaus in the world, the United States, and their own locality.

3. Distribute copies of Master 28a, Landscape Regions Worksheet. Project the transparency of the same master. Ask students to use a purple pencil or crayon to color in every region on their worksheets that has a 1. These are the mountain regions. Ask them to color the areas with 2s, the plains regions, in green; and the 3s, the plateau regions, in brown.

4. Project Master 1, U.S. Map, the landscape map. Help students locate their own state and the two or three neighboring states and label them either on the map itself or at the sides. Ask the class:

What kind of landscape region do you live in?

Where is the mountain landscape region nearest to your area?

Where is the nearest plains region? What about plateaus?

5. Allow students to discuss their answers until they arrive at a consensus.

Master 28a. Landscape Regions Worksheet

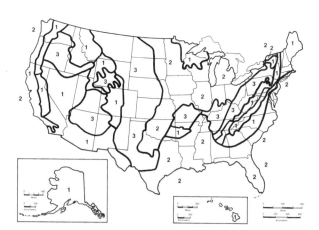

From Master 21, Formation and
Breakup of the Pangaea

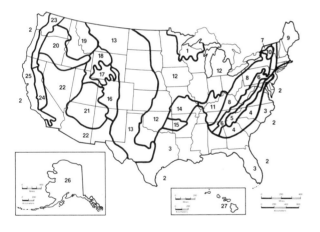

Master 28b. Landscape Regions of
the U.S. See Master 28c for a
complete list of the regions
numbered. The four mentioned in
the text include (6) Folded
Appalachians, (15) Ouachita
Mountains, (22) Basin and Range
Region, and (24) Sierra Nevadas.

Activity Two:
The Folding Mountains Mystery

Materials for the teacher
- Transparency made from Master 28b, Landscape Regions of the U.S.
- Transparency made from Master 19, Plate Boundaries Map
- Transparency made from Master 21, Formation and Break-up of Pangaea
- Overhead Projector
- A Classroom map of U.S.

Materials for each student or small group
- Three to five half-sheets of colored construction paper, cut lengthwise

Procedure

1. On a classroom map of the United States, and on Master 28b, locate the Folded Appalachians, the Ouachita Mountains, the Sierra Nevada Mountains, and the Basin and Range regions of the United States. Explain that each of these regions has been molded by earthquakes or activity associated with earthquakes.

2. Tell students that the Folded Appalachians and the Ouachita Mountains were formed largely by a process called folding. Distribute colored paper so that each student or group has several half-sheets of different colors. Explain that the colors will represent rock layers of the lithosphere in the simulation they are about to do. Give these directions:

a. Stack the sheets of paper, then pick up the stack by its two ends.

b. Making sure the sheets of paper stay together, push them toward the center from both sides.

What happened? (The paper folded into several ridges.)

If the sheets of paper were layers of rock, what would provide the push to fold them? (the pressure of earthquake movements and convergent plate movements, or the squeezing of rock layers from opposite sides)

3. Project Master 19, the plate boundaries map, and ask: Do you see evidence of plates converging anywhere near either the Folded Appalachians or the Quachitas? Challenge students:

How could these layers have been folded? (Do not provide any answer yet.)

4. After some discussion, project Master 21, The Formation and Breakup of Pangaea, and let students observe that plate boundaries were converging in those places hundreds of millions of years ago, when these old mountains were formed.

Activity Three: Mountain Modeling

Materials for each student or pair of students
- Dull table knife or scissors
- Rectangular block of plastic foam or furniture foam, at least 10 cm long and wide and 5 cm thick
- Newspapers to cover desks or work surfaces

Teacher Take Note: This procedure can be done with any of several kinds of material, but you'll want to experiment with whatever you select. You'll see what kind of cutting tool works best and know what to expect when you do the activity with your class.

Procedure

1. Distribute materials. Tell students that they are going to model another type of mountain building which formed the Sierra Nevadas and the Basin and Range areas of the United States. Give these directions:

a. Cut a wedge-shaped section out of the middle of the block, lift it out, and then replace it in its original position.

b. Hold the sides of the block in two hands and pull them apart slightly, allowing the inner wedge to drop.

Examples of mountain building action

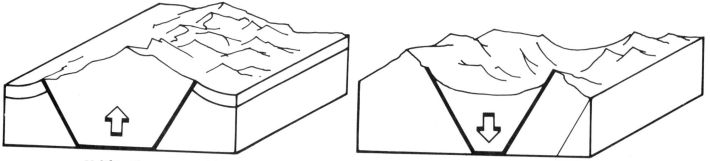

Uplifting (or upwarping) may be caused by convergence.

Downdropping may be caused by convergence or divergence.

What do the tops of the two cut surfaces represent? (faults)

What do the slopes along which the wedge slipped represent? (fault cliffs)

What could cause something like this to happen to the Earth's lithosphere? (There are several possible answers. An earthquake could cause two portions of the lithosphere to separate. Plates could be diverging. Convergence could also cause this kind of movement, however, and is a likely explanation in the case of the Sierra Nevadas and the Basin and Range mountains.)

2. Ask students to put the wedge back in its original position to prepare for another simulation. Direct them to hold the three sections together with their two hands and push on the outsides, causing the wedge to move up. Ask:

What could happen in the lithosphere to cause this kind of movement? (compression resulting from the convergence of plates or convergence due to fault movement)

How could a small movement like this result in mountains thousands of meters high? (Mountains would be formed by a series of earthquakes, or many series over many thousands of years.)

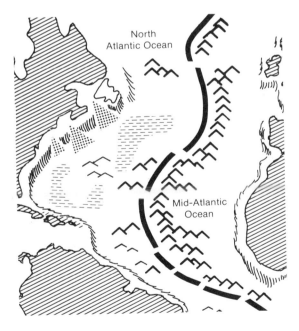

Activity Four: Underwater Avalanche

Materials for the teacher
- Transparency made from Master 29, Ocean Bottom
- Overhead projector

Materials for each small group
- A trough 50 cm to one meter long (This could be a section of PVC rain gutter or a shipping tube cut and lined with plastic. Halves of quart milk cartons would also work.)
- 2 L container filled with water
- Trough supports (blocks of wood or old books)
- Sandy soil or mixture of sand and dry pottery clay (kaolin) to simulate sediment
- Plastic shoe box or baking pan to hold water and sediment
- Corrugated cardboard strips with the grooves exposed (Tear off the outer layer of paper.)
- Tape

Procedure

1. Project the transparency of the ocean bottom, Master 29. Orient students by pointing out the eastern United States, the Mid-Atlantic Ridge in the Atlantic Ocean, and the abyssal areas in the underwater delta. Inform students that the abyssal areas are one of the largest landscape features of the Earth. Ask the class why they suppose there are such extensive flat areas on the ocean bottoms, and why the underwater deltas exist. Also ask why the deltas and abyssal areas are located where they are. (Accept various answers for now.)

2. Point out the angled underwater landscape of the continental slope and the rough topography near the mid-ocean ridge. Explain that earthquakes under the continental slopes can cause sediment on the ocean bottom to loosen, mix with water, and slide down the slope at speeds up to 100 km an hour. We call this movement a turbidity current.

3. Tell the class that they are going to build a model to demonstrate turbidity currents and their effects on the features of the ocean bottom. Give these directions:

a. Set up the trough, making sure it can hold water.

b. Place one end of the trough so that it overhangs the collecting pan.

c. Prop up the high end with books or blocks of wood, so that there is about a 10- to 20-degree slope to the trough, representing the topography of the ocean slope.

d. Place some corrugated cardboard in the collecting pan and tape it in place. If necessary, hold the cardboard in place during the next steps. It represents the rough landscape east of the abyssal areas on the ocean bottom.

e. Cover the bottom of the trough with soil or sand and clay.

f. Slowly and continously pour water into the upper end of the trough. While one student is pouring, another will shake the trough.

a • bys • sal   plain

An abyssal plain is a plain under the ocean between a continent and a mid-ocean ridge.

tur • bid • i • ty cur • rent

A turbidity current is a downward flow of water and sediments, such as mud or sand, along the ocean bottom. These swirling currents may be caused by earthquakes.

2-liter bottle filled with water for pouring

Trough one meter long

Shake the collecting pan to hold sand and water in suspension.

Corrugated cardboard

Sediment forms over the corrugated ribs of cardboard as sand settles out of the sand and water mixture.

4. Have students create different kinds of turbidity currents by repeating steps e–f above, possibly pouring at different speeds and shaking with different intensities. Ask:

What does the shaking of the trough represent? (an earthquake)

What has happened to the rough surface (corrugated cardboard) of the ocean bottom? (It has become smoother because sediments have filled it in.)

What has been produced? (An abyssal plain is produced by the deposition of sediment from the turbidity current.)

What has been formed where the trough overhangs the collecting pan? (An underwater delta has been formed. If students don't know what a delta is on land—an area where sediments are deposited at the mouth of a river—explain and give examples—the Nile Delta, the Mississippi Delta.)

5. To sum up, project the transparency of the ocean bottom again and reinforce the meaning and origin of abyssal plains and underwater deltas, and how they are produced (at least in part) by turbidity currents generated by earthquakes.

Extensions

1. Use a stopwatch to calculate the speed of the turbidity currents.

2. Tie string across the trough to represent underwater communication cables, then observe and record what happens to these model cables in a turbidity current.

3. Show some other diagrams or maps of ocean bottoms, and discuss several other features and how their origin is related to earthquakes. (Other ocean features related to earthquakes include ocean trenches, rift valleys, mid-ocean ridges, island arcs, lava flows, and volcanoes of the mid-ocean ridges.)

Unit III. Physical Results of Earthquakes

Materials List

Grades K-2
empty shoe box
colored pencils
markers
crayons
drawing paper
masking tape
overhead projector
scissors

Grades 3-4
scissors
colored pencils
unlined paper
paper clips
light cardboard
glue stick
metric measuring
   cup/beaker
small plastic tub
sand
newspapers
foam tray
soil
overhead projector
gravel
aluminum foil
cake mix
cake ingredients
13 x 9 foil cake pan

Grades 5-6
scenic photographs
crayons
colored pencils
construction paper
2-liter soda bottle
foam block
furniture foam
newspapers
permanent markers
PVC rain gutter, shipping
   tube, or milk carton
plastic shoe box
blocks of wood
sandy soil, or sand, or clay
   (kaolin)
corrugated cardboard
dull table knife or scissors
overhead projector
notebook
tape

Instructional Resources (Books, maps, pamphlets, slides)

Cazeau, C. J. (1977, February). Earthquake. *Instructor*, 86, pp. 76-82.

Duschl, R. S. (1987, September/October). Causes of Earthquakes: An Inquiry into the Plausibility of Competing Explanations. *Science Activities*, 24, pp. 3, 8-14.

Fradin, D. B. (1982). *Disaster! Earthquakes*. Chicago: Children's Press.

Lauber, P. (1972). *Earthquakes*. New York: Random House, Inc.

Rueter, M. (1977). *Earthquakes: Our Restless Planet*. Milwaukee, Wisconsin: Raintree Publishers, Ltd.

Walker, B., and others. (1982). *Planet Earth Earthquake*. Alexandria, Virginia: Time-Life Books. pp. 140-147.

Teacher packets containing leaflets and reference list: (free)

Geologic Inquiries Group, United States Geological Survey, 907 National Center, Reston, VA 22092.

35-mm slide sets: (Request current prices.)

National Geophysical Data Center; NOAA, Code E/GC4, Dept. F11; 325 Broadway; Boulder, Colorado 80303.

Available sets include

- Earthquake Damage Slide Set
- New Earthquake Damage Slide Set for San Francisco, California, April 18, 1906
- Earthquake Damage, San Francisco, California, April 18, 1906
- Earthquake Damage to Transportation Systems
- Earthquake Damage, Mexico City, Mexico, September 1985
- Earthquake Damage General
- Earthquake Damage to Schools
- Tsunami General

Poster of world epicenters:
Earth's Dynamic Crust. (1985, August). Washington, DC: National Geographic Society.

References

Alaska's Good Friday Earthquake, March 27, 1964. Reston, Virginia: United States Geological Survey. Circular 491.

Bolt, B.A. (1988). *Earthquakes.* San Francisco: W.H. Freeman and Co.

Brownlee, S. (1986, July). Waiting for the big one. *Discover,* 7, pp. 52-71.

Earthquake Country: A Teachers Workshop. (1978, February 25-26). Far Western Section of National Association of Geology Teachers and California Science Teachers Association.

Earthquakes: A National Problem. Washington, DC: Federal Emergency Management Agency.

Iacopi, R. How, Why and Where Earthquakes Strike in California. *Earthquake Country,* pp. 42-154.

Gere, J., and H. Shan. (1984). *Terra Non Firma: Understanding and Preparing for Earthquakes.* New York: W.H. Freeman and Co.

Muir, R. (1987). *Earthquakes and Volcanoes: Causes, Effects, and Predictions.* New York: Weidenfeld and Nicolson.

National Oceanic and Atmospheric Administration. (1976). *Catalog of Earthquake Photographs—Key to Geophysical Records,* Documentation No. 7. Boulder, Colorado: National Geophysical Data Center.

Press, F., and R. Siever. (1986). *Earth.* New York: W.H. Freeman and Co. 4th edition.

Schnell, M. L., ed. (1984). *National Earthquake Hazards Reduction Program: Overview Report to The United States Congress.* Reston, Virginia: United States Geological Survey. Circular 918.

Tarbuck, E.J., and F.K. Lutgens. (1987). *The Earth: An Introduction to Physical Geology,* 2nd ed. Columbus, Ohio: Merrill Publishing Co.

Van Rose, S. (1986). *Earthquakes.* New Rochelle, New York: Cambridge University Press.

Fault Movements

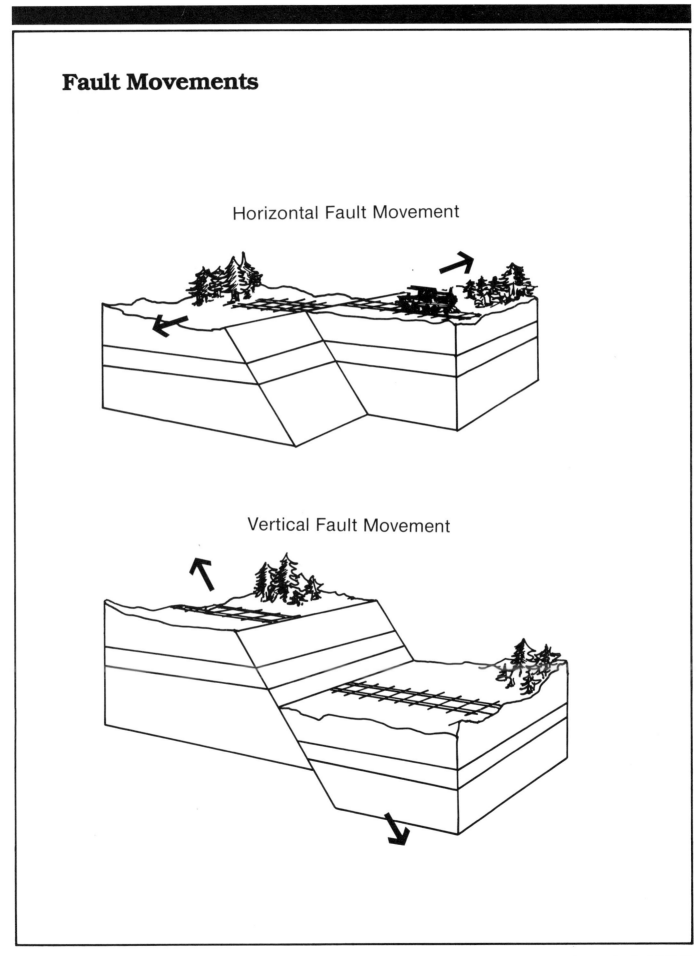

Horizontal Fault Movement

Vertical Fault Movement

Rural Community After an Earthquake

Name

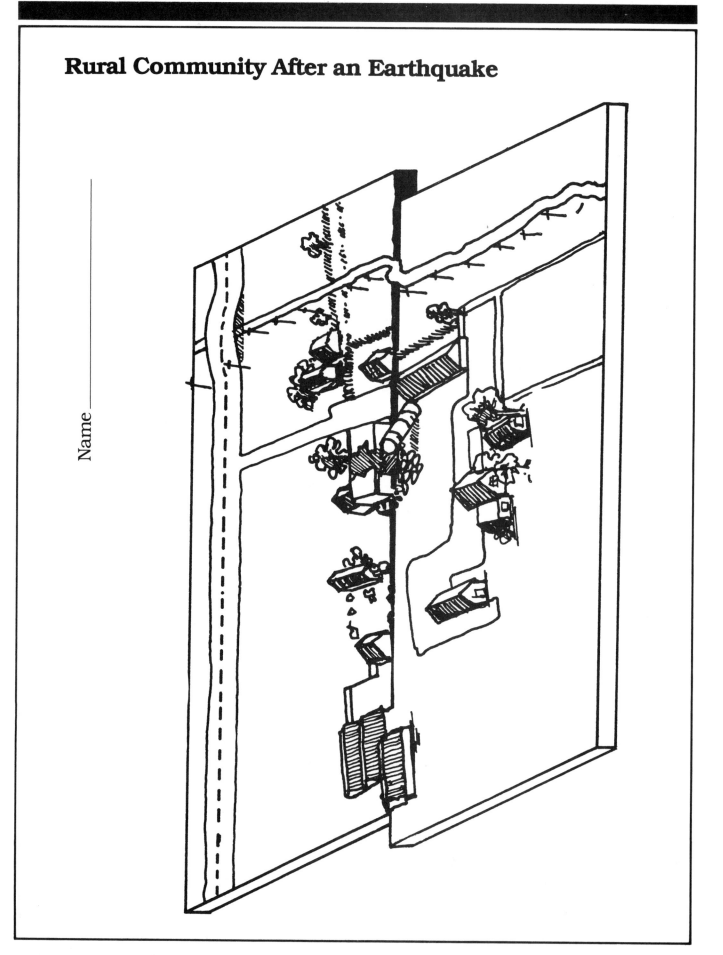

Fault Model

Name _____

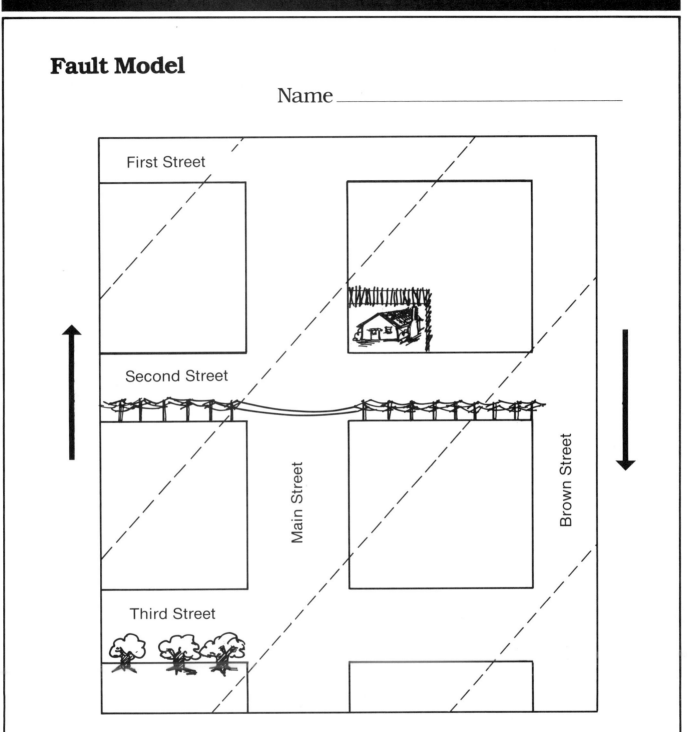

This is a map of a town.

1. Make more houses, trees, poles, and fences on the map.

2. Cut into five pieces on the dotted lines.

3. Put your pieces of paper on your desk and slowly slide them beside each other to see what can happen during an earthquake.

Fault Worksheet Name _____

fault

Here are some words with the same vowel sound as fault. Write the word under the picture.

caught   taught   haul   laundry   faucet   daughter

Earthquake Math Facts

Name _____

1. Do the problems. Watch the signs.

$\begin{array}{r} 9 \\ -5 \\ \hline 4 \end{array}$ = E	$\begin{array}{r} 3 \\ +4 \\ \hline \end{array}$ = T	$\begin{array}{r} 6 \\ -1 \\ \hline \end{array}$ = R	$\begin{array}{r} 5 \\ +1 \\ \hline \end{array}$ = K
$\begin{array}{r} 9 \\ -7 \\ \hline \end{array}$ = Q	$\begin{array}{r} 3 \\ +5 \\ \hline \end{array}$ = A	$\begin{array}{r} 5 \\ -1 \\ \hline \end{array}$ = E	$\begin{array}{r} 8 \\ -5 \\ \hline \end{array}$ = U
	$\begin{array}{r} 4 \\ -3 \\ \hline \end{array}$ = H	$\begin{array}{r} 6 \\ +2 \\ \hline \end{array}$ = A	

2. What is the big word that means the sudden shaking of the earth?

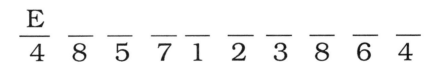

$$\frac{E}{4} \quad \frac{}{8} \quad \frac{}{5} \quad \frac{}{7} \quad \frac{}{1} \quad \frac{}{2} \quad \frac{}{3} \quad \frac{}{8} \quad \frac{}{6} \quad \frac{}{4}$$

Fault Planes

Name _____

Diagram A

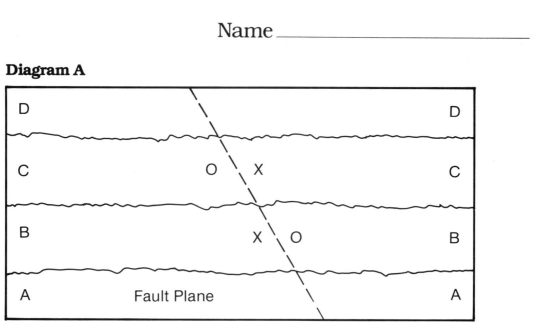

D		D
C	O X	C
B	X O	B
A	Fault Plane	A

1. Color each layer, A-D, in a different color.

2. Cut out diagram first on solid lines, then cut on dashed line.

Diagram B

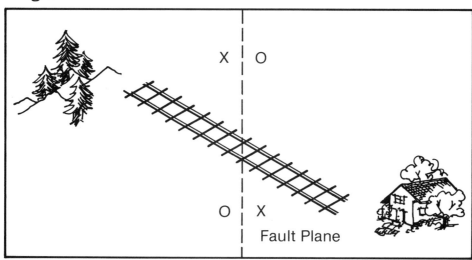

1. Color the surface features.

2. Cut out diagram on solid lines, then cut on dashed line.

Landscape Regions Worksheet

Name _____

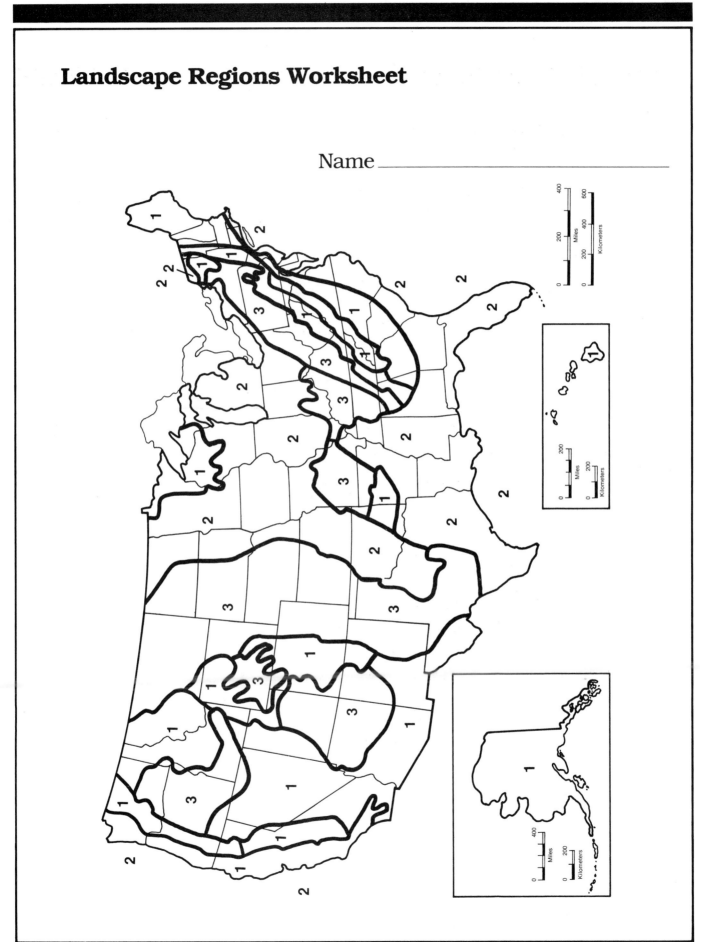

Landscape Regions of U.S.

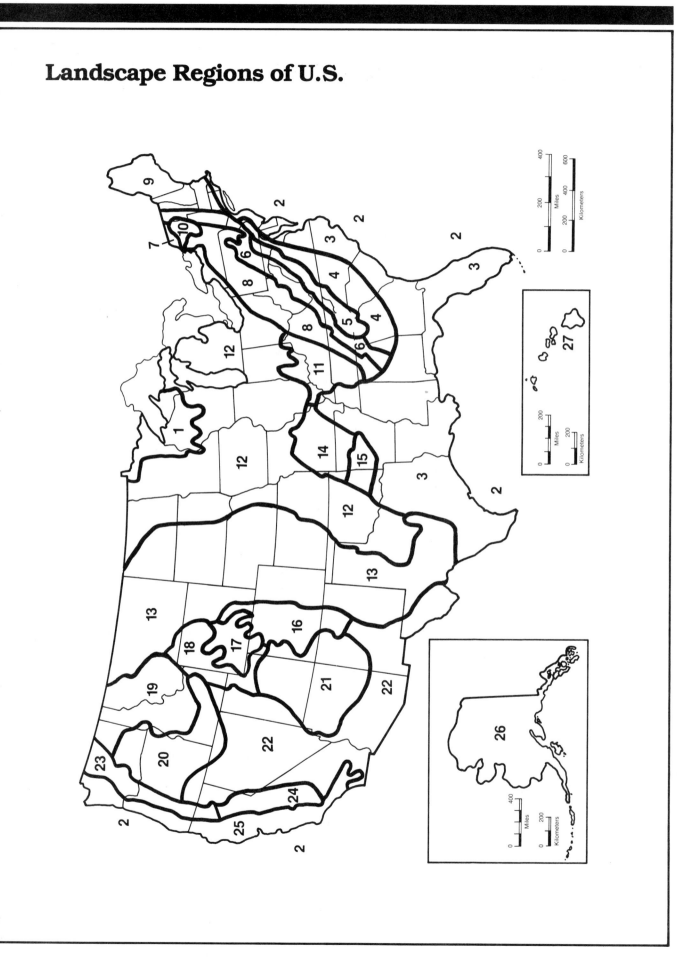

Landscape Regions Key

1. Superior Uplands-mountains **(1)**
2. Continental Shelf-plains **(2)**
3. Coastal Plain-plain **(2)**
4. Appalachian Piedmont-mountains **(1)**
5. Blue Ridge Appalachians-mountains **(1)**
6. Folded Appalachians-mountains [folded] **(1)**
7. St. Lawrence Valley-plain **(2)**
8. Appalachian Plateaus-plateau **(3)**
9. New England Uplands-mountains **(1)**
10. Adirondack Mountains-mountains **(1)**
11. Interior Low Plateaus-plateau **(3)**
12. Central Lowlands-plain **(2)**
13. Great "Plains"-plateau **(3)**
14. Ozark Plateau-plateau **(3)**
15. Ouachita Mountains-mountains [folded] **(1)**
16. Southern Rocky Mountains-mountains **(1)**
17. Wyoming Basin-plateau **(3)**
18. Middle Rocky Mountains-mountains **(1)**
19. Northern Rocky Mountains-mountains **(1)**
20. Columbia Plateau-plateau **(3)**
21. Colorado Plateau-plateau **(3)**
22. Basin and Range-mountains [fault block] **(1)**
23. Cascade Mountains-mountains **(1)**
24. Sierra Nevada Mountains-mountains **(1)**
25. Pacific Coastal Ranges-mountains **(1)**
26. Alaska (mostly mountains)-mountains **(1)**
27. Hawaii (composed of volcanoes)-mountains **(1)**

Ocean Bottom

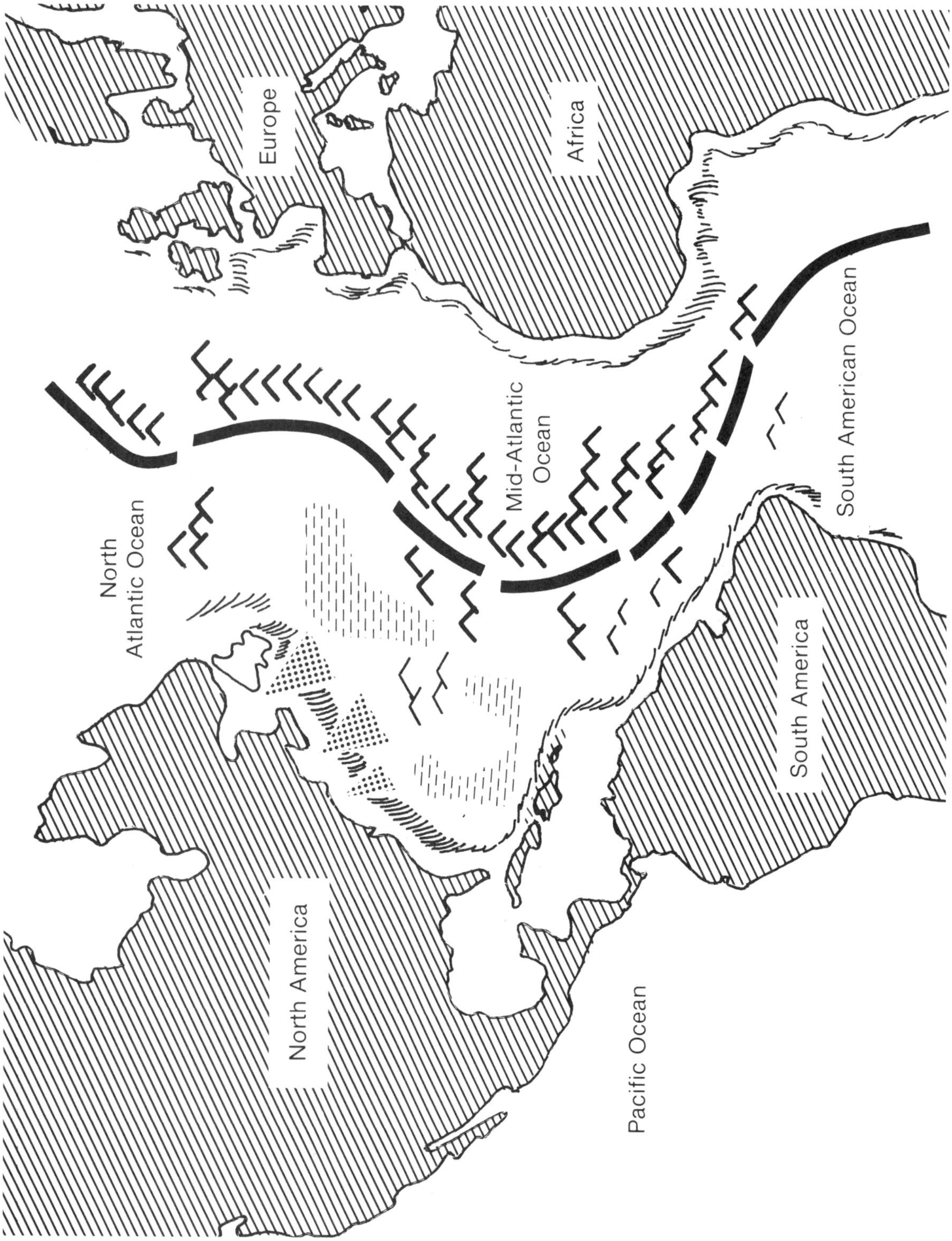

Europe

Africa

North Atlantic Ocean

Mid-Atlantic Ocean

South American Ocean

South America

North America

Pacific Ocean

IV

Measuring Earthquakes

EARTHQUAKE CURRICULUM, K-6
SCOPE AND SEQUENCE CHART

Unit IV: Measuring Earthquakes

Level	Concept	Laboratory	Mathematics	Language Arts	Social Studies	Art
K-2	Earthquakes have different strengths. Earthquakes cause different amounts of damage.	Simulation of relative strengths of earthquakes	Ordinal numbers Concepts of most and least	Vocabulary development of earthquake words Label reading, picture matching Sequencing events	Effects of earthquakes on buildings and people	Coloring earthquake pictures
3-4	Earthquakes differ in the amount of energy they release. Earthquakes may be measured by their effects (intensity) or by the amount of energy they release (magnitude).	Coffee grounds simulation of earthquakes Seismograph simulation	Measurement of distances Graph of measurement data Roman numerals	Vocabulary development of earthquake words Written descriptions of Mercalli illustrations	Impact of earthquakes on society Biographical study of earthquake scientists	Illustrations of the Mercalli scale
5-6	Earthquake waves are either surface or body waves. Earthquake body waves are either primary or secondary. Earthquake waves detected by a seismograph are recorded as seismograms.	Slinky™ simulation of earthquake waves Shoebox and rubber band simulation of earthquake waves Seismograph simulation Earthquake wave simulation game	Ratio of earthquake wave speed Metric measurement of wave amplitude Computation, reducing fractions	Vocabulary development of earthquake words	Impact of earthquakes on society	Model designing

IV

Measuring Earthquakes

Two scales are commonly used to measure earthquakes, the Mercalli and the Richter. The Mercalli scale,
the older of the two, measures the impact of a quake on
people and their property. The Richter scale measures
the magnitude of the waves released in an earthquake.
Earthquake vibrations are transmitted as energy waves.
Surface waves cause the most damage at the surface,
while body waves travel in all directions through the
lithosphere, and even the core and mantle. Body waves—
which we divide into P- (Primary) and S- (Secondary)—
are important because they allow us to locate the point
where a quake originates (its *focus*) and also to study
the Earth's interior.

Measuring Earthquakes

With few exceptions, earthquakes occur because of the release of energy stored in the rocks of the Earth's lithosphere. In order to understand how this release of energy is measured, however, we must first understand how it occurs.

Stress and Strain

Compressional Stress

When rocks are squeezed we say that they are under *compressional stress*. The rocks will behave elastically. That is, they will absorb the stress by changing their shape, like the soles of good running shoes. This change in shape is called *strain*. But, just like rubber soles, or rubber balls that are squeezed, strained rocks will rebound to their original shapes when the stress is removed. When the rocks rebound we say that their strain energy has been released.

Tensional Stress

Alternatively, if lithospheric rocks are being pulled apart, we can say that they are under *tensional stress*. In this case the rocks will tend to stretch like a stretching rubber band. They will rebound to their original shapes when the tensional stress is removed.

Earthquake!

However, if the stress exceeds what the material can bear, the material will rupture, or break. What happens when you pull too hard on a rubber band?

When rocks are strained too much, they break, and the original pieces rebound to their original shapes. In the Earth's lithosphere this rebounding and release of strain energy is accompanied by rubbing, grinding, and crashing, as the rock masses move past each other. The result is what we call an earthquake.

California

North American Plate

Pacific Plate

San Andreas Transform Fault

Faults

A fault is a break in the Earth's rocky surface along which the two sides have been displaced relative to each other. Faults that are near the Earth's surface can be seen firsthand, on aerial photographs, or in geologic maps. Most of the larger and more active faults have names, like the San Andreas fault of California or the Wasatch fault of Utah.

Some faults lie well below the surface and are difficult to locate with existing technology. These may be the foci for unexpected earthquakes, such as the New Madrid, Missouri earthquake of 1811 or the Charleston, South Carolina earthquake of 1886.

Waves and Vibrations

Regardless of the depth of the focus, vibrations from the release of strain energy travel in all directions. The earthquake vibrations are transmitted through the surrounding lithosphere, and even through the Earth's mantle and core, by a variety of wave-like motions. Earthquake waves are of two kinds, body waves and surface waves.

Body Waves

Body waves that travel through the Earth are either P- (for Primary) waves or S- (for Secondary) waves. P-waves travel faster than S-waves. The two types together are called *body waves* because they travel through the body of the Earth. Body waves are important because they allow us to locate the epicenters of earthquakes. They also enable us to study the structure and composition of the Earth's interior.

Surface Waves
Earthquake waves that travel at or near the surface of
the Earth are called *surface waves*. The two main varieties are Love waves, which move sidewise, and Rayleigh
waves, which have an up-and-down (rotary) motion. Surface waves spread for thousands or tens of thousands of
square kilometers around an earthquake's epicenter.
They are responsible for the strongest shaking of the
ground and most of the damage to buildings that occur
in large earthquakes.

Two Ways of Measuring Earthquakes

The Mercalli Scale: A Measure of Intensity
Earthquake intensity is a measure of the effects of an
earthquake at a particular place. Intensity is determined
from observations of an earthquake's effects on people,
structures, and the Earth's surface. A ten-value intensity
scale which had been in use in Europe since 1883 was
refined in 1902 by an Italian seismologist, Giuseppe
Mercalli. The Mercalli scale we use today is a modifica-
tion of Mercalli's 12-value scale developed by two Americans, H. O. Wood and Frank Neumann, in 1931. The
scale uses Roman numerals from I to XII to rank relative
levels of destruction, ground motion, and human
impact.

The intensity (or impact) of an earthquake in a given
area will depend on the type of geological structures in
the area as well as the type of buildings. Houses built on
rock, for example, will receive less damage than houses
built on sediments at the same distance from a quake's
epicenter. Poorly built houses will receive more damage
than those that have been reinforced to withstand
earthquakes. In general, though, the further a site is
from the earthquake's focus, the lower the amount of
damage it will sustain.

The Richter Scale: A Measure of Magnitude
Another method of rating the size of earthquakes is by
using scientific instruments to measure the *amplitude*
of body waves and surface waves recorded on *seismograms*. The amplitude is the height of the wave tracing
above the center line on the seismogram. The instrument's reading indicates the amount of strain energy
released by an earthquake. This measure is called the
earthquake's *magnitude*. The greater the wave ampli-
tute, the greater the magnitude.

Table: Earthquake World Records

Location	Date	Magnitude
Ecuador	January 31, 1906	8.9
Assam, India	June 12, 1897	8.7
Alaska	March 28, 1964	8.6
Alaska	September 10, 1899	8.6
Southern Chile	May 21-30, 1960	8.5
San Francisco	April 18, 1906	8.2
Kwanto, Japan	September 1, 1923	8.2
Erzincan, Turkey	December 27, 1939	8.0
Indonesia	August 19, 1977	8.0
Mexico	September 19, 1985	7.9

A magnitude scale was devised by the American seismologist Charles Richter in 1935. It uses Arabic numerals. Richter's scale is logarithmic and open-ended; that is, there is no upper or lower limit to Richter magnitudes. Each whole-number increase in the magnitude of an earthquake represents about a thirty-fold increase in the amount of energy released.

The original Richter magnitude scale was devised to measure earthquakes in southern California. Later, however, Richter and his colleague Beno Gutenberg devised a scale to measure distant earthquakes. This scale is based on the amplitudes of surface waves. Body waves from distant earthquakes can also be used to determine magnitude.

The Seismograph
The instrument used to record earthquakes is called a *seismograph*. The first seismographs were designed by British scientists working in Japan between 1880 and 1890. The most famous of these early seismographs was a horizontal pendulum model built by John Milne.

Pendulum seismographs rely on a simple principle of physics, the principle of inertia. A heavy weight that is allowed to move freely will tend to remain in its original position when the ground beneath it begins to move in response to earthquake waves.

This is a reproduction of an actual seismogram, recorded during the Mexico City earthquake, September 19, 1985, reading 8.1 on the Richter Scale.

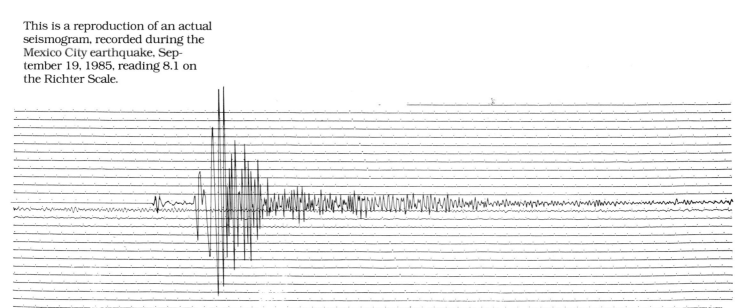

Mechanical or electrical devices can be used to sense the motion of the ground relative to the heavy pendulum of the seismograph. Up-and-down or sideways ground motion sends a mechanical or electrical signal to a pen attached to a paper-covered drum. As the drum turns, the pen wiggles, producing an amplified recording of the ground motion. This recording is called a *seismogram*. Scientists use the amplitudes of earthquake waves recorded as seismograms to determine the magnitude ratings of earthquakes.

Over the years other types of seismographs have been developed. Precision in locating distant earthquakes and accuracy in determining their magnitudes have improved as the number and sophistication of seismograph designs have increased. Today computers are being used to analyze seismographic data—something your students may want to research on their own.

From Master 32, Seismographs

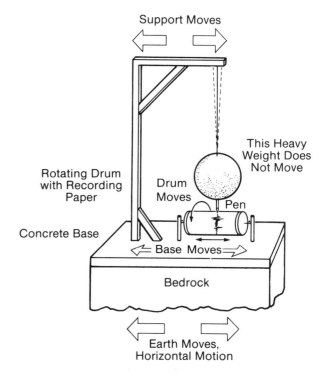

Earthquakes Great and Small

Content Concepts

1. Earthquakes have different strengths.

2. Earthquakes cause different amounts of damage.

Vocabulary

energy
damage
cause
effect
most
least

Objectives

Students will
—construct a model to simulate earthquakes and earthquake damage.
—demonstrate that earthquakes have different levels of strength.
—compare the movement in the earthquake model to ground movement during a quake.
—compare different levels of earthquake strength in terms of their effects on people and property.
—rank descriptions of earthquake damage from least to most.
—match descriptions of earthquake damage with pictures of quake effects.

Learning Links

Language Arts: Discussion/oral communication, vocabulary building, reading (optional), sequencing events, matching descriptive sentences to pictures

Social Studies: Discussing effects of earthquake damage on people and their property

Math: Using ordinal numbers

Art: Choosing colors and applying them to illustrations, working within defined areas

Activity One: Shakes Make Quakes

Materials for the teacher
• An audiovisual cart on wheels or a small table or desk that moves easily

Materials for each small group of students
• A shallow box partially filled with sand or soil
• An assortment of paper plates, cups, and small boxes that can be stacked to form a building

Procedure

1. Conduct a class discussion on the concept of energy. Establish that energy has many forms (such as mechanical energy, heat, sound, and light) and many different strengths.

2. Have students demonstrate two familiar types of energy.

a. Ask them to clap their hands loudly and describe the sound, then to clap them softly and describe the sound.

Do you hear a difference? (Yes.)

Why is there a difference? (Soft clapping releases a smaller amount of sound energy than loud clapping does.)

b. Ask them to rub their hands together slowly and describe how they feel, then rub them together quickly and describe how they feel.

Do you feel a difference? (Yes.)

Why do you feel a difference? (Quick rubbing releases a greater amount of heat energy than slow rubbing does.)

3. Tell students that earthquakes are caused by the release of energy stored in rocks, and invite them to make a model for demonstrating earthquakes.

4. Ask a small group of students to pile plates, cups, and small boxes on top of each other in the filled box to form a tall structure, as they did in Unit I. (Either have enough materials for each group to construct one model, or have the groups take turns.)

5. Place the large box on the cart, table, or desk.

6. Shake the cart, table, or desk very gently, so that nothing happens to the structure.

7. Shake it three more times, increasing the amount of force each time, so that you end by destroying the structure completely. Adjust or rebuild the structure after the second and third simulations.

8. After each of the four simulations ask the students to comment on what they are seeing. At the end of the activity, lead the students to compare and comment.

en • er • gy

Energy is power to move or change things.

dam • age

Damage is harm. Things are damaged when they are changed in ways we do not like.

What caused the buildings to fall down? (the shaking of the table)

What caused the table to shake? (the students who shook it)

What did the students give to the table? (energy)

How much energy did we use to shake the table the first time? (a small amount)

What happened to the buildings? (Nothing happened.)

How much energy did we use the last time? (a large amount)

What happened to the buildings? (They broke apart.)

Are earthquakes always the same? (No. Some are weak and some are strong.)

Summarize: Different earthquakes have different amounts of energy, and cause different amounts of *damage*.

Activity Two: Quakes of All Sizes

Materials for the teacher
- Transparencies of Master 30 a-d
- Overhead projector

Materials for each student
- Worksheets made from Master 30 a-e
- Scissors
- Paste
- Pencils and crayons

Procedure

1. Display transparencies 30 a–d on the projector, one at a time.

2. Help the students to analyze the pictures with the following questions:

What do you see in this picture?

What is damaged?

Which picture shows the *most* damage?

What *caused* the damage? (the energy of the earthquake)

Which of our earthquake demonstrations is it most like? (the last one)

Which picture shows the *least* damage?

Why did this earthquake have less effect? (This earthquake had less energy or happened farther away, so that less of its energy reached this place.)

Which of our demonstrations is it most like? (the first one)

Can we put the pictures in order, from the one that shows the least damage to the one that shows the most?

3. Hand out worksheets made from Masters a–e. Read the descriptions aloud, then instruct students to number the pictures in 1–4 order. Readers can match the written descriptions with the pictures, cut them out, and paste them on the correct pages. Then students may color the pictures.

Extensions

1. Invite students to tell, draw, or write a story about the earthquake simulation activity.

2. Invite students to describe imaginatively what they might feel, see, and hear if they were watching their model building when an earthquake occurred.

Indoor Damage, Light

Outdoor Damage, Heavy

Different Shakes for Different Quakes

Content Concepts

1. Earthquakes differ in the amount of energy they release.

2. Earthquakes may be measured by their effects (intensity) or by the amount of energy they release (magnitude).

Vocabulary

damage
energy
earthquake wave
amplitude
earthquake intensity
earthquake magnitude
landslide
moderate
modified Mercalli scale
Richter scale
Roman numerals
seismograph
seismogram

Objectives

Students will
—demonstrate by a simulation that earthquakes differ in the amount of energy they release.
—construct drawings to illustrate the Mercalli scale as a measure of earthquake effects on people, structures, and the Earth's surface.
—identify the Richter scale as a measure of energy released by earthquakes.
—construct and use a seismograph to demonstrate the measurement of earthquakes.

Learning Links

Language Arts: Reading sentences, sequencing ideas, discussing, building vocabulary, constructing paragraphs
Social Studies: Discussing the human impact of earthquakes
Math: Using Roman numerals, interpreting data
Art: Making illustrations

Activity One: Coffee Quake

Materials for the teacher or for each small group
- Dry coffee grounds
- Two flat wooden sticks or strips of softwood lattice about the size of a ruler—30 cm long, 2.5-3 cm wide, and 4-7 mm thick
- One flat wooden stick of the same width and thickness but about 1 meter long
- Large sheets of white paper or newspapers to cover desks (optional, but speeds cleanup and makes coffee grounds easier to see)
- Measuring sticks (optional—see Extensions)
- Goggles to protect students' eyes

Procedure

1. Demonstrate the effects of different earthquakes with the activity that follows. You may do it either as a class activity or as a teacher demonstration.

a. Divide students into small groups and distribute one short stick to each group.

b. Direct each group to place its stick flat on a desk so that half extends over the edge. A student will use one hand to hold the half that is on the desk and the other to bend the extended end, but not hard enough to break it.

c. While still holding the end that is on the desk, the student will release the bent stick. It will snap back. Ask students to describe what they feel. (The vibration that results from the release of energy should be felt along the length of the stick.)

d. Ask: Where did the energy come from? (The student transferred energy to the stick.)

e. Have students repeat the bending, but this time apply even more force. The stick will break, releasing energy. Ask students to describe what they observe.

f. Distribute the second short sticks. A student will hold each in place on a desk as in step a. Before the stick is bent, however, someone will place a small amount of coffee grounds on the end that is on the table. This time the energy that is released will scatter the coffee. Leave the broken stick and coffee where they are and have students move to another desk for the next activity.

earth • quake in • ten • si • ty

Earthquake intensity is a measure of ground shaking based on damage to structures and changes felt and observed by humans. It is expressed in Roman numerals on the Mercalli scale.

earth • quake mag • ni • tude

Earthquake magnitude is a measure of the amount of energy released by an earthquake. It is expressed in Arabic numberals on the Richter scale.

seis • mo • graph

A seismograph is an instrument for recording the motion of earthquake waves.

seis • mo • gram

A seismogram is a recording of the wavy lines produced by a seismograph.

Teacher Take Note: You may have to visit a lumberyard to find wooden strips the right size. Try this procedure out before you do it in class, to make sure that the wood you've chosen isn't too soft (so it won't snap) or too hard (so it snaps with excessive force.) Also, be sure to dispose of the broken sticks as soon as the exercise is done, so they won't be a safety hazard.

Extensions

1. Measure the farthest distance that the coffee grounds traveled from the short stick and the long stick. Compare the two, and compare both measurements among the different groups of students.

2. If you use paper on the desks, students can draw an outline of the area covered by the coffee grounds from the short and long sticks. Again, groups can compare their results.

Shortened Mercalli Scale

I. Only instruments detect it.

II. People lying down might feel it.

III. People on upper floors of buildings will feel it, but may not know it is an earthquake.

IV. People indoors will probably feel it, but those outside may not.

V. Nearly everyone feels it, and wakes up if they are sleeping.

VI. Everyone feels the quake. It's hard to walk.

VII. It's hard to stand.

VIII. People will not be able to drive cars. Poorly built buildings may collapse; chimneys may fall.

IX. Most foundations are damaged. The ground cracks.

X. Most buildings are destroyed. Water is thrown out of rivers and lakes.

XI. Rails are bent. Bridges and underground pipelines are put out of service.

XII. Most things are leveled. Large objects may be thrown into the air.

g. Distribute the longer sticks and have students use them to repeat the steps above. Measure and compare the distance the coffee grounds moved from the two sticks. Also compare the amount of energy required to break the two sticks.

2. Conduct a follow-up discussion around the following questions:

What is an earthquake? (Answers should include the idea that energy is released which displaces objects.)

What did the sticks in this activity represent? (rock layers)

What did the breaking of the sticks represent? (the buildup and release of energy that moves rock layers in an earthquake)

Do all earthquakes release the same amount of energy? (No, they differ.)

If the amount of energy released by different earthquakes differs, what about the amount of damage they can cause? (It will also differ.)

Activity Two: Measuring with Mercalli

Materials for the teacher
• Master 31, Modified Mercalli Scale
• Large Roman numerals I through XII

For each student or group
• A copy of the Mercalli scale made from Master 31
• A large sheet of drawing paper
• Art supplies—colored pencils, crayons, felt markers
• Scissors
• Tape

Procedure

1. Introduce the Mercalli scale by explaining its purpose—to measure the intensity of the damage an earthquake causes. You might want to add other information from the unit introduction. Explain that the use of Roman numerals distinguishes Mercalli measurements from those on another scale (the Richter, to be introduced in Activity Three).

2. Teach or review Roman numerals.

3. Distribute copies of the Mercalli scale and have students take turns reading the descriptions aloud.

4. Divide students into groups and ask them to draw scenes illustrating the Mercalli numbers. Provide art supplies. Intensity I may only require one drawing, but the higher numbers may require more.

5. Distribute large Roman numerals I through XII around the classroom wall in order from lowest to highest. As students bring up their illustrations, the class will try to assign each to its correct numeral. Students may hang their pictures on the wall under the correct numeral.

6. Either before or after a class discussion about the social impact of each step on the scale, have students write paragraphs describing their illustrations and add them to the wall display.

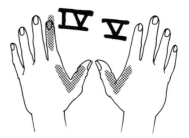

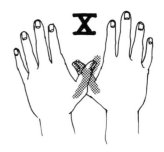

Activity Three: Rocking with Richter

Materials for the teacher
- Transparencies made from Master 32, Several Seismographs; Master 33, Seismogram Worksheet; Master 34, Richter Scale; and Master 38, Seismogram Showing Amplitude
- Overhead projector

Materials for each small group
- Free-flowing overhead marker with fine tip for marking transparency
- Blank transparency sheet
- A chair or cart with wheels

Materials for each student
- Worksheet of seismogram tracings made from Master 33

Teacher Take Note: It's easy to do a finger drill on Roman numerals. The space between the pointer and the thumb is V, or 5. The V plus the I's on the other hand stand for the numerals 6 through 8. The 9 (IX) is made with one finger and the crossed thumbs. The crossed thumbs make an X. Also remind students that Roman starts with a capital R, and all the numbers it uses (I, V, X, etc.) are upper case.

Procedure

1. Place a stationary chair, table, or desk next to another object of approximately the same height that has wheels.

2. Place a blank overhead transparency on the movable object.

3. Have students take turns as holders and shakers. The first student rests an elbow on the stationary object and holds the marker lightly with thumb, index, and middle fingers so it just touches the surface of the transparency sheet. As he or she holds the pencil suspended, the other student shakes the movable object back and forth, varying the intensity of the shaking as much as possible. The markings that result will be similar to a seismogram. Show students the transparency of several types of seismographs (Master 32) and then Master 38, Seismogram Showing Amplitude.

4. Discuss the concepts of magnitude and amplitude. (Refer to the teacher background if necessary.) Explain that the amplitude of the earthquake waves (their height measured from a fixed reference line) reflects the amount of Earth movement, and therefore the magnitude of the earthquake. This magnitude is expressed as a Richter number, in honor of Charles Richter, who developed the scale in 1935. Project the transparency of Master 34, the Richter Scale, and discuss.

5. Distribute the worksheets made from Master 33, and ask students to rank the seismograms from A to D, least amplitude to greatest.

Answers to Master 33
Least_____B	
_____A	
_____C	
Greatest_____D	

Sizing Up Earthquake Waves

Content Concepts

1. Earthquake waves are either surface waves or body waves.

2. Earthquake body waves are either primary or secondary.

3. Earthquake waves detected by a seismograph are recorded as seismograms.

Objectives

Students will

—distinguish between body and surface waves and between primary and secondary body waves (P-waves and S-waves).

—construct a model to simulate S-wave motion.

—identify the focus in a simulated earthquake.

—construct a model seismograph and identify its parts.

—identify different amplitudes of simulated earthquake waves by using the seismograph.

Activity One: Popping P-Waves

Materials for the teacher
- Transparencies made from Master 35, P-Wave Motion and S-Wave Motion, and Master 10, Earthquake Terms
- Overhead projector

Vocabulary

earthquake wave
wave amplitude
earthquake intensity
earthquake magnitude
seismograph
seismogram
fault
focus
epicenter
surface waves
body waves
P- (primary) waves
S- (secondary) waves
expansion
compression

Learning Links

Language Arts: Discussing, following directions, taking notes

Social Studies: Observing and discussing effects on people at various stages on the Mercalli Scale

Math: Metric measurement, computation, reducing fractions, computing ratios

Art: Creating models

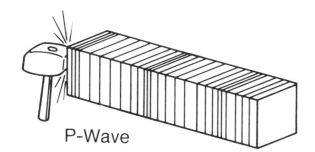

P-Wave

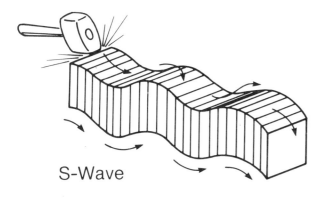

S-Wave

Teacher Take Note: Metal Slinkies will be more effective than plastic ones for this activity. Mark one spot on each coil with bright permanent marker or a bit of white tape, to make it easy for students to see the wave motion.

Materials for the students

- Slinky™ toys (One for every two students is ideal.)
- Signpost labeled Focus (Teacher or student volunteers can make it ahead of time.)
- Safety goggles

Procedure

1. Elicit from class the definition of an earthquake. Review or explain that the energy of an earthquake is released in the form of waves. (Use Master 10, Earthquake Terms.) Point out that all the energy moves out from the focus.

2. Divide students into pairs or groups of even numbers, depending on the number of Slinkies available. Distribute Slinkies.

3. Two students will hold each Slinky, one on either end. Instruct them to stretch it to a length between 2 and 3 meters on the floor or a wide work surface.

4. Ask one of each pair to compress between ten and twenty coils and then release them rapidly. Both students continue to hold the Slinky during compression and release.

5. Ask students to describe what they see, and let this lead into your explanation of body waves, P-waves, and S-waves (see unit overview). Be sure to point out that the Slinky's motion simulates the expansion and compression of P-waves.

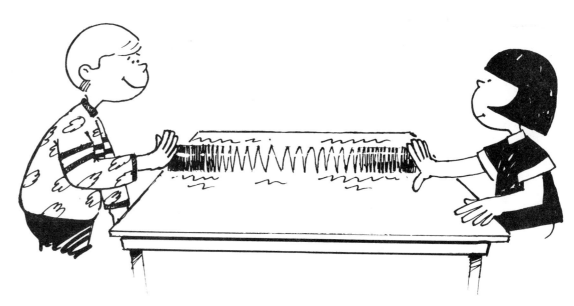

Also note that P-waves vibrate in the direction in which they travel. Use the transparency of Master 35, P-Wave Motion and S-Wave Motion.

6. Place the signpost labeled Focus in an open area of the classroom. Have all the students compress and release their Slinkies in this one area at the same moment. This demonstration will help students to realize that earthquake waves radiate in all directions from the focus.

Activity Two: The S-Wave Machine

Materials for the teacher
- Handout or transparency made from Master 36, The S-Wave Machine
- Transparency made from Master 35, P-Wave Motion and S-Wave Motion
- Overhead projector

Materials for each group
- 1 shoe box without its top, or a 1- or 2-qt. paper milk carton, cut as shown
- Compass point or other punching tool
- A rubber band long enough to stretch the length of the box or carton
- Scissors
- 2 metal washers 2 cm or larger
- 5-7 metal paper clips

fault

A fault is a crack in rock or soil along which movement has taken place.

fo • cus

The focus, or *hypocenter*, is the place inside the lithosphere where an earthquake's energy is first released.

sur • face   waves

Surface waves are earthquake waves that travel only on the surface of the Earth.

bo • dy   waves

Body waves are earthquake waves that travel through the body of the Earth. They are of two types, P-waves and S-waves.

P-waves

P- (or Primary) waves are the fastest body waves, which travel by compression and expansion.

S-waves

S- (or Secondary) waves are body waves which travel more slowly than P-waves, and create elastic vibrations in solid substances.

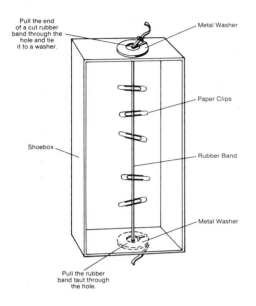

Pull the end of a cut rubber band through the hole and tie it to a washer.

Metal Washer

Paper Clips

Shoebox

Rubber Band

Metal Washer

Pull the rubber band taut through the hole.

Master 36. The S-Wave Machine

Procedure

1. Gather students in pairs or small groups and distribute materials. Inform students that they are going to build and operate a device to illustrate the type of body waves called S-waves. Project Master 36 or hand out copies.

2. Instruct students to assemble their machines, referring to the projected illustration or the handout.

a. Stand box on end and punch a small hole in the top and bottom, near the center.

b. Cut open a rubber band and thread it through the top hole, tying the end to a washer to keep it from pulling through.

c. While another student holds the band stretched, thread the free end through the bottom hole and fasten it with the second washer. (The rubber band should be taut enough to twang when it is plucked.)

d. Attach 5 to 7 paper clips evenly along the length of the band so they are centered horizontally and they all face in the same direction. Allow the band and clips to come to rest.

e. Pluck the band and observe the motion of the clips.

3. Ask students to describe what they see. (They'll see paper clips swinging in all directions, at right angles to the movement of the wave up and down the rubber band.)

4. Project the wave transparency, Master 35, and explain the motion of S-waves through the Earth in terms of the demonstration. Point out that S-waves cause vibrations perpendicular to the direction of their movement. Compare this movement with the movement of P-waves.

Activity Three: Traveling Tremors

Materials for the teacher
- Transparencies made from Masters 31, Modified Mercalli Scale, and 34, Richter Scale
- Transparency made from Master 32, Several Seismographs
- Overhead Projector

Materials for the students
- Slinky™ toys, one for every two students if possible
- Photographs, slides, newspaper clippings, and other material to illustrate actual earthquakes and compare their intensities

Procedure

1. Distribute Slinkies to pairs of students.

2. Ask each pair to stretch their Slinky to about a meter in length.

3. While one student moves the Slinky up and down, ask the other to move it in a sideways motion. Explain that this demonstration simulates surface earthquake wave motion.

4. Ask students to observe the Slinkies, and describe the effect on people and things of such a wave moving through the Earth's surface. Students should have observed both up and

One child moves the spring up and down and the other side to side.

down and sideways movements of the model surface waves. Make sure students understand that these surface waves cause the damage and most of the events humans associate with earthquakes.

5. Review the concept that quakes vary in Richter magnitude and Mercalli intensity, using the transparencies on the Mercalli and Richter scales, Masters 31 and 34. Discuss the human impact of earthquake activity at each level of intensity, drawing first on students' own experiences, and then on photographs, slides, newspaper clippings, and other illustrative material.

Activity Four: Set Up a Seismograph

Materials for the teacher
- Transparencies made from Masters 37, Student Seismograph; 32, Several Seismographs; and 38, Seismogram Showing Amplitude
- Overhead projector

Materials for each small group of students
- 7 to 9 heavy books
- 3 rubber bands 5–10 cm long
- A thin-line felt pen or marker
- A large metal nut or washer
- A ball of clay (about 50 g)
- 3 strips of paper, at least 35 cm long
- A standard wooden ruler or flat stick 20–30 cm long
- A metric ruler with millimeter divisions
- Scissors

Master 37. Student Seismograph

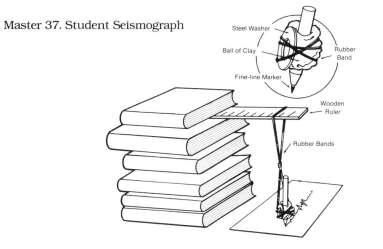

Steel Washer
Ball of Clay
Rubber Band
Fine-line Marker
Wooden Ruler
Rubber Bands

Procedure

1. Inform students that they are going to build and operate a simple seismograph. Display transparency of student seismograph (Master 37), then the several seismographs on Master 32. Point out the basic parts they have in common—weight, support stand, pen, and recording paper—and give students these directions:

a. Stack the books in one pile.

b. Insert the ruler between the top two books, with about two thirds of its length protruding.

c. Tie two rubber bands together the long way, and tie one end of the double length to the nut or washer.

d. Remove the cap from the pen and connect the washer to its inky end, just above the tip, with another rubber band.

e. Use the ball of clay to bind the washer to the pen and weight your seismograph.

f. Hang this arrangement from the ruler by the top end of the rubber band chain so that the tip of the pen just touches the table. Add or remove books as needed to adjust the height.

g. Place the beginning of the paper strip just under the tip of the pen.

2. Have pairs of students sit on opposite sides of each desk that holds a seismograph. Instruct one of each pair to hold onto the desk, while gently and steadily pulling the paper under the marker. The other gently shakes the desk until the length of the paper has run out (from 5–10 seconds).

Children can experiment with their own designs for making seismographs.

Richter Scale

Richter Magnitude 1.0	TNT Energy Equivalent 6 ounces	Example (approximate) Small Blast at a Construction Site
1.5	2 pounds	
2.0	13 pounds	
2.5	63 pounds	
3.0	397 pounds	
3.5	1,000 pounds	
4.0	6 tons	Small Atomic Bomb
4.5	32 tons	Average Tornado
5.0	199 tons	
5.5	500 tons	Massena, NY Quake, 1944
6.0	6,270 tons	
6.5	31,550 tons	Coalinga, CA Quake, 1983
7.0	199,000 tons	Hebgen Lake, MT Quake, 1959
7.5	1,000,000 tons	
8.0	6,270,000 tons	San Francisco, CA Quake, 1906
8.5	31,550,000 tons	Anchorage, AK Quake, 1964
9.0	199,999,000 tons	

3. Have them label the strip of paper Gentle Shaking, and tell students that they have made a seismogram.

4. Make two more seismograms, but ask students to shake the desk harder each time than the time before. Have them number the seismograms that result from 1 to 3, with 1 being the most gentle shaking.

5. Explain and define *wave amplitude*, using Master 38, Seismogram Showing Amplitude. Help students to measure the amplitude of their own seismograms and relate them to the degree of force with which they shook their desks. Ask:

How does the amplitude of the wave on the seismogram (Master 38) relate to the Richter magnitude of the earthquake it records? (The higher the wave amplitude, the higher the Richter magnitude.)

Which of your own seismograms would have the highest Richter magnitude? (the one with the highest amplitude, or the one which received the hardest shaking)

Activity Five: Drum Rumbles

Materials for the teacher
- A drum (any type that's portable—a coffee can will do)
- 2 posters, one labeled S-wave and one labeled P-wave
- A watch that indicates seconds (Most digitals would work.)

Materials for each student
- A pencil and a notebook

Procedure

1. Line students up single file in a long corridor indoors, or outdoors along a wall or fence.

2. Choose three volunteers: two to hold the S-Wave and P-Wave posters at a starting point (call it the *focus*) and one to beat the drum.

3. At a signal from the teacher, the drummer will begin a steady beat of one tap per second, to indicate that an earthquake has begun at the focus, and the P- and S-wave students will begin to walk the length of the line of students. The P-wave student must take one step per second and the S-wave student one step every two seconds. Both students should loudly count out the seconds to the beat of the drum so the students in line can hear them.

4. Instruct students to write down the number that each marcher calls out in passing them. This is the arrival time of the simulated earthquake wave.

5. Students return to the classroom with their data. Ask them to write down the two arrival times as a fraction (P/S) and reduce it to the lowest terms.

6. Ask them to share their data. The answers may vary, but if care has been taken with counting, pacing, and reducing of fractions, most answers should be about 1/2. This 1:2 ratio *approximates* the 3:5.5 ratio of the P- and S-waves' traveling times.

Extensions

1. Students may keep a scrapbook of references to earthquakes in newspapers and magazines, and correlate them with their Mercalli and Richter ratings.

2. Students may wish to build other types of seismographs, such as those described in the references. Master 32 suggests some possible designs, but you might be surprised at what students can do on their own, without following a pattern.

Unit IV. Measuring Earthquakes

Materials List

Grades K-2
audiovisual cart on wheels
shallow box
sand or soil
paper plates & cups
small boxes
overhead projector
scissors
paste
pencils
crayons

Grades 3-4
chair or cart with wheels
drawing paper
rulers
wooden sticks (30 cm)
colored pencils
markers
wooden stick (1 meter)
crayons
tape
large sheet of white paper
dry coffee grounds
scissors
blank transparency sheet
goggles
transparency markers
overhead projector

Grades 5-6
watch with second indicator
Slinky™
paper
photographs of earthquakes
punching tool
shoe box
rubber bands
metal washers
scissors
paper clips
large metal nut
flat stick
clay
ruler
metric ruler
drum or coffee can
thin-line markers
heavy books
overhead projector
goggles
pencils
notebooks

Instructional Resources (Books, maps, pamphlets, slides)

Brown, B.W., and W.R. Brown. (1974). *Historical Catastrophes: Earthquakes*. Reading, Massachusetts: Addison-Wesley Publishers Co.

Cazeau, C. J. (1977, February). Earthquake. *Instructor*, 86, pp. 76-82.

Markle, S. (1987). Hands-on Science: Earthquake! *Instructor*, 96, pp. 7, 97-99.

Reuter, M. (1977). *Earthquakes: Our Restless Planet*. Milwaukee, Wisconsin: Raintree Publishers, Ltd.

Walker, B., and others. (1982). *Planet Earth Earthquake*. Alexandria, Virginia: Time-Life Books.

Poster of earthquake damage:

Hopper, M. G., and S. T. Algermissen. (1984). *Types of Damage That Could Result from a Great Earthquake in the New Madrid, Missouri, Seismic Zone*. Reston, Virginia: United States Geological Survey.

State seismicity maps: (Request current prices.)

Map Distribution Division; U.S. Geological Survey; Federal Center, Box 25286; Denver, Colorado 80225. (These maps show earthquake location, year, and maximum Modified Mercalli intensity. The maps are revised and updated from time to time.)

References

Bolt, B. A. (1988). *Earthquakes*. San Francisco: W. H. Freeman and Co.

Bolt, B. A. (1978). *Earthquake: A Primer*. San Francisco: W. H. Freeman and Co.

Brownlee, S. (1986, July). Waiting for the big one. *Discover*, 7, pp. 52-71.

Earthquake Country: A Teachers Workshop. (1978, February 25-26). Far Western Section of National Association of Geology Teachers and California Science Teachers Association.

Earthquakes: A National Problem. Washington, DC: Federal Emergency Management Agency.

Gere, J,. and H. Shan. (1984). *Terra Non Firma: Understanding and Preparing for Earthquakes*. New York: W.H. Freeman and Co.

National Oceanic and Atmospheric Administration. (1976). *Catalog of Earthquake Photographs—Key to Geophysical Records*, Documentation No. 7. Boulder, Colorado: National Geophysical Data Center.

Muir, R. (1987). *Earthquakes and Volcanoes: Causes, Effects, and Predictions*. New York: Weidenfeld and Nicolson.

Press, F., and R. Siever. (1986). *Earth*. New York: W.H. Freeman and Co. 4th edition.

Richter, C. F. (1958). *Elementary Seismology*. San Francisco: W. H. Freeman and Co.

Schnell, M. L., ed. (1984). *National Earthquake Hazards Reduction Program: Overview Report to The United States Congress*. Reston, Virginia: United States Geological Survey. Circular 918.

Severity of an Earthquake, The. (1986). Reston, Virginia: United States Geological Survey.

Tarbuck, E. J., and F. K. Lutgens. (1987). *The Earth: An Introduction to Physical Geology*, 2nd ed. Columbus, Ohio: Merrill Publishing Co.

Van Rose, S. (1986). *Earthquakes*. New Rochelle, New York: Cambridge University Press.

Yanev, P. (1974). *Peace of Mind in Earthquake Country: How to Save Your Home and Your Life*. San Francisco: Chronicle Books.

Earthquake Activity Worksheet

Earthquakes happen all the time.
People do not feel most earthquakes.

Some earthquakes make things move.

Earthquakes can make things move,
fall, and break.

Very large earthquakes cause great damage.

1. Cut out sentences.

2. Paste a sentence under the correct picture.

3. Color the pictures.

Modified Mercalli Scale

I. People do not feel any Earth movement.

II. A few people might notice movement if they are at rest and/or on the upper floors of tall buildings.

III. Many people indoors feel movement. Hanging objects swing back and forth. People outdoors might not realize that an earthquake is occurring.

IV. Most people indoors feel movement. Hanging objects swing. Dishes, windows, and doors rattle. The earthquake feels like a heavy truck hitting the walls. A few people outdoors may feel movement. Parked cars rock.

V. Almost everyone feels movement. Sleeping people are awakened. Doors swing open or close. Dishes are broken. Pictures on the wall move. Small objects move or are turned over. Trees might shake. Liquids might spill out of open containers.

VI. Everyone feels movement. People have trouble walking. Objects fall from shelves. Pictures fall off walls. Furniture moves. Plaster in walls might crack. Trees and bushes shake. Damage is slight in poorly built buildings. No structural damage.

VII. People have difficulty standing. Drivers feel their cars shaking. Some furniture breaks. Loose bricks fall from buildings. Damage is slight to moderate in well-built buildings, considerable in poorly built buildings.

VIII. Drivers have trouble steering. Houses that are not bolted down might shift on their foundations. Tall structures such as towers and chimneys might twist and fall. Well built buildings suffer slight damage. Poorly built structures suffer severe damage. Tree branches break. Hillsides might crack if the ground is wet. Water level in wells might change.

IX. Well built buildings suffer considerable damage. Houses that are not bolted down move off their foundations. Some underground pipes are broken. The ground cracks. Reservoirs suffer serious damage.

X. Most buildings and their foundations are destroyed. Some bridges are destroyed. Dams are seriously damaged. Large landslides occur. Water is thrown on the banks of canals, rivers, lakes. The ground cracks in large areas. Railroad tracks are bent slightly.

XI. Most buildings collapse. Some bridges are destroyed. Large cracks appear in the ground. Underground pipelines are destroyed. Railroad tracks are badly bent.

XII. Almost everything is destroyed. Objects are thrown into the air. The ground moves in waves or ripples. Large amounts of rock may move.

Seismographs

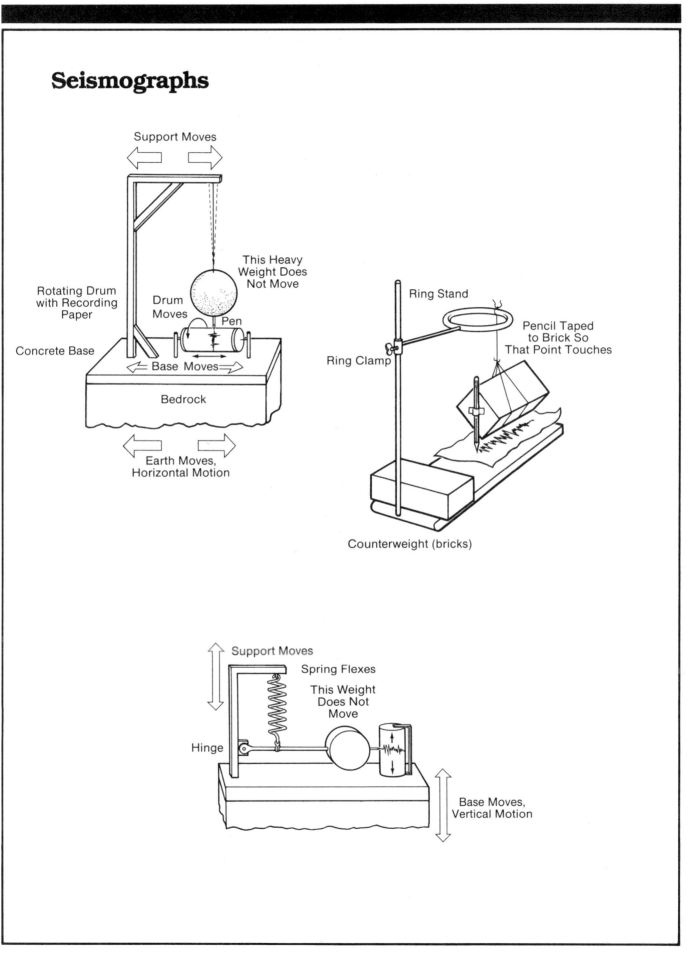

Seismogram Worksheet

Name_____

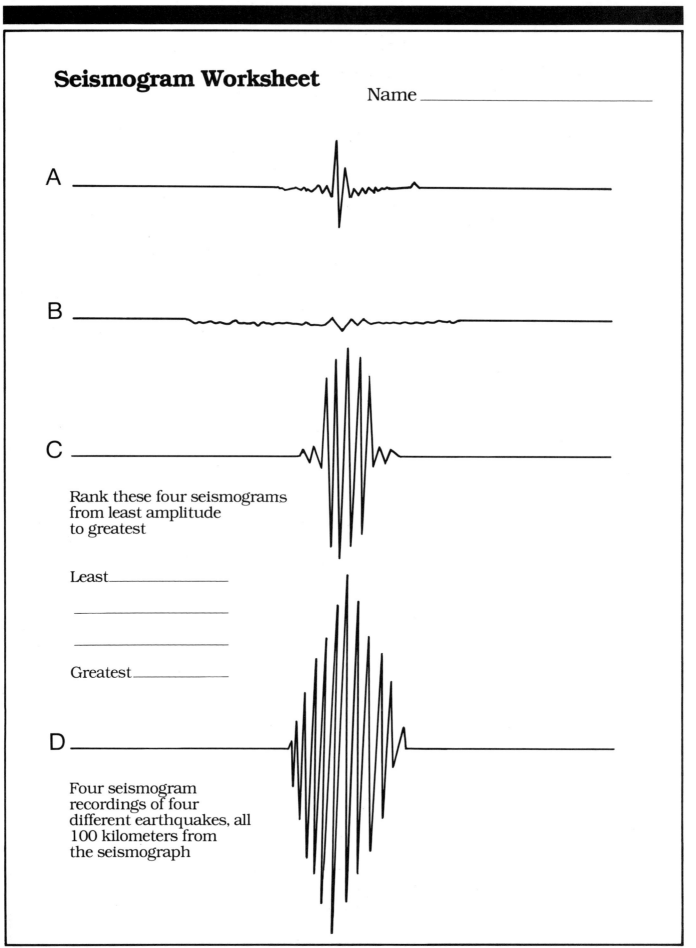

A

B

C

Rank these four seismograms
from least amplitude
to greatest

Least_____

_____

_____

Greatest_____

D

Four seismogram
recordings of four
different earthquakes, all
100 kilometers from
the seismograph

The Richter Scale

Richter Magnitude 1.0	TNT Energy Equivalent 6 ounces	Example (approximate) Small Blast at a Construction Site
1.5	2 pounds	
2.0	13 pounds	
2.5	63 pounds	
3.0	397 pounds	
3.5	1,000 pounds	
4.0	6 tons	Small Atomic Bomb
4.5	32 tons	Average Tornado
5.0	199 tons	
5.5	500 tons	Massena, NY Quake, 1944
6.0	6,270 tons	
6.5	31,550 tons	Coalinga, CA Quake, 1983
7.0	199,000 tons	Hebgen Lake, MT Quake, 1959
7.5	1,000,000 tons	
8.0	6,270,000 tons	San Francisco, CA Quake, 1906
8.5	31,550,000 tons	Anchorage, AK Quake, 1964
9.0	199,999,000 tons	

P-Wave Motion and S-Wave Motion

P-Wave

S-Wave

The S-Wave Machine

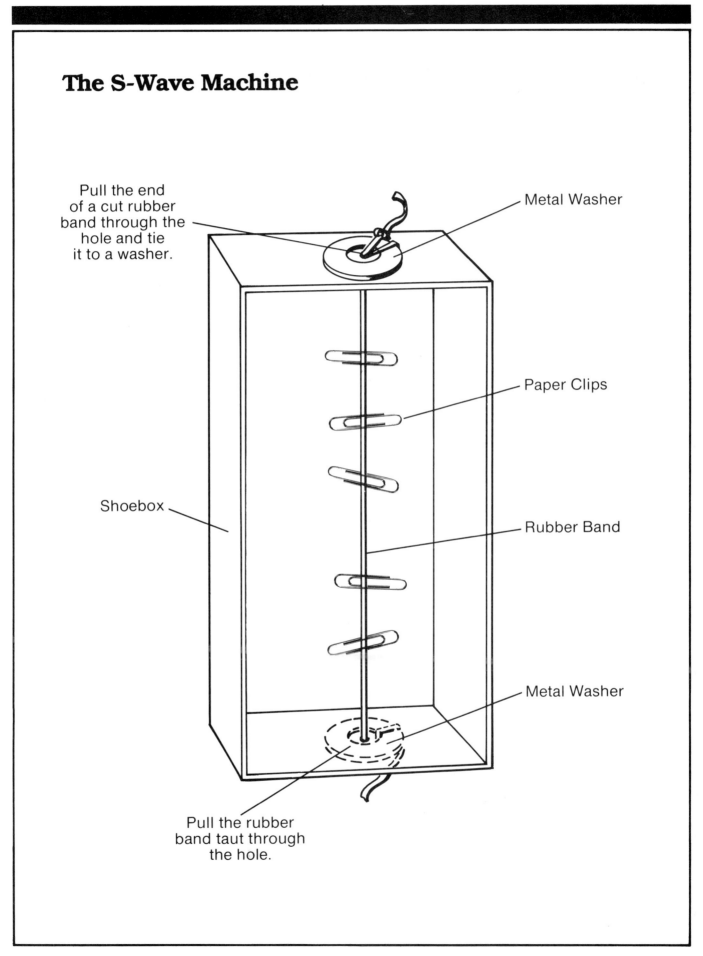

Pull the end of a cut rubber band through the hole and tie it to a washer.

Metal Washer

Paper Clips

Rubber Band

Shoebox

Metal Washer

Pull the rubber band taut through the hole.

Student Seismograph

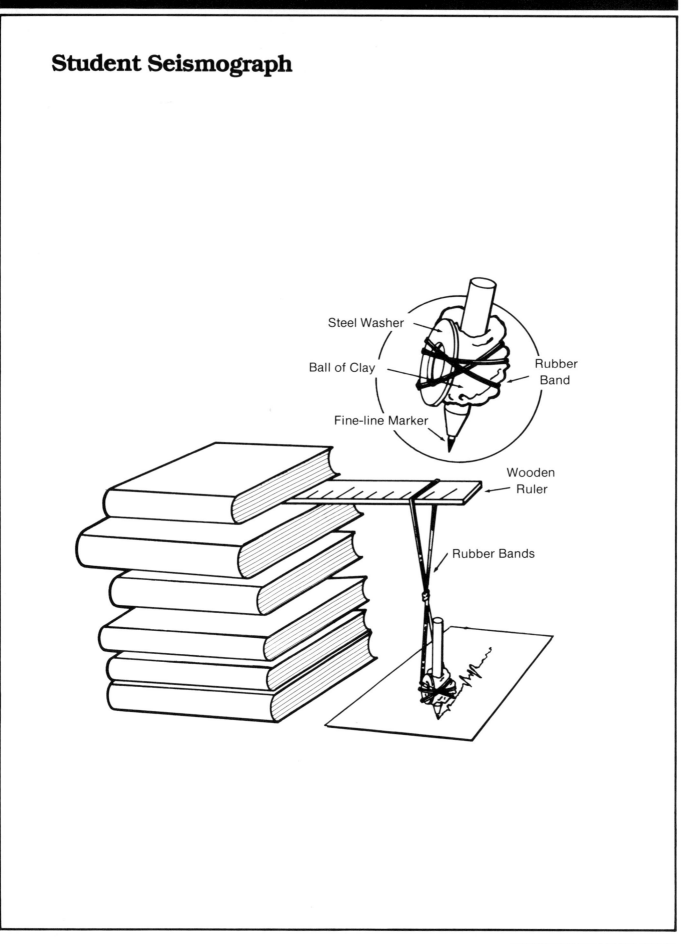

Steel Washer

Ball of Clay

Rubber Band

Fine-line Marker

Wooden Ruler

Rubber Bands

Seismogram Showing Amplitude

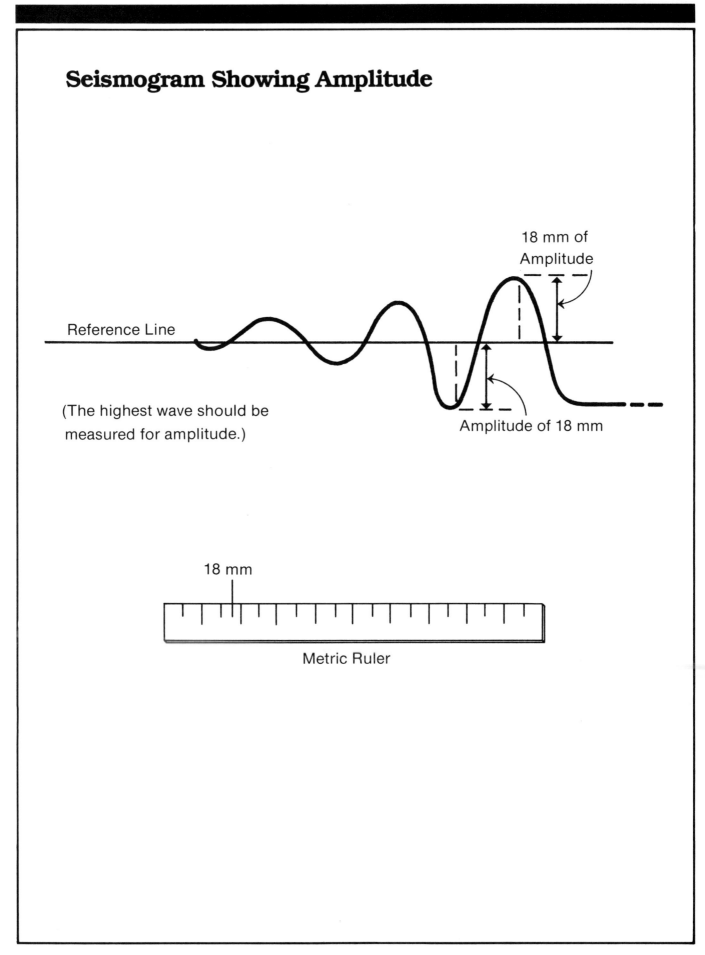

Reference Line

18 mm of Amplitude

Amplitude of 18 mm

(The highest wave should be measured for amplitude.)

18 mm

Metric Ruler

Recognizing
an Earthquake

EARTHQUAKE CURRICULUM, K-6
SCOPE AND SEQUENCE CHART

Unit V: Recognizing an Earthquake

Level	Concept	Laboratory	Mathematics	Language Arts	Social Studies	Art
K-2	Earthquake and earthquake activity are relatively unpredictable. People may feel, see, hear, and smell the signs of an earthquake. Earthquakes affect people in many ways.	Singing and playing instruments Earthquake simulation		Earthquake songs and lyrics Earthquake vocabulary Feelings vocabulary	U.S. map study of earthquake locations Earthquake damage Quake-safe actions Quake simulation	Cut, paste, and color earthquake effects
3-4	Earthquakes and earthquake activity are relatively unpredictable. People may feel, see, hear, and smell the signs of an earthquake. Earthquakes affect people in many ways.	Earthquake simulation Evacuation drill	Time span associated with earthquakes Estimating Concept of one million Interpreting charts	Descriptions of earthquake effects Vocabulary development of earthquake words	Map study of earthquakes and locations of damage risk Earthquake damage and effects on people Discussing community response	Color keys on maps
5-6	Earthquakes and earthquake activity are relatively unpredictable. Some earthquakes result in large dollar amounts of damage. Scientists use isoseismals to compare the effects of different earthquakes. Earthquakes on the ocean floor sometimes cause giant seismic waves, or tsunamis.	Tsunami simulation	Graphing earthquake damage Scale and map distances	Earthquake effects descriptions Vocabulary development of earthquake words Comparison and discussion	Events during and after an earthquake Earthquake damage Map study of earthquakes	Construction of seashore environments for tsunami simulation

V

Recognizing an Earthquake

Scientists cannot accurately predict when and where an earthquake will occur. We can teach our students what to expect, however, and how to protect themselves. They will learn that earthquakes are relatively brief, but their effects range far and wide. Foreshocks and aftershocks may spread over days and even months. The impact of a quake may be felt hundreds of miles from its epicenter. A severe quake may trigger a chain of events, such as landslides, fires, floods, and pollution, that extend the damage and add to the panic and the casualties. Teaching our students to recognize an earthquake and take immediate positive action can help them and those around them to come through the disaster safely.

Recognizing an Earthquake

Earthquake Prediction

The destructive impact of earthquakes could be greatly reduced if we knew where and when they were going to happen. Unfortunately, all scientists have been able to derive so far are a few scattered clues. One of the most intriguing is animal behavior. Many eyewitnesses have reported seeing animals strangely agitated just before a quake. Cockroaches, for example, seem to sense the onset of even small quakes before they register on any of our instruments. Scientists remain sceptical about the significance of these reports.

The emission of natural gases, changes in elevations of the Earth's surface, and changes in the speed of seismic waves offer other clues. The strain movements of rocks which build up to a quake may cause increased release of natural gases. In low-lying areas, a strong smell of marsh gas has been noted before some major earthquakes.

In other areas, strain and fault movement causes deformation at the surface of the Earth. Scientists are using sensitive instruments to measure these motions and see if surface elevations change when strain energy is released in nearby earthquakes.

The buildup of strain energy over large portions of the Earth's crust also affects the speed of body waves inside the Earth. This change has enabled scientists to predict some earthquakes successfully, but its application appears to be limited.

Some scientists look to the historical record as a basis for prediction. Because written records for the U.S. only go back about 200 years, scientists use tree ring evidence of landsliding and radioactive dating to chart earthquake activity before the 18th century. Some repeat patterns are beginning to emerge, but we are still a long way from predicting earthquakes.

Shortened Mercalli Scale

I. Only instruments detect it.

II. People lying down might feel it.

III. People on upper floors of buildings will feel it, but may not know it is an earthquake.

IV. People indoors will probably feel it, but those outside may not.

V. Nearly everyone feels it, and wakes up if they are sleeping.

VI. Everyone feels the quake. It's hard to walk.

VII. It's hard to stand.

VIII. People will not be able to drive cars. Poorly built buildings may collapse; chimneys may fall.

IX. Most foundations are damaged. The ground cracks.

X. Most buildings are destroyed. Water is thrown out of rivers and lakes.

XI. Rails are bent. Bridges and underground pipelines are put out of service.

XII. Most things are leveled. Large objects may be thrown into the air.

The Onset of an Earthquake

Since the science of earthquake prediction is still in its infancy, we can't usually count on more than a few seconds advance warning. Some earthquakes are preceded by a low rumbling sound. Observers say it sounds like the passing of heavy vehicles, freight trains, jet engines, or thunder. At a distance from the epicenter the sound becomes smoother and more regular, like the low roll of distant thunder.

During the Earthquake

The first thing we might feel is likely to be a jolt or shaking of the ground we are on or the building we are in. We may not even realize we are in an earthquake at first, but if it is a sizable quake the fact will soon be unmistakable. One survivor of the 1906 San Francisco earthquake compared the physical sensation to riding down a long flight of stairs on a bicycle. Fortunately, ground movement in that quake only lasted for about 40 seconds. The Fort Tejon earthquake of 1857 is reported to have shaken Los Angeles for two minutes—an unusually long time for an earthquake.

Far-Ranging Effects

Even though the main shock lasts for such a short time, the effects of a major earthquake may reach a long way in both space and time. People hundreds of miles away from the epicenter may experience shaking or damage. This is especially true in the eastern United States, where quakes are felt over a much larger area than they are in the West.

An *isoseismal* map shows zones or bands of the Earth where earthquake waves of the same intensity have been reported. For example, the U.S. map on the next page shows the areas that reported Modified Mercalli intensities of VI or greater for two major earthquakes. All of the areas between the isoseismal line labeled VI and the line labeled VII could experience effects of Mercalli intensity VI. The effects would be less strong in the area outside the line labelled V. The San Francisco earthquake of April 18, 1906, and the New Madrid earthquake of December 16, 1811, had roughly the same magnitude on the Richter scale. However, the area which registered VII or above on the Mercalli scale was *twenty times larger* for the New Madrid quake than for the one in San Francisco.

The main shocks in the New Madrid area were followed by fifteen strong aftershocks. All were felt strongly enough to waken sleepers in Washington, D.C. In the three months following the main shock, nearly 2,000 aftershocks were reported at Louisville, Kentucky, 320 km (or 200 miles) from the New Madrid fault zone.

The Charleston earthquake of August 31, 1886, had a Richter magnitude of 7 and a Mercalli intensity of X at the epicenter. Events of Mercalli intensity II to III were reported as far north as upper New York state and western New England and as far south as the tip of Florida.

Secondary Disasters

Even near the epicenter of a disastrous quake, much of the damage that occurs is due to secondary events. An earthquake may trigger landslides, fires, floods, chemical spills, and the release of nuclear wastes and other dangerous wastes. It may cause train wrecks and collisions of other vehicles. Power sources and water supplies may fail.

Earthquakes on the ocean bottom may result in the up or down shifting of large blocks of the crust. Such motion can generate a special kind of ocean wave called a *tsunami*, or seismic sea wave. A series of these waves may travel at speeds up to 800 km/hr in the deep ocean, where they are too small to be seen. But, when they reach land, they mount to heights of tens of meters and break against the shore and its buildings. Low coastal areas can be flooded, and much loss of life can result.

Dreadful as these events are, they can all be made worse by fears born of ignorance. The information you give your students will help them and those around them to cope safely if a natural disaster does occur in their area.

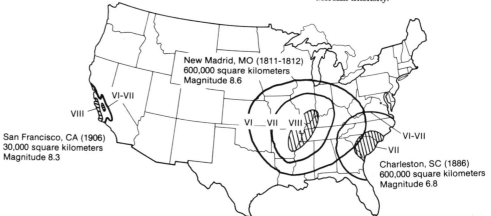

Isoseismal map of three U.S. earthquakes. Areas with lines show Modified Mercalli Intensity.

New Madrid, MO (1811-1812)
600,000 square kilometers
Magnitude 8.6

San Francisco, CA (1906)
30,000 square kilometers
Magnitude 8.3

Charleston, SC (1886)
600,000 square kilometers
Magnitude 6.8

VI-VII

VIII

VI — VII — VIII

VI-VII

VII

What Happens During an Earthquake?

Content Concepts

1. Earthquakes and earthquake activity are relatively unpredictable.

2. You might feel, see, hear, and smell the signs of an earthquake.

3. Earthquakes affect people in many different ways.

Vocabulary

epicenter
emergency
landslide
tsunami
drop and cover

Objectives

Students will

—identify events that occur during an earthquake.

—identify hazards caused by earthquakes.

—demonstrate safe behavior during an earthquake simulation.

Learning Links

Language Arts: Identifying and listing feeling words

Social Studies: Observing the locations of epicenters on the U.S. map, discussing the effect of earthquakes on people and their property, experiencing a simulation of an earthquake

Art: Cutting, pasting, and coloring pictures

Music: Singing and playing accompaniment, improvising rhythmic movements

Activity One: Know What Might Happen

Materials for the teacher
• Transparencies made from Master 11, U.S. Map with Epicenters; Master 39, Where Earthquakes Happen; and Master 40, Parts a–f, the Earthquake Events Set
• Overhead projector

Materials for each student
• Handout made from Master 39
• Glue
• Scissors
• Crayons

Procedure

1. Lead an introductory discussion reviewing Earth plates. Help students to understand that earthquakes can happen without warning. Project the transparency of Master 11, U.S. Map with Epicenters, and examine the distribution of earthquakes throughout the U.S.

2. Project Master 39, Where Earthquakes Happen. Discuss the different kinds of locations where earthquakes occur, emphasizing that earthquakes where people live are our greatest concern. Distribute copies of Master 39. Direct students to cut and paste the sentences to match the appropriate pictures, then color the pictures.

3. Tell the students that an earthquake can shake, damage, or destroy buildings. Earthquakes can cause emergencies where many people are injured and killed, and their homes and towns destroyed. However, the Earth does not split open and swallow people and homes. Point out that we can avoid or reduce our chances of being hurt if we know what to expect and what to do during an earthquake.

4. Ask students to describe what they think they would see, hear, feel, and smell if an earthquake occurred nearby. Allow time for them to respond, and then display transparencies of Master 40, Parts a–f, the Earthquake Events Set. Use the pictures to direct the discussion, supplementing the students' ideas with some or all of the information that follows.

Teacher Take Note: Be sure students understand that in an actual earthquake they must take cover. From their safe positions they would feel, hear, and smell much more than they will see. Right now we are imagining what we *might* see *if* we could watch from a perfectly safe place.

Master 50, U.S. Map with 14 Epicenters

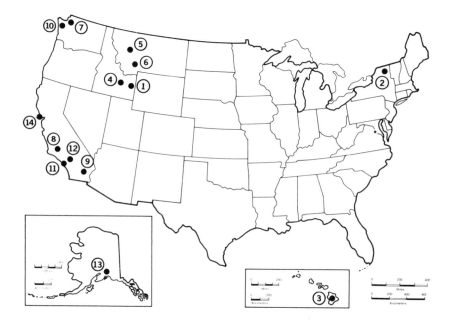

U.S. Map with 14 Epicenters

   1. Pocatello Valley, ID
   2. Massena, NY
   3. Hilo, HI
   4. Borah Peak, ID
   5. Helena, MT
   6. Hebgen Lake, MT
   7. Seattle, WA
   8. Coalinga, CA
   9. Imperial Valley, CA
   10. Olympia, WA
   11. Long Beach, CA
   12. Whittier, CA
   13. Prince Wm. Sound, AK
   14. San Francisco, CA

ep • i • cen • ter

An epicenter is a point on the Earth's surface directly above the place where an earthquake's energy is released.

e • mer • gen • cy

An emergency is an unexpected event or situation that calls for quick action.

Master 40a. Living Room

You might become aware of gentle movement which grows stronger, or you might be jarred by a sudden jolt.

You would see hanging objects swing and sway, and possibly fall from their hooks or nails. Mirrors and pictures might fall and break. Plaster may drop, windows may shatter, ceilings and walls may crack. Electric lights may flicker and go out.

You would hear a low rumbling noise that quickly grows louder. You might also hear creaking and grumbling from the house itself, and from other buildings.
You might smell odors from spilled food and liquids of various kinds.

Master 40b. Bedroom

You might see tall, heavy pieces of furniture topple over. Things in drawers and on shelves might spill. Water would slosh out of fishbowls.

You might hear the sound of tree branches hitting against the house. You might hear crashes from things that fall and break.

Master 40c. Neighborhood

Animals may make loud, excited noises. Babies may cry; adults and children may shout.

The cement that holds bricks together may come loose, allowing bricks to tumble from chimneys and brick buildings. Ladders and other tools may fall if nothing is holding them in place.

Master 40a

Living Room

EARTHQUAKES-NSTA/FEMA

Master 40b

Bedroom

EARTHQUAKES-NSTA/FEMA

Master 40c

Neighborhood

EARTHQUAKES-NSTA/FEMA

Master 40d. Downtown

Reservoirs, sewer systems, and water pipes might begin to leak.

You may hear church bells ringing, cars honking, and sirens screaming.

Separate parts of buildings such as ledges, signs, and decorations may fall and cause damage. Sometimes walls and roofs may collapse, or even whole buildings. Sometimes large objects might be thrown into the air.

Gas lines might break and leak gases. You may smell gas, or smoke from gasoline fires and other fires.

Master 40e. Tsunami

When an earthquake occurs under the ocean, the vibrations may set large waves of water in motion. These waves are called *tsunamis*. If they reach a shore where people live, they may cause great damage.

If a tsunami warning is in effect, stay away from the shore, and listen to the radio for safety information.

Master 40f. Landslides

When earthquake waves pass through wet soil, it may lose its firmness and collapse. This process is called *liquefaction.* Quakes may also cause rocks or soil to tumble rapidly downhill.

If you could see a landslide from your window, you would see rocks and soil tumbling at a great rate of speed. Trees and plants would travel with them. You might hear a rumbling noise.

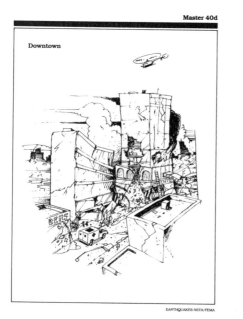

Master 40d

Downtown

EARTHQUAKES-NSTA/FEMA

Master 40e

Tsunami

EARTHQUAKES-NSTA/FEMA

Teacher Take Note: Do not excuse children with special needs from participating in earthquake drills. Children who are blind, deaf, or have impaired mobility especially need experiences which build confidence in their ability to avoid and cope with dangers. Plan with other teachers and the school nurse to determine quake-safe actions for these children.

It may not be possible for children with impaired mobility to get under a desk or table. They can, however, learn to react quickly and turn away from windows; move away from light fixtures and unsecured bookcases; and use their arms or whatever is handy to protect their heads.

Activity Two: Practice What to Do

Materials for the teacher
- Master 41, Earthquake Simulation Script
- Transparency made from Master 42, Drop and Cover
- Overhead Projector

Materials for the students
- Pencils, books, and other objects to drop
- Chairs to rattle and slide
- Desk or table to get under
- Pencils and cardboard or other hard objects to provide the scratching noise of the trees
- Handout made from Master 43, Earthquake Feelings

Procedure

1. Explain that you are going to talk through an imaginary earthquake to help students understand what might happen during a real one. Display the transparency of Master 42, call out "Drop and Cover," and direct students to practice the following actions:

Get under the table or desk.
Turn away from the windows.
Put both hands on the back of your neck.
Tuck your head down.
If your desk or table moves, hold onto the legs and move with it.

2. Before you begin reading, ask several students to demonstrate what they should do when they hear "Drop and Cover." As a group, discuss which of the demonstrations were most effective for protection, and what might be done to improve some of the others.

3. Appoint student helpers for the simulation. Ask one student to flick the lights on and off several times, and then turn them off. Appoint another to act as timer for this activity. Designate students to help create earthquake sound effects, such as:

rattling glass	trees scraping the building
scraping desks	people shouting
scraping tables	babies crying
opening drawers	bricks falling (drop several pencils)
barking dogs	doors banging shut
meowing cats	hanging plant falling
books falling	(drop a dish or pan)

4. Read the simulation on Master 41. Direct the students at their desks to follow Drop and Cover instructions during the simulation, while helpers provide effects as indicated.

Repeat the simulation a second time, selecting different students to provide the effects, so that each student has an opportunity to practice the Drop and Cover procedure.

5. Take time after the simulation to let students respond to the experience. Encourage them to ask questions and discuss their fears and concerns, including the unpleasant, worried and frightened feelings that they might experience.

6. Distribute the handout of Master 43, and direct students to color only the letters with stars. Discuss the feelings of the children in the picture.

Teacher Take Note: Although doorways have traditionally been regarded as safe locations during an earthquake, it's important to anticipate some problems. Doors may slam shut. Door jambs may be bent. Automated safety doors will probably close. You will need to use your own best judgment in choosing where to position yourself for the simulation. Local safety officials can answer your specific questions.

Activity Three: Sing it Out!

Materials
- Transparency made from Master 44, Shimmy—Shimmy—Shake
- Optional: Rhythm band instruments

Procedure

1. Sing the song with the students to the tune of "Old MacDonald's Farm." Invite them to suggest sound effects and movements to accompany the singing.

2. Repeat the song several times, until all the students are familiar with the words. This activity will do a great deal to dispel the tension produced by the earthquake drill, as well as to reinforce the concepts of the lesson.

They're Strong, But Not for Long

Content Concepts

1. Earthquakes and earthquake activity are relatively unpredictable.

2. Students might feel, see, hear, or smell the signs of an earthquake.

3. Earthquakes affect people in many different ways.

Objectives

Students will
—identify which parts of the United States are most at risk from earthquake damage.
—demonstrate how long an average earthquake lasts.
—demonstrate safe behavior during an earthquake simulation.
—chart the numbers of earthquakes that occur each year in different damage categories, mild to severe.
—demonstrate the concept of a million through a counting exercise.
—graph some recent major earthquakes.

Vocabulary

minor
moderate
major
million
evacuate
aftershock

Learning Links

Language Arts: Following directions, class discussion

Social Studies: Locating states, identifying countries, discussing disaster relief

Math: Counting to a million, timing a minute, constructing a bar graph, estimating injuries

Art: Coloring an earthquake risk map

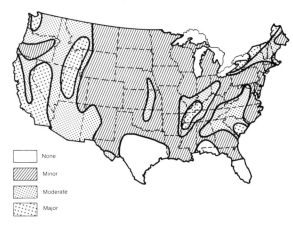

None

Minor

Moderate

Major

Master 45, Earthquake Risk Map

Teacher Take Note: This map is based on earthquakes that have happened in the past. Major Risk on the map does not necessarily indicate that a particular area will experience a damaging earthquake in the near future, and None does not mean that earthquakes are impossible in that area.

Activity One: Size Up Your Risk

Materials for the teacher
- Transparency made from Master 45, Earthquake Risk Map, colored according to directions in step 3 below
- Overhead projector

Materials for each student
- Copy of Master 45
- Crayons or colored pencils

Procedure

1. Discuss with students the following question: Are all regions of the U.S. equally likely to receive earthquake damage?

2. Tell students that they are going to work with a map that divides the United States into zones by different degrees of potential earthquake intensity, as measured on the Mercalli scale. All 50 states and all U.S. territories are at some risk from earthquakes. At least 39 states are at moderate to high risk.

3. Distribute the maps, ask students to take out their crayons or colored pencils, and give these instructions:

a. Use yellow to color in the sections of the United States that have no shading in them. In the legend, use yellow to color in the box in front of the word None.

b. Skip the Minor box for now. Use blue to color in the sections that have dots and color in the box in front of the word Moderate.

c. Use red to color in the sections marked with X. In the legend, color the box in front of the word Major red.

d. Color the rest of the United States green, and also the box in front of the word Minor.

4. After the maps have been colored, project the overhead and conduct a class discussion around the following questions:

What is the risk for damage from earthquakes in the area where we live? (Answers will vary.)

Is the risk factor the same for our entire state? (Again, answers will vary.)

How many states in the U.S. are believed to be totally free from earthquake risk? (none of them)

Activity Two: Shake a Minute

Materials for the teacher
• Large clock with a second hand
• Blackboard and chalk

Materials for each student
• Pencils
• Paper

Procedure

1. Ask students to estimate on a piece of paper how long they think an earthquake lasts. (How long will the ground shake?)

2. Collect the estimates and list them on the board.

3. Explain to students that in most earthquakes, shaking rarely lasts for as long as a minute in any one area. Strong shaking from a major quake usually lasts from 30 to 60 seconds. The 1906 San Francisco earthquake lasted about 40 seconds. In the 1964 Alaskan earthquake, the shaking lasted 3 to 4 minutes—an extremely long time. This does not happen very often.

4. Tell students that they are going to estimate how long a one-minute earthquake is without looking at a clock. Have them break up into pairs. One of each pair will be the time-keeper and recorder, while the other is the "earthquake."

5. When you give the signal, the earthquakes are to begin shaking, and the timers are to begin timing. Ask the quakes (whose backs are to the chalkboard) to continue shaking until they think that a minute has passed.

mi • nor

A minor risk is a relatively small possibility of harm.

mod • e • rate

A moderate risk is a possibility of harm that is neither small nor great, but in between.

ma • jor

A major risk is a serious and significant possibility of harm.

e • vac • u • ate

To evacuate a building is to empty it of people.

Teacher Take Note: Instruct students to shake with care, so they do not hurt themselves or anyone around them.

6. Once the timing and shaking start, write the time elapsed on the board every five seconds. The timers, who can see the board, should record the last time listed when their partners stop shaking. Instruct the timers not to share the time with the earthquake students yet.

7. Ask the timers to report the actual times that each "quake" lasted. Write all of the times on the board. Have the class compare the times:

> How long was the shortest "earthquake"?
>
> How long was the longest?
>
> What was the average time for this group?

8. Have partners switch roles and repeat steps 5 and 6, then step 7. Ask the class:

> Did the second group come closer to one minute than the first?
>
> If the answer is yes, why? (perhaps because the second pair of students had the advantage of observing the first pair)

9. Now have everyone in the class shake for one minute at the same time. Tell them when to start and stop, but ask them not to watch the clock. Then ask:

> Did the time you shook seem like more or less than a minute? (Explain that even though an earthquake is over in a short time, it usually seems much longer to those people experiencing it.)
>
> What might happen to objects in this classroom if the ground shook strongly for a minute? (Answers will vary.) Explain that we will learn more about this in our next activity.

Activity Three: Earthquake Simulation

Materials for the teacher
- Master 41, Earthquake Simulation Script
- Transparency made from Master 42, Drop and Cover
- Master 48, Coalinga Schools Report (teacher background only)
- Overhead Projector

Materials for the students
- Pencils, books, and other objects to drop
- Chairs to rattle and slide
- Desks or tables to get under
- Pencils and cardboard or other hard objects to provide the scratching noise of the trees
- Copies of Master 44, Shimmy—Shimmy—Shake

Procedure

1. Follow the directions in Unit V, Level 1, Activity Two for the simulation drill. When you have finished, tell students that it would be necessary to leave the building after an earthquake.

2. Ask them to estimate how long it takes to evacuate the building when there is a fire drill.

3. Go through an actual fire drill procedure with your students and record the time it takes to complete this evacuation. Tell students that fire drill exits are often the best way to evacuate a building after an earthquake. Then ask:

How long did it take us to get out of the building? (probably 5 minutes)

How did this compare with your estimates? (Answers will vary.)

How long does a moderately severe earthquake last? (about one minute)

Would it be possible to evacuate the building during a quake of that length? (Students will probably answer no.) Why or why not? (There isn't time.)

What would be some of the hazards along the way if we tried to leave the building during a quake? (falling objects, fires, gas leaks, broken windows, other items mentioned in the simulation)

4. You may want to read and discuss the Coalinga Schools Report, Master 48, with your students.

5. Explain to students that they will have a chance to practice earthquake evacuation in a later lesson. Answer any further questions they have about the experience of an earthquake. You may want to finish by singing "Shimmy—Shimmy— Shake," on Master 44. (See Unit V, Level 1, Activity 3.)

Activity Four:
Little Shakes and Big Quakes

Materials for the teacher
- Overhead projector
- Transparency made from Master 46, Earthquake Severity Worksheet

Materials for each student
- Worksheet of Master 46
- Pencils

Procedure

1. Tell students that seismographs record close to 1 million earthquakes every year. They are going to estimate how many of those cause serious damage.

2. Distribute worksheets. Have students place the numbers from the answer section at the bottom of the sheet where they think they belong in the right hand column, Estimated Number per Year.

3. Project the transparency and invite students to compare their answers with the actual figures. Discuss their reactions. Ask them to write in the correct figures on their own sheets.

4. Have students add the four lower numbers to see how many earthquakes cause slight to serious damage every year. (about 620)

Activity Five: How Much is a Million?

Materials for the teacher
• Classroom clock with second hand

Materials for each student
• Paper
• Pencil

Procedure

1. Review with students the information from Activity Four that about 1 million earthquakes occur every year. Write the number 1,000,000 on the board.

2. Tell the students they are going to get a better idea of how big a million is by doing a counting exercise.

3. Have students estimate how long it would take to count to a million and write their estimates down on a piece of paper. Collect the papers.

4. Have one student count at a steady rate to 100 while you or another student keeps time. It should take a little longer than a minute.

5. Tell students that for the purpose of this activity, we are going to pretend that we can count a hundred numbers every minute. At this rate, we are going to figure out how long it would take to count to a million. Ask:

How many minutes would it take to count to a million at the rate of 100 numbers a minute? (Divide 1,000,000 by 100: the answer is 10,000.)

How could we calculate how many hours this is? (Divide 10,000 by 60: the answer is 167.)

How could we calculate how many days this is? (Divide 167 by 24: the answer is 7 days.)

Could a person really count to a million this quickly? (Remind students that this is non-stop counting, with no pauses for food or sleep; also point out that counting large numbers such as 333,333 would take longer than counting small numbers such as 1, 2, and 3. The 7 days is just an approximate answer; actual time would be much longer.)

6. Compare student estimates with the answer of 7 days.

Activity Six: Killer Earthquakes

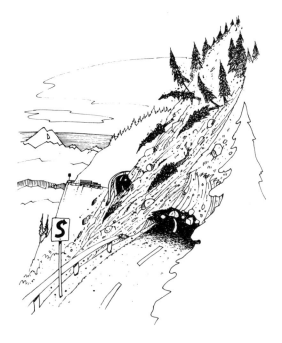

Materials for the teacher
• World Map, or transparency made from Master 5
• Transparency made from Master 7, World Map with Epicenters
• Overhead projector

Materials for each student
• Worksheet made from Master 47, Killer Earthquakes
• Pencil

Procedure

1. Discuss with students that although there are only about 20 major earthquakes each year that inflict serious damage, some of these earthquakes kill many people when they occur.

2. Distribute the worksheet and have students graph the earthquakes listed on the sheet. These are some of the major "killer earthquakes" that have occurred in the last 20 years.

3. Point out that the 1978 Iran earthquake with a Richter magnitude of 7.7 killed 15,000 people, while the 1970 Peru earthquake with a Richter magnitude of 7.8 killed 67,000 people. Ask the class to give some possible reasons for the great difference in fatalities, considering that the magnitudes for the two quakes were similar. (Possible answers: location of the epicenter—a populated area versus a non-populated area; local geology—in the Peru earthquake 18,000 people were buried in a landslide; the type of buildings that people live in; the type of soil; the depth of the soil; the time of day.)

4. Have students locate the quakes listed on the worksheet on a world map.

5. Refer back to the World Map with Epicenters, Master 7. Did these earthquakes happen in areas where earthquakes had occurred in the past? (Yes)

6. Tell students that one of the greatest killer earthquakes of all time is not on their tables. It happened on July 28, 1976, in Tangshan in the Hebei Province of China. Estimates of the number of people killed vary between 200,000 and 800,000. Ask:

How much longer would your graph have to be to show that quake? (2-8 times longer)

7. Have students compare the number of people killed in each of these earthquakes to the number of people in their school and/or community, in order to put the numbers of deaths in context.

8. There is a general relationship between the number of people killed in a disaster such as an earthquake and the number hospitalized for injuries. The number hospitalized usually averages about four times the number killed. Have the students determine the number of injuries for each of these earthquakes on the basis of this rough rule of thumb.

Master 7, World Map with Epicenters

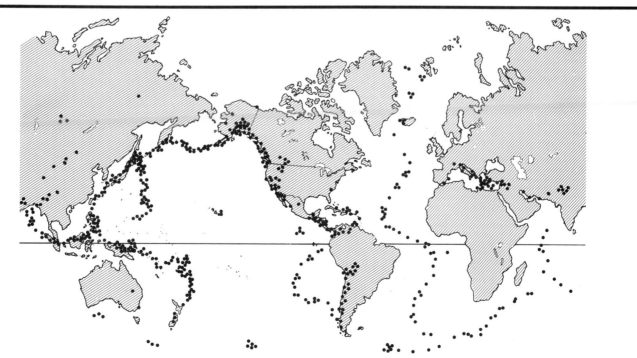

9. Ask students to think about what survivors of a major earthquake like the ones graphed in this activity would have to face and deal with. You may want to show pictures of earthquake damaged areas at this point so students can have realistic ideas of what a locality might look like after a quake. Students can work in small groups or brainstorm as an entire class. Some of the items that need to be mentioned include:

a. Immediately after an earthquake:

first aid

evacuation

checking for fire

checking for building damage—gas, water, sewer, electricity, structural damage, chimneys and other attachments

finding temporary shelter

finding food and water supplies

bringing in government and private organizations to help

b. In the days and weeks ahead:

cleaning up the mess

fixing gas, water, sewer lines; telephone lines; electrical lines

reopening essential stores (food, etc.)

rebuilding roads and bridges

raising money for the rebuilding effort

rebuilding homes

rebuilding public buildings

Extensions

1. Research how long some famous earthquakes lasted.
2. Have students graph some other "killer" earthquakes that have happened in the past.

Quake Events Range Far and Wide

Content Concepts

1. Earthquakes and earthquake events are relatively unpredictable.

2. Some earthquakes result in large dollar amounts of damage.

3. Scientists can use isoseismals to compare the effects of different earthquakes.

4. Earthquakes on the ocean floor sometimes cause giant seismic sea waves, or *tsunamis*.

Vocabulary

isoseismal
tsunami

Objectives

Students will
—review the events of an earthquake.
—demonstrate safe behavior during a quake simulation.
—demonstrate awareness of the relative unpredictability of earthquakes.
—interpret data about the costs of some specific earthquakes.
—draw isoseismals on a map which includes Mercalli intensity data.
—identify tsunamis as an earthquake event, and demonstrate their mechanism and effects on shore features.

Learning Links

Language Arts: Comparing and discussing written worksheets

Social Studies: Discussing effects of earthquakes on individuals, schools, and communities; rehearsing earthquake drill; locating states and cities on a map of the United States

Math: Interpreting isoseismals, drawing isoseismals from numerical data of Mercalli intensity ratings, using map scales to estimate distance

Art: Constructing seashore environments for tsunami simulation

Activity One: Quake Events

Materials for the teacher
- Transparencies made from Masters 40 a–f, Earthquake Events Set
- Eyewitness accounts of an earthquake, film footage, or similar materials, including transparency made from Master 48, Coalinga Schools Report
- Transparency made from Master 31, Modified Mercalli Scale
- Master 41, Earthquake Simulation Script
- Overhead projector
- Blank transparency
- Transparency marker

Materials for students
- Class notebooks
- Handouts made from Master 42, Drop and Cover
- Pencils or pens
- Notebooks, books, and other objects to drop
- Chairs to rattle and slide
- Desks or tables to get under
- Combs and hairbrushes (scrape on desks to simulate the sound of trees scratching buildings)

i • so • seis • mal

An isoseismal is a line drawn on a map of the Earth's surface to contain points registering the same intensity in a single earthquake.

tsu • na • mi

A tsunami is a giant ocean wave caused by movements of the ocean floor, such as earthquakes and volcanic eruptions.

★Coalinga, CA

Procedure

1. Project the Mercalli scale, Master 31, and review its events, with their varying degrees of damage. Read Master 48, Coalinga Schools Report, and discuss it with the class. Present any other background materials that you have, and compare the intensities of the earthquakes they describe.

2. Tell students that they are going to simulate an earthquake and practice what they would do if an earthquake occurred while they were in school. Explain that they will not be able to simulate a quake higher than VI or VII on the Mercalli scale.

3. Pass out the Drop and Cover sheet (Master 42) and go over it with the class. Use Master 41 and follow the directions in Unit Five, Level 1, Activity Two to conduct the simulation drill.

4. Using the transparencies and other materials as a springboard, create a class list of events that occur during and immediately after an earthquake. Write them on a blank transparency or on the blackboard. Discuss the list until the students are satisfied it is complete.

Activity Two: Earthquakes Are Expensive

Materials for the teacher
- Transparency made from Master 49, Selected U.S. Earthquake of the 20th Century
- Transparency made from Master 50, U.S. Map with 14 Epicenters

- Transparency made from Master 54, Cascade of Disasters
- Overhead projector
- Transparency marker
- Classroom wall map of U.S. with states and major cities marked
- Atlas of the United States, including Alaska and Hawaii

Materials for each student
- Handouts made from Masters 49 and 50
- Pencils and pens

Teacher Take Note: If you have studied any recent earthquakes or quakes of local interest, be sure to mark their locations on the map with additional dots before copying and distributing Master 49, Selected U.S. Earthquakes of the 20th Century.

Procedure

1. Invite students to estimate how much they think a major earthquake might cost the communities affected, in terms of property damage. Discuss the kinds of damage a quake might do, and the expenses involved in repair and rebuilding.

2. Distribute copies of Master 49, Selected U.S. Earthquakes of the 20th Century. Ask students:

Would you have expected amounts to be smaller than this? Larger? (Answers will vary.)

Do the damage figures rise or fall along with the magnitudes? (No, there are discrepancies.)

Why don't they? (The number and type of structures will vary from one location to another. So will the type of rock and soil in the area and other factors.)

3. Distribute copies of Master 50, U.S. Map with 14 Epicenters and give these directions.

a. On the map of the United States, locate the first earthquake on Master 49. The location of each quake is marked with a dot.

b. Place a 1 next to the dot, then write the name of the location on the first blank line beneath the map.

c. Make the next dot 2, and continue until you have labeled all the dots and filled in a blank for each dot.

U.S. Map with 14 Epicenters

1. Pocatello Valley, ID
2. Massena, NY
3. Hilo, HI
4. Borah Peak, ID
5. Helena, MT
6. Hebgen Lake, MT
7. Seattle, WA
8. Coalinga, CA
9. Imperial Valley, CA
10. Olympia, WA
11. Long Beach, CA
12. Whittier, CA
13. Prince Wm. Sound, AK
14. San Francisco, CA

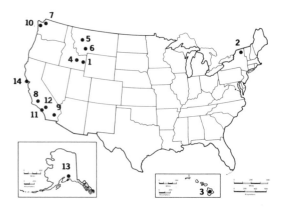

Each dot marks the site of a quake that caused serious property damage.

Teacher Take Note: Do not expect the student's isoseismal lines to look exactly like the ones on this page. The scientists who construct these maps also produce varying interpretations of the same data.

4. Let students check their own maps as you go through the work in class. You may fill in the map transparency with the class or display completed versions for students to check against.

5. Discuss with the class the economic impact major earthquakes would have on their community, state, and nation. Put the numbers on Master 49 in perspective by comparing them to some typical salaries in the community, or to the annual school budget.

6. Distribute the Cascade of Disasters handout, Master 54. Explain that the damage earthquakes cause is due to more than just the shaking of the ground. A long chain of disasters may be set off by a major quake, as the diagram illustrates. Discuss these events and their impact on a community.

Activity Three: Sizing up Isoseismals

Materials for the teacher
- Transparency made from Master 31, Modified Mercalli Scale
- Transparency made from Master 51, Isoseismal Map, San Fernando, 1971
- Transparency made from Master 52, Isoseismal Worksheet
- Overhead projector
- Transparency marker

Materials for the student
- Handouts made from Master 51 and Master 52
- Pencils

An isoseismal map illustrates the impact of an earthquake on areas around its focus.

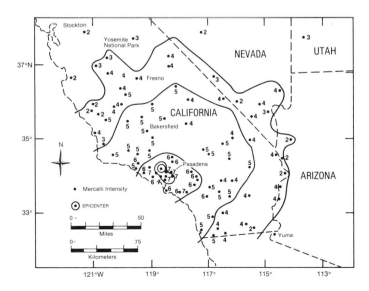

Procedure

1. Project the Mercalli scale and review it if necessary. Distribute the isoseismal map, Master 51, and explain how and why isoseismals are produced. (See unit background.)

2. Have students practice using the map scale to estimate the distances from the San Fernando epicenter to Bakersfield, Fresno, Stockton, Yuma, and Yosemite. (If any location near your home can be seen on the map, add that.) Write the answers on the board or a transparency sheet on the overhead.

3. Ask these questions about the isoseismal map:

How many solid lines (isoseismals) do you see on the map? (five)

What is their general shape? (curves centered around the epicenter)

How does Mercalli intensity relate to distance from the epicenter? (The isoseismals show Mercalli intensity generally decreasing with distance from the epicenter.)

On this map, what is the shortest distance from the epicenter to the isoseismal marked IV? (about—km; answers will vary somewhat.)

Why is there variation in the pattern of the Mercalli numbers, with lower numbers sometimes closer to the epicenter than high numbers? (Remind students that Mercalli ratings measure the effects of the quake on people and their property. These effects may vary greatly because of soil conditions, types of construction, population density, and other factors. Data collecting methods may also vary.)

4. Now distribute copies of the second map, Master 52, Isoseismal Worksheet. Ask students to draw isoseismals by using curved lines to connect identical numbers.

5. After students have been working for a few minutes, let them get together in small groups to compare their results. Project the transparency of the worksheet and draw the isoseismals as the class directs. If differences arise, point out that often in science there may be different and equally correct interpretations of the same data. Work toward consensus.

6. End by inviting questions. This may be an opportunity to reinforce some of the points in the questions under step 3.

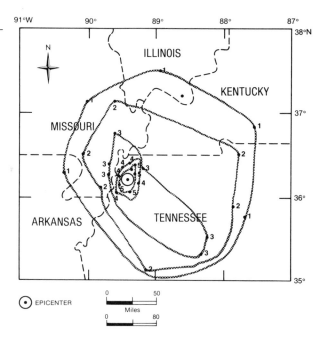

Completed Isoseismal Worksheet, Master 52

Activity Four: Tsunami!

Materials for the teacher
- Transparencies made from the two isoseismal maps, Master 51 and Master 52
- Transparency made from Master 53, Tsunami Facts
- Overhead projector

Materials for each pair or group of students
- Glass or metal baking pan or plastic shoe box
- About 1 liter of water
- Plastic lid of the type used to reclose coffee or margarine containers
- Punching tool or drawing compass
- Scissors
- String
- Sand
- Erasers, toothpicks, popsicle sticks, and other small objects to represent shore features
- Book or block of wood to serve as wedge
- Metric ruler

Procedure

1. Show students the two isoseismal maps from Activity Three, Masters 51 and 52. Point out that the lines they drew on the worksheet ring the epicenter completely, while those on the San Fernando map are incomplete circles. Ask:

Why aren't these circles finished? (because they reach the ocean and stop)

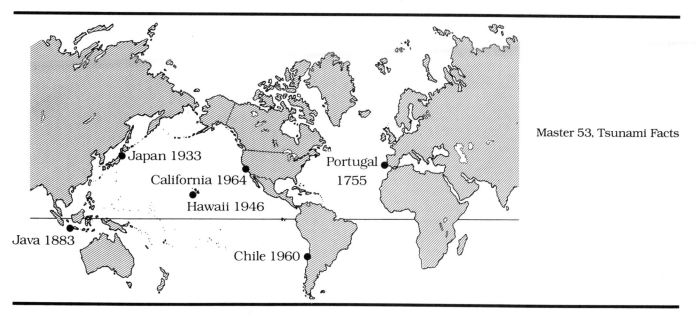

Master 53, Tsunami Facts

Japan 1933
California 1964
Hawaii 1946
Java 1883
Portugal 1755
Chile 1960

Do earthquakes occur under the ocean? (Yes; students should know this from Unit III.)

Why don't we have Mercalli numbers for these earthquakes? (because Mercalli numbers measure the impact on people and structures, and most people live on land)

Do earthquakes under the ocean ever affect people? (Some students may think of tsunamis. If not, introduce the topic.)

2. Project the transparency of Master 53. Begin with what students already know about tsunamis, and share the information on the master. Then tell class that they are going to build a model of a tsunami.

3. Divide students into pairs or small groups, distribute materials, and give these directions:

a. Use the wedge to tilt the pan at an angle of about 20 degrees.

b. Pour water into the pan to cover the lower end, leaving about a third of the pan at the upper end dry.

c. Pack a layer of sand 2–3 cm thick on the dry end of the pan to simulate a beach or coastline. Use your hands to mold dunes or drifts. Draw roads parallel to the shore with a stick or your fingers. Build docks and other small, lightweight structures to complete the shore environment. Be creative.

d. Punch the plastic lid on one end near the rim to make a hole, and thread it with a piece of string 20 cm long. Tie knots to hold the string in place.

e. Gently (in order not to make waves) place the plastic onto the bottom at the deep end of the pan. Trim it to fit if necessary. The string should be next to the low side of the pan.

f. Have one student use several fingers to hold the plastic down tightly on the shallow end, while another student pulls the string up at the deep end with a rapid movement. Tsunami!

4. When all groups have completed the simulation, ask them to describe what happened and discuss their observations.

Extensions

1. For extra credit, assign interested students to learn more about the various factors that account for differences in Mercalli intensity, including composition of the soil, saturation of the soil, slope of the land, types of building construction, and local building codes.

2. Invite students to prepare a class report on one of the tsunamis listed on Master 53. See the reference list for some possible sources of information.

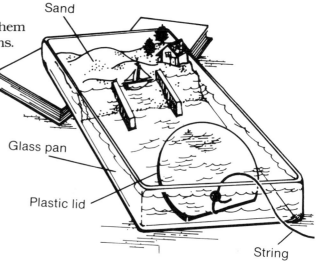

Sand

Glass pan

Plastic lid

String

Unit V. Recognizing an Earthquake

Materials List

Grades K-2
glue
scissors
crayons
objects for sound effects
rhythm band instruments
overhead projector

Grades 3-4
crayons or colored pencils
clock with second hand
paper
objects for sound effects
overhead projector
pencils

Grades 5-6
objects for sound effects
flexible plastic lid
string
baking pan or plastic shoe
  box
punching tool
scissors
small building materials
sand
metric ruler
book or block of wood
overhead projector
blank transparency
transparency markers
class notebooks
pencils or pens
U.S. wall map
U.S. atlas

Instructional Resources (Books, maps, pamphlets, slides)

Cazeau, C. J. (1975). *Earthquakes*. Chicago: Follett Corp.

References

Alaska's Good Friday Earthquake, March 27, 1964. Reston, Virginia: United States Geological Survey. Circular 491.

Bolt, B. A. (1988). *Earthquakes*. San Francisco: W. H. Freeman and Co.

Brownlee, S. (1986, July). Waiting for the big one. *Discover*, 7, pp. 52-71.

Earthquake Country: A Teachers Workshop. (1978, February 25-26). Far Western Section of National Association of Geology Teachers and California Science Teachers Association.

Earthquakes: A National Problem. Washington, DC: Federal Emergency Management Agency.

Gere, J. and H. Shan. (1984). *Terra Non Firma: Understanding and Preparing for Earthquakes*. New York: W.H. Freeman.

HELP: Hands-on Earthquake Learning Package. (1983). Palo Alto: California. Environmental Volunteers, Inc.

Herndon, S. *Second Grade Earthquake Safety*. Conway, Arkansas Disaster Mitigation Planning Section.

Muir, R. (1987). *Earthquakes and Volcanoes: Causes, Effects, and Predictions*. New York: Weidenfeld and Nicolson.

Murty, T. S. (1977). Seismic Sea Waves: Tsunamis, Bulletin 198 of Fisheries and Research Board of Canada. Ottawa, Canada: Minister of Supply and Services.

National Oceanic and Atmospheric Administration. (1976). *Catalog of Earthquake Photographs—Key to Geophysical Records*, Documentation No. 7. Boulder, Colorado: National Geophysical Data Center.

Press, F. and R. Siever. (1986). *Earth.* New York: W.H. Freeman and Co. 4th edition.

Richter, C. F. (1958). *Elementary Seismology.* San Francisco: W. H. Freeman and Co.

Safety and Survival in an Earthquake. (1983). Reston, Virginia: United States Geological Survey.

Safety and Survival Earthquake. (1984). Kiwanis Club of Coalinga, California.

Tarbuck, E. J., and F. K. Lutgens. (1987). *The Earth—An Introduction to Physical Geology,* 2nd. ed. Columbus, Ohio: Merrill Publishing Co.

Tsunami! (1974, January). NOAA, 4.

Tsunami! The Great Waves. (1975). U.S. Department of Commerce, National Oceanic and Atmospheric Administration, National Weather Service.

Van Rose, S. (1986). *Earthquakes.* New Rochelle, New York: Cambridge University Press.

Watkins, J. T. (1981, December). The 1906 San Francisco Earthquake. *California Geology.* pp. 260-266.

Where Earthquakes Happen

Earthquakes happen under the ocean.

Earthquakes happen where people live.

Earthquakes happen in the forest.

Earthquakes begin inside the Earth's crust.

1. Cut out the sentences.

2. Paste the correct sentence with its picture.

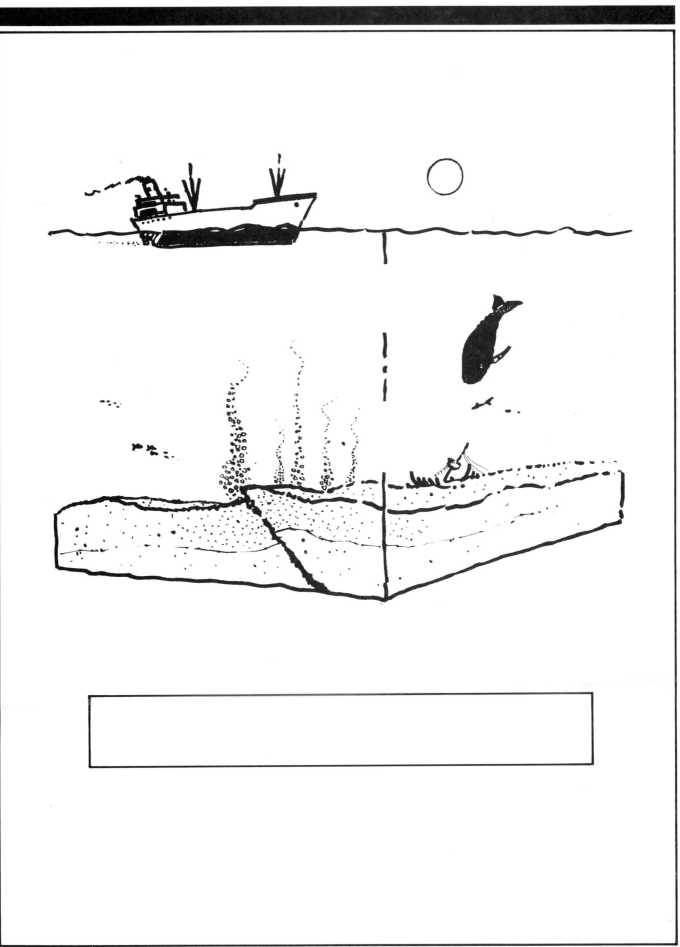

Living Room

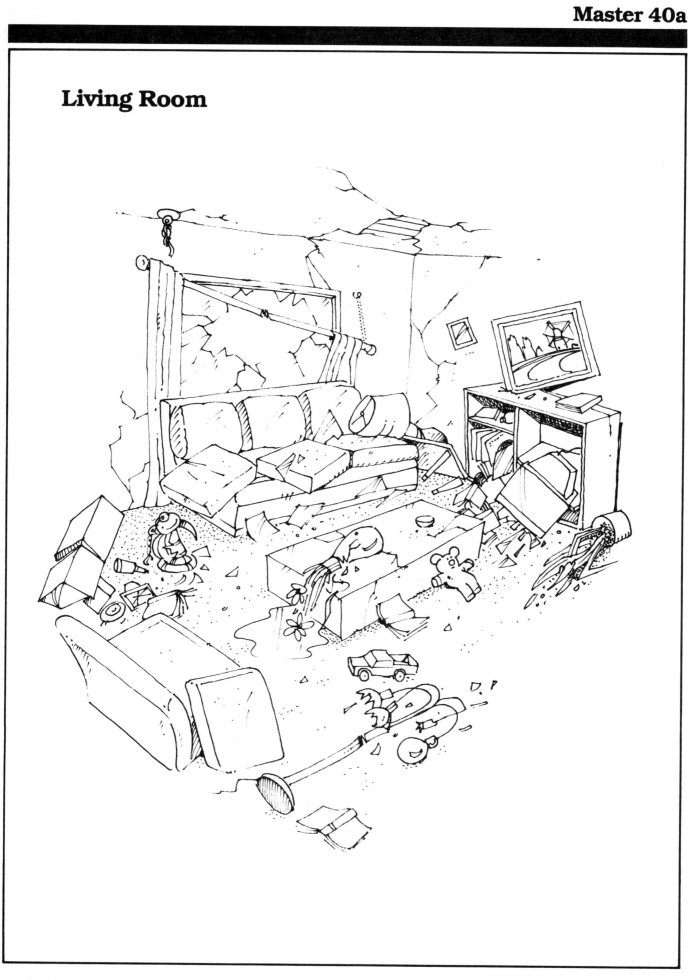

Bedroom

Neighborhood

Downtown

Tsunami

Landslides

Earthquake Simulation Script

Imagine that you hear a low, rumbling, roaring sound. The noise builds, getting louder and louder, for about ten seconds. Then, Wham! There's a terrific jolt. You feel like someone suddenly slammed on the brakes in the car, or like a truck just rammed into the side of the building.

The floor seems to be moving beneath you. It's hard to stand up, or even stay in your seat. If you do stand up, you might feel like you're riding a raft down a fast river. When you walk, it's like trying to walk on a trampoline or a waterbed. You hear someone say, "Earthquake! Drop and cover!"

I want all of you at your desks to take cover as quickly and quietly as you can, right now. Please listen very carefully.

The shaking and commotion may last about 60 seconds or a little longer. We'll have our timer count off the seconds for as long as this earthquake lasts. *[The timer may begin counting softly now.]*

The building is creaking and rattling. Books are falling from the bookcase. Hanging lamps and plants are swaying. Suddenly a pot falls to the floor and smashes, and the plant spills. A windowpane just shattered, and glass is falling to the floor. The table is sliding, too.

Be sure to stay in the drop and cover position under your desk. If your desk is moving, grab the legs and move with it.

You hear noises outside. Dogs are barking. Cats are meowing. A baby is crying. People are shouting and screaming. The shaking is making church bells ring. You hear crashing sounds, from brick chimneys and other loose parts of the building falling to the ground. Trees outside are swaying and scraping against the walls.

Inside the room, pictures are moving on their nails. Oh! That one just fell off the wall and crashed to the floor. The desk drawers are sliding open. The lights begin to flicker on and off . . .they just went out! Now the door swings back and forth on its hinges. Bang! It slams shut. There's silence now. Just as suddenly as the noise and shaking began, the room grows quiet. *[The timer can stop counting now.]*

Please, everyone, get back in your seats. It is important to remain very quiet and wait for instructions. When it is safe to leave the building, I am going to lead you outside to an open space. Stay together, and be ready to take cover again at any moment, because the shaking may start again. Sometimes other quakes, called aftershocks, begin after the first earthquake has stopped.

HELP: Hands-on Earthquake Learning Package, California Edition. (1983). Environmental Volunteers, Inc.

Drop and Cover

1. Turn away from windows.

2. Crouch under a desk or table.

3. Put both hands on the back of your neck and tuck your head down.

4. If the desk or table moves, hold the legs and move with it.

Earthquake Feelings

Name _____

Some of the letters below contain
stars. Color the letters with the stars to
see some ways people might feel after
an earthquake.

Shimmy--Shimmy--Shake!

(To the tune of Old McDonald's Farm, lyrics adapted from Sylvia Herndon)

Verse 1
Rumble, rockin', shakin' ground
Shimmy - shimmy - shake!
Whoops! it's hard not to fall down . . .
Shimmy - shimmy - shake!

With a rattle rattle here
And a rumble tumble there

Here a rattle - there a rumble . . .
Everywhere a rumble tumble.
Rumble, rockin', shakin' ground . . .
Shimmy - shimmy - shake!

Verse 2
Someone says It's an earthquake!
Shimmy - shimmy - shake!
Best to hurry, don't you wait . . .
Shimmy - shimmy - shake!

With a rattle rattle here
And a rumble tumble there

Here a rattle - there a rumble
Everywhere a rumble tumble.
Rumble, rockin', shakin' ground . . .
Shimmy - shimmy - shake!

Verse 3
Get under something near and safe
Shimmy - shimmy - shake!
You must be fast, now don't you wait . . .
Shimmy - shimmy - shake!

With a rattle rattle here
And a rumble tumble there

Here a rattle - there a rumble
Everywhere a rumble tumble.
Rumble, rockin', shakin' ground . . .
Shimmy - shimmy - shake!

Verse 4
Hold on tight and 'fore you know
Shimmy - shimmy - shake!
Rockin's over, you can go . . .
No more shimmy - shake!

No rattle rattle here
No rumble tumble there

Here no rattle - there no rumble
Gone is all the rumble tumble,
Rumble, rockin', shakin' ground . . .
No more shimmy - shake!

G G G D   E E D   B B A A   G

* Developed by Disaster Mitigation Planning Section, Office of Emergency Services,
P.O. Box 758, Conway, AR 72032-0758

Earthquake Risk Map

Name _____

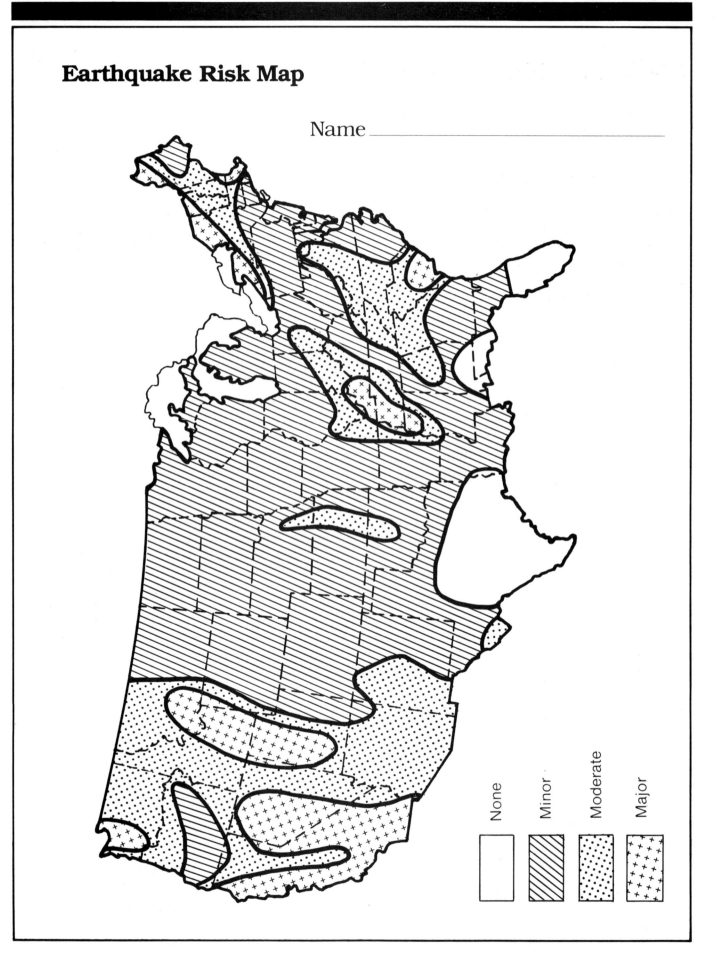

None

Minor

Moderate

Major

Name _____

Earthquake Severity Worksheet

Richter Magnitudes	Earthquake Effects	Estimated Number Per Year Worldwide
Less than 3.5	Generally not felt, but recorded.	
3.5-5.4	Often felt, but only minor damage.	
5.5-6.0	Slight damage to buildings.	
6.1-6.9	Can be destructive in areas where people live.	
7.0-7.9	Major earthquake. Causes serious damage.	
8 or greater	Great earthquake. Total destruction to nearby communities.	

Choose which answers belong in the last column.

Answers:	20	30,000	500
	100	900,000	1

Killer Earthquakes

Name _____

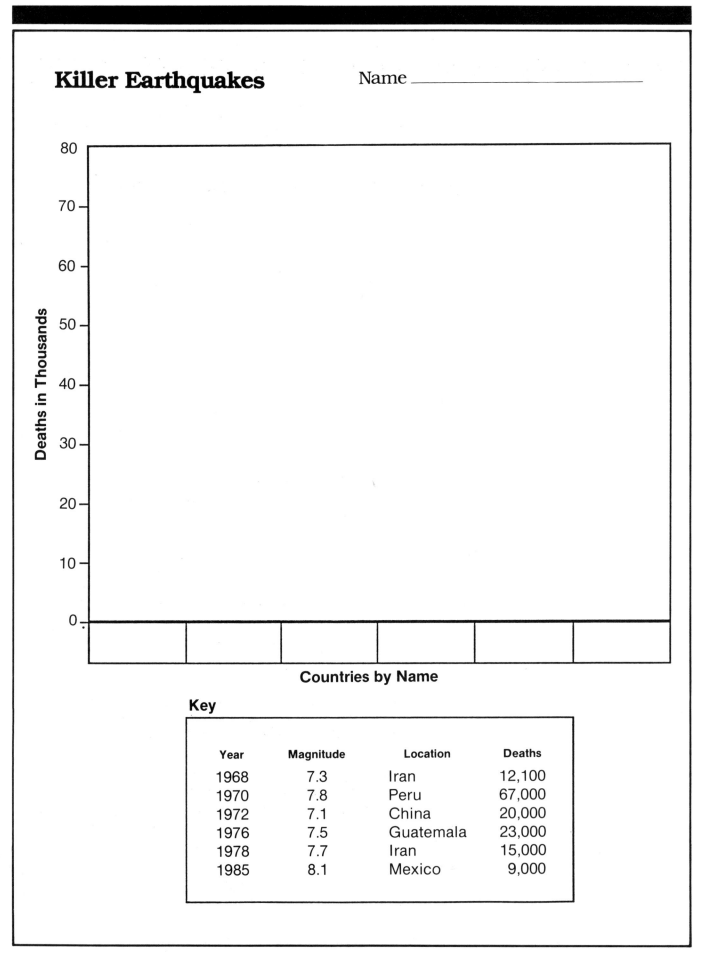

Deaths in Thousands

80

70

60

50

40

30

20

10

0

Countries by Name

Key

Year	Magnitude	Location	Deaths
1968	7.3	Iran	12,100
1970	7.8	Peru	67,000
1972	7.1	China	20,000
1976	7.5	Guatemala	23,000
1978	7.7	Iran	15,000
1985	8.1	Mexico	9,000

Coalinga Schools Report

At 4:42 p.m. on Monday, May 2, 1983, an earthquake registering 6.5 on the Richter scale struck the Coalinga area. Seconds later there was an aftershock of 5.0 Richter magnitude.

Coalinga has three elementary schools, one junior high, and one high school, serving approximately 1,900 students. The school buildings were constructed between 1939 and 1955. They contain 75 classrooms, plus gymnasiums, auditoriums, libraries, and multipurpose rooms.

Superintendent Terrell believes that death and serious injury would have occurred if school had been in session. The following is an account of the nonstructural damage to these schools:

Windows
Large windows received and caused the most damage. The 31-year-old junior high library had glass windows approximately 2.40 m × 3.04 m (8×10 ft) on the north and south walls. The glass was not tempered. All the windows imploded and littered the room with dagger-shaped pieces of glass. Floor tiles and wooden furniture were gouged by flying splinters.

Lighting Fixtures
Approximately 1,000 fluorescent bulbs fell from their fixtures and broke. All of the fixtures in the elementary schools came down, and many in other buildings. None of the hanging fixtures had safety chains. Glass in the older recessed fixtures was shaken out and broken.

Ceilings
Improperly installed T-bar ceilings came down. Glued ceiling tiles also fell, especially around vent ducting and cutouts for light fixtures.

Basements and Electrical Supply
Water pipes which came into the buildings through concrete walls were severed by the movement of the walls. Basements were flooded to five feet.

Since all the electrical supply and switching mechanisms for these buildings were in the basements, all of them were destroyed by water.

Chemical Spills
In the second-floor high school chemistry lab, bottles of sulfuric acid and other chemicals stored in open cabinets overturned and broke. Acid burned through to the first floor. Cupboard doors sprang open and glass cabinet doors broke, allowing chemicals to spill. Because there was no electric ventilation, toxic fumes permeated the building.

Furnishings and Miscellaneous Items
File cabinets flew across rooms; freestanding bookcases, cupboards, cabinets, and shelves fell over.

Machine shop lathes and presses fell over.

Typewriters flew through the air.

Metal animal cages and supplies stored on top of seven-foot cabinets crashed to the floor.

Movie screens and maps became projectiles.

Storage cabinets in the high school had been fastened to the wall with molly bolts, but they were not attached to studs. They pulled out of the wall and fell to the floor with their contents.

(based on a report prepared by E. Robert Bulman for Charles S. Terrell, Jr., superintendent of schools for San Bernardino County, California)

Selected U.S. Earthquakes of the 20th Century

Location	Date	Dollar Damage (1979 dollars)	Magnitude
1. Pocatello Valley, ID	March 28, 1975	$1,000,000	6.1
2. Massena, NY	September 5, 1944	$8,000,000	5.6
3. Hilo, HI	April 26, 1973	$9,000,000	6.2
4. Borah Peak, ID	October 2, 1983	$15,000,000	7.3
5. Helena, MT	October 19, 1935	$19,000,000	6.2
6. Hebgen Lake, MT	August 18, 1959	$26,000,000	7.1
7. Seattle, WA	April 29, 1965	$28,000,000	6.5
8. Coalinga, CA	May 2, 1983	$31,000,000	6.7
9. Imperial Valley, CA	May 19, 1940	$33,000,000	6.4
10. Olympia, WA	April 13, 1949	$80,000,000	7.0
11. Long Beach, CA	March 11, 1933	$266,000,000	6.3
12. Whittier, CA	October 1, 1987	$350,000,000	6.0
13. Prince Wm. Sound, AK	March 27, 1964	$1,020,000,000	8.4
14. San Francisco, CA	April 18, 1906	$2,000,000,000	8.2

U.S. Map with 14 Epicenters

Name _____

1. _____ 9. _____

2. _____ 10. _____

3. _____ 11. _____

4. _____ 12. _____

5. _____ 13. _____

6. _____ 14. _____

7. _____ 15. _____

8. _____ 16. _____

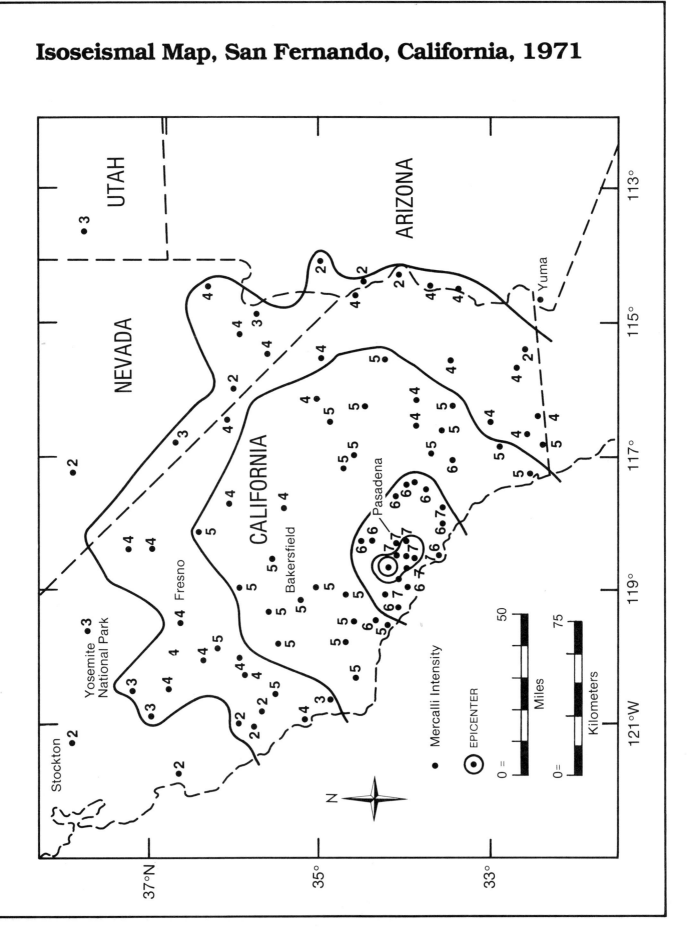

Isoseismal Map, San Fernando, California, 1971

Isoseismal Worksheet

Name _____

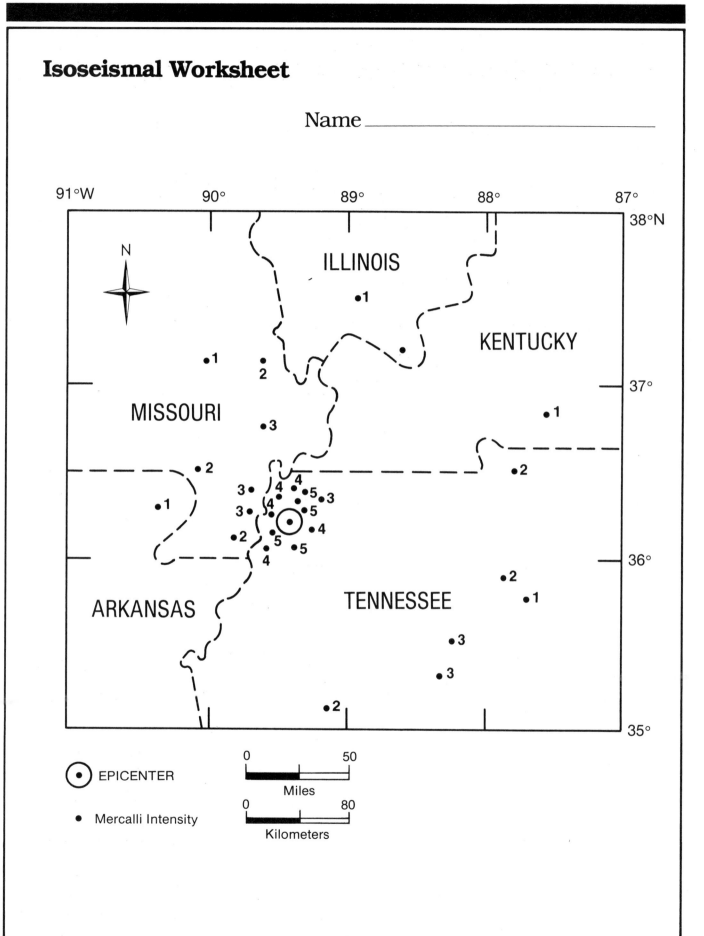

N

91°W   90°   89°   88°   87°

38°N

ILLINOIS

•1

KENTUCKY

•1
•2

37°

MISSOURI

•1

•3

•2

•1

•2

4

3• •4
•4 5 •3
3• •4 •5
•5 •4

•2 5
4 •5

36°

ARKANSAS

TENNESSEE

•2
•1

•3

•3

•2

35°

⊙ EPICENTER

• Mercalli Intensity

0   50
Miles

0   80
Kilometers

Tsunami Facts

Tsunami (pronounced soo • nah • me) is a Japanese word that means "wave in the harbor."

Tsunamis are caused by earthquakes and other movements of the ocean floor, such as volcanic eruptions and landslides. These movements generate waves that travel at speeds up to 800 km (500 miles) per hour.

In deep water, on the open ocean, tsunamis cause no damage and are hardly noticed. When they meet shallow water, however, they can batter coastlines with waves as high as 60 meters, or 100 feet.

Tsunami damage is very similar to the damage caused by hurricanes and other kinds of storm waves. Since 1946, nations in the Pacific region have shared data from the Tsunami Warning Center in Honolulu, through an international Seismic Sea Wave Warning System. This center sends out Pacific-wide warnings when an earthquake of tsunami potential occurs.

Tsunamis are often misnamed *tidal waves*. This is incorrect because they have nothing to do with the tides, which are caused by the gravitational pull of the Moon and Sun.

Notable Tsunami
November 1, 1755. A Lisbon, Portugal earthquake generated tsunamis that hit the west coasts of Spain, Portugal, and Morocco.

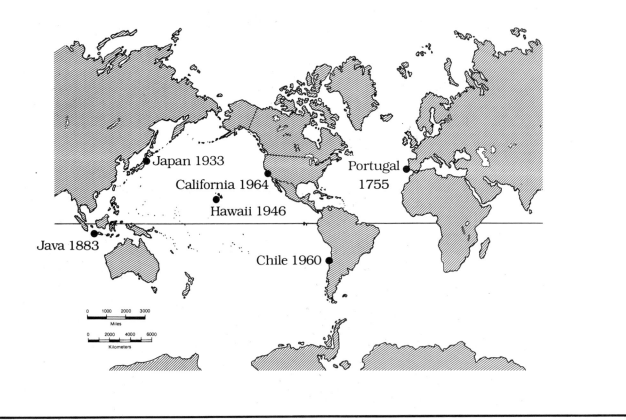

August 27, 1883. The volcanic eruption and explosion on the island of Krakatoa (west of Java in the East Indies) generated a tsunami that sent 100-foot (about 30 meters) waves crashing into Java and Sumatra, drowning 36,500 people.

March 2, 1933. An earthquake along a submarine fault in the Japan trench (subduction zone) generated a tsunami that struck the Japanese coast with wave crests as high as 25 meters, killing 3,000 people.

April 1, 1946. An earthquake on the sea bottom near the Aleutian Islands generated a tsunami that struck Hilo, Hawaii killing 159 people.

May 22, 1960. An earthquake in Chile generated a tsunami, killing 1,000 people in Chile, Hawaii, the Philippines, and Japan.

March 28, 1964. The powerful Alaskan earthquake caused a tsunami that came ashore in many places, including Crescent City, California. It caused a total of 122 deaths, and $104,000,000 in damage, overall. Waves were 52 meters (about 170 feet) high in Valdez, Alaska.

A Cascade of Disasters

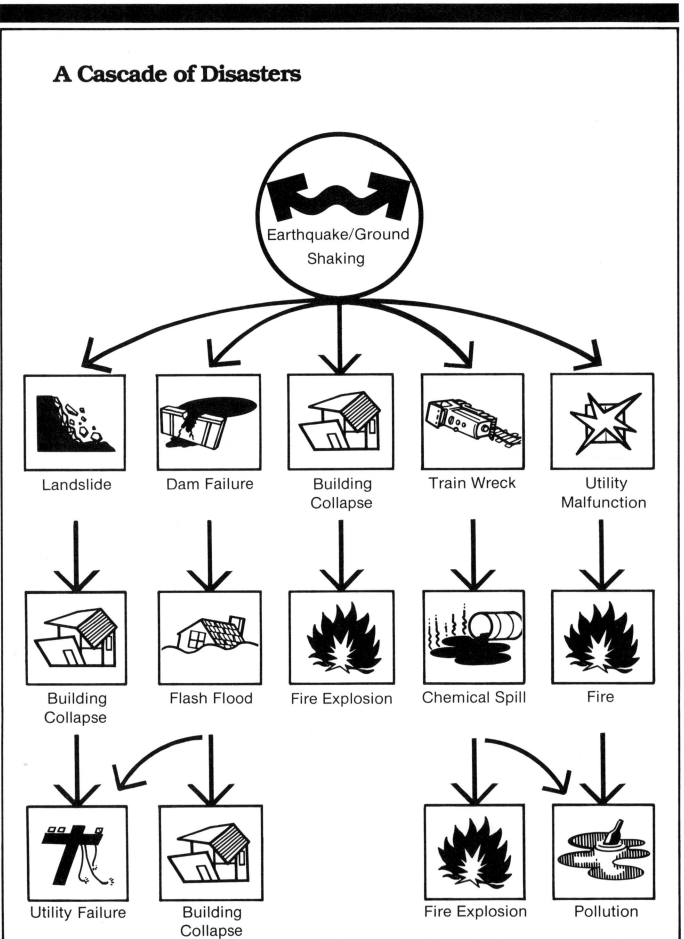

Reprinted from (1975) *Hazards Evaluation For Disaster Preparedness Planning.* Published by ABAG
(Association of Bay Area Governments), Oakland, CA.

VI

Earthquake Safety
and Survival

EARTHQUAKE CURRICULUM, K-6
SCOPE AND SEQUENCE CHART

Unit VI: Earthquake Safety and Survival

Parts	Concept	Laboratory	Mathematics	Language Arts	Social Studies	Art
1	Every environment contains potential earthquake hazards.	Classroom hazard hunt		Discussion and list making	Discussion of damage to buildings caused by earthquakes	Illustrations of earthquake hazards in classrooms
	Students can identify hazards and eliminate them or reduce their impact.	Home hazard hunt			Hazard hunt and ways to reduce danger	
2	Students can increase their chances for survival in an earthquake by having essential supplies before they are needed.	Safety kit preparation		Disseminating information to family and neighbors	Discussion of essential items needed during evacuation	Earthquake safety posters
	Students can help to assemble emergency kits of supplies for their classroom, home, and family vehicle.				Earthquake safety kits	
				Group solutions	Poster distribution	
	Students can help to inform others about earthquake safety and survival.			Slogan writing		
3	Students can cope with hazards during evacuation.	Evacuation drill		Hazard descriptions	Discussion of hazards during evacuation	Safety kit decorating
	Students are responsible first for their own safety and can then help if others are injured.				Giving aid to the injured	
	Students can cope with the disturbed environment and their own emotional reactions.				Feelings and events after an earthquake	
					Drop and cover procedures	

VI

Earthquake Safety and Survival

There is a great deal that you and your students can do to take care of yourselves during and after an earthquake. This unit goes through three essential steps: planning, preparation, and practice. We start with what students have learned in Unit V about the events of an earthquake, and ask them to list hazards in their classroom, home, and community. Students cooperate with adults to eliminate some of these hazards, and learn to avoid those that cannot be eliminated. They prepare an emergency kit to take with them in evacuating the classroom, and list ingredients for kits to be used in other settings. They share what they have learned with other children and adults in the community. Finally, they practice the Drop and Cover drill in several settings and evacuate their classroom. Class discussions provide opportunities for students not only to express their negative feelings, but also to develop pride in the positive competency they have gained.

Earthquake Safety and Survival

Earthquake Safety and Survival

Most people caught in earthquakes have a feeling of helplessness. Especially if they have never experienced a quake before, they have no idea how long it is going to last or what will happen next. In this unit you will take your students through several steps that will help them know what to expect and what to do if an earthquake occurs.

Hazard Hunts

Unit V stressed the unpredictability of earthquakes and the many kinds of events a quake can trigger. This unit reviews those events with students and invites them to take an active role in making their own environment a safer place to be during an earthquake.

Contrary to popular imagination, an earthquake does not cause the Earth to open up and swallow people. Especially in the smaller earthquakes, which make up the vast majority of all quakes, most injuries and fatalities occur because the ground shaking dislodges loose objects in and on buildings.

Classrooms, homes, and all the other places where children spend time indoors contain objects that could cause injury or damage during a quake. Because students have already learned a great deal about earth-

Teacher Take Note: This unit is structured differently from Units I through V. All three parts of Unit VI are meant to be used with all levels of elementary students.

quakes in the previous lessons, they are able to identify many of these objects themselves. They make class lists of the hazards in different settings and then work with teachers, parents, and other adults to eliminate as many hazards as they can.

Students can remove objects that could fall and cause injury during earthquake shaking. Those objects that cannot be removed should be securely fastened. In the classroom these may include fish tanks and animal cages, wall maps, models, and wheeled items such as pianos and rolling carts for audiovisual equipment. At home, bookcases, china cabinets, and other tall furniture should be secured to wall studs. Hanging lamps, heavy mirrors, framed pictures, and similar ornaments should be removed or permanently fastened.

There will be some hazards in the classroom, home, and community that students will not be able to eliminate. Be sure they know how to avoid those things they cannot change.

Emergency Kits
After a quake you and your students may spend several days together, cut off from many of the normal sources of community support. In the second part of this unit the class will devise emergency kits for several settings and make one for the classroom. Students will also make posters as a way of sharing their knowledge of earthquake preparedness.

Earthquake Simulation and Drill
During an earthquake, the most important thing for any child or adult to remember is the Drop and Cover drill: crouch under a desk or table, tuck your head, and keep

your hands on the side of your neck unless you need them to hold onto the legs of your shelter and move with it. After the quake, however, it is important to get out of the building and into a clear space, taking the emergency kit along. Students will point out various hazards that might occur in the course of leaving the building and discuss ways of dealing with various obstacles.

Aftershocks may occur without warning, minutes or even months after the major earthquake. Practice Drop and Cover on the way out of the building, and in as many other settings as possible, until the drill becomes second nature to you and your students. You may want to time how long it takes for everyone in the class to get into a safe position. Then challenge students to cut down that time, and let them know they're getting faster.

In teaching this last lesson, be sensitive to your students' fears and concerns, and give them chances to talk and ask questions. Recognize their negative feelings, and share your own, but also emphasize their competencies and the things they are able to do for themselves and each other.

Congratulate your students, and yourself. You're learning to be quake-safe!

Hunt for Hazards

Vocabulary

hazard
secure

Learning Links

Music: Create movements to accompany a chant

Language Arts: Discussing hazards and making lists, using and applying action verbs, sharing information with parents and families

Social Studies: Identifying hazards throughout the community on several levels: school, home, and beyond

Art: Drawing home hazards that are not on the Home Hazard Hunt worksheet

Content Concepts

1. Every environment contains potential earthquake hazards.

2. Students can identify hazards and eliminate them or reduce their impact.

Objectives

Students will

—identify potential hazards in their classroom that may cause damage, injury, or death during an earthquake.

—list, and, if possible, make changes in their classroom to reduce potential hazards.

—identify potential earthquake hazards in their homes.

—list, and, if possible, make changes in their homes to reduce potential hazards.

Activity One: Classroom Hazard Hunt

Materials for the teacher
• Transparency made from Master 55, Fourth Grade Classroom
• Overhead projector
• Transparency marker

Materials for each student
• Handout made from Master 55
• Crayons or colored pencils
• Handout made from Master 56, Classroom Hazard Hunt
• Drawing paper (optional)

Procedure

1. Ask students what they think is the direct cause of most earthquake deaths and injuries. Listen to their ideas. After some discussion, tell students that the movement of the ground during an earthquake seldom causes death or injury. Most deaths and injuries are caused by falling debris from damaged buildings.

2. Review materials from Units Four and Five about the ways in which ground shaking from earthquakes can damage buildings.

a. Building damage can include:

   toppling chimneys

   falling brick from walls and roof decorations, such as parapets and cornices (Show pictures or draw pictures of these decorations; or if they're attached to your school building, point them out to the students.)

   collapsing exterior walls

   falling glass from broken windows

b. Damage inside the building can include:

   falling ceiling plaster and light fixtures

   overturned bookcases and other furniture and appliances

   falling objects from shelves and walls

c. Damage to the building and damage inside the building can also cause:

   fires from broken chimneys, gas lines, and electrical wires

   flooding from broken water pipes

   spilled chemicals

d. In the community, earthquake ground shaking can cause:

   downed power lines

   damage to bridges, highways, and railroad tracks

   flooding from dam failures, damage to reservoirs and water towers

   fires from spilled gasoline and other chemicals

   liquefaction and landslides

   water sloshing in ponds, pools, etc.

   tsunami (in coastal areas)

haz • ard

A hazard is any object or situation which contains the potential for damage, injury, or death.

se • cure

We *secure* (V.) objects when we fasten them so that they cannot move. Then we can feel *secure* (Adj.), or safe from harm.

Teacher Take Note: This activity will take about 60 to 90 minutes, or longer if students modify their classroom to make it safer during an earthquake. You may want to divide the procedure between two separate sessions.

3. Sum up: There are many things in our environment (home, school, and community) that could cause us harm during an earthquake. We refer to these things as *hazards*. Potential hazards include objects that might fall, break, or catch fire during an earthquake. There will be many hazards that we cannot correct. But identifying these hazards will help us to anticipate them and avoid danger and injury.

4. Tell students they are going to conduct a hazard hunt in their classroom to identify things that might hurt them during an earthquake. Refer to Master 56, the Classroom Hazard Hunt, to help students identify hazards.

5. Distribute Master 55, Fourth Grade Classroom. Have students circle or color those hazards which are found in their classroom. Ask them to make a list of any other hazards that are in their classroom but are not included in the picture, or to draw their own classroom and point out additional hazards.

6. Conduct a class discussion about the hazards you have identified and how they might cause harm. Use the overhead of Master 55 in your discussion.

7. Ask students to decide what they can do as a group to make the room safer. Actions might include tying down objects, moving hanging objects, placing objects on lower shelves, and so on. You may want to write the following action verbs on the blackboard:

move anchor
relocate replace
attach remove
fasten eliminate
secure change
tie down

8. If appropriate, have students spend time changing the things they can change to make their room safer.

9. Have students make a list of things that could be changed, but not without adult help. These might include putting latches on cabinets, blocking wheels on the piano, and attaching cabinets to walls.

10. If appropriate, have students help to make these changes. They might want to meet with the principal or work with the custodians to help make their room safer.

11. When changes can't be made, be sure students are aware of the remaining hazards, and know they must avoid or move away from them if an earthquake occurs.

Teacher Take Note: How you use the Quake-Safe Home Checklist will depend on the grade level of your students. K–2 teachers may want to adapt this sheet.

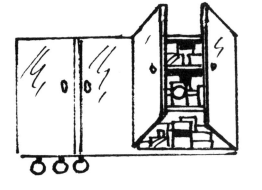

Activity Two: Home Hazard Hunt

Materials for the teacher
- Transparencies made from Master 57 a, b, and c, Home Hazard Hunt Worksheets
- Overhead projector

Materials for each student
- Handouts made from Master 57 a, b, and c
- Handout made from Master 58, Quake-Safe Home Checklist
- Pencil or pen

Procedure

1. Explain to students that there may be many possible earthquake hazards in their homes—objects that can fall, break, spill, or cause damage and injury in other ways.

2. Conduct a brainstorming session with your students and see how many home hazards they can think of. List these on the board.

3. Tell students that they are going to conduct a hazard hunt at home to identify things that might hurt them or their families during an earthquake. Distribute the student worksheets made from Master 57. Discuss each of the pictures with the students and ask why the item pictured could be a hazard. Remind students that this sheet does not include all the possible home earthquake hazards—just some of them.

4. Instruct students to take the worksheets home and have other children and their parents or guardians join them in looking through the house for hazards. Some hazards may exist in more than one place. Give these instructions:

a. Put a check in the box beneath every hazard you find in your home. (If the hazard occurs more than once, students may write a total number in the box instead of a check.)

b. If you can, write the name of the room(s) in which the hazard is located.

c. On a separate piece of paper or on the back of the worksheets, list or draw any potential earthquake hazards that are found in your home but are not on the list.

d. Bring your completed worksheets back to class.

5. Conduct a classroom discussion about the hazards that students found in their homes. Especially discuss hazards they identified that were not on the list. You may want to use transparencies of the home hazard worksheets during your discussions.

6. Explain to students that now they have identified earthquake hazards in their homes, they can take action to reduce their danger. Emphasize that there are some actions they can take which cost little or no money, while other actions will cost quite a bit and will have to be done by adults.

7. Distribute copies of the Quake-Safe Home Checklist (Master 58) to students. Discuss the items on the list. Determine which changes can be made easily and which will be more difficult. Again, emphasize that this list does not include everything that can be done to make a home safer.

8. Have students take the list home to discuss with their families. Families may decide which changes could be made immediately in their homes and which ones will have to wait. Encourage students to help their parents in any way possible to make the changes that can be made. As you did in Activity One, remind students that they will have to be responsible for avoiding the hazards they cannot remove.

9. You may want the children to bring back the completed checklists so they can have a follow-up discussion in class.

Extensions

1. Since homes without young children also need to be prepared for earthquakes, you and the class might explore ways of disseminating the Quake-Safe Home Checklist to other members of your community. What about grocery stores, community centers, libraries, and churches? Students may have other ideas.

2. Make a transparency and student copies from Master 59, Neighborhood Hazard Hunt. Show the picture and ask students to use red pencils to circle everything they see that could come loose and cause damage during an earthquake. Share answers. This could be either a class activity or homework.

3. Distribute copies of Master 60, Safety Rules for Shoppers. Discuss the rules in class, then ask students to take the page home and share it with their families.

4. (older students) Distribute student copies of the Community Hazard Map, Master 61. Challenge students to identify the hazards on the map. Follow up with a class discussion.

Prepare and Share

Vocabulary

essential
responsibility

Learning Links

Language Arts: Reaching consensus in a group, copying lists of kit materials, writing preparedness slogans

Social Studies: Sharing kit lists with families, discussing ways to inform the community about quake-safe actions, distributing posters

Art: Planning and decorating the classroom kit, making safety posters

Content Concepts

1. Students can increase their chances for safety and survival in an earthquake by having essential supplies assembled before they need them.

2. Students can help to assemble emergency kits of supplies for their classroom, home, and family vehicle.

3. Students can help to inform others about earthquake safety and survival.

Objectives

Students will

—demonstrate an awareness of responsibility for their own well-being and the well-being of others during an emergency.

—list items to include in classroom, home, and vehicle emergency kits.

—list uses for the kits in emergencies other than an earthquake.

—prepare an emergency kit for their classroom.

—take home lists of suggestions for home and vehicle kits.

—make posters illustrating what they have learned, and distribute them around the school and community.

Activity One: Brainstorming

Materials for the teacher
• Blackboard and chalk

Procedure

1. Review the earthquake hazard hunts in Part 1 of this unit to be sure students have a clear idea of the most common earthquake hazards.

2. Remind the students that they may have to evacuate their school, home, or other location after an earthquake. If this happens, they will want to have some essential items in a convenient place, ready to pick up and take.

3. Invite students to name some things they could *not* take with them if they had to leave their houses in a hurry. Take suggestions for only about five minutes, keeping the mood light. This exercise should help young children, in particular, to see the difference between essential and nonessential items.

4. Now invite students to name some things they really need to have in order to live. Write suggestions on the blackboard

Teacher Take Note: Taking an active role in preparedness will help students to deal with their natural and reasonable fear of earthquakes. Nevertheless, fears and anxieties are inevitable, even among older children who have learned to hide their emotions. Express your own concerns openly, and let students know that it's normal to be afraid.

es • sen • tial

Essential items are those we need to stay alive and healthy.

re • spon • si • bil • i • ty

A responsibility is a task or a set of tasks someone is able to do and expected to do.

or overhead. After food and water have been named, there will be differences of opinion on the remaining items. Remind them to choose things that can be easily carried and have more than one use.

5. Ask the class:

Which of these things should we have ready in the classroom? (Make a classroom list.)

Which of them should we have at home? (Make a home list.)

Which of them should we have in the family car, van, or other vehicle? (Make a vehicle list.)

6. When the class has reached agreement on a number of items, invite them to brainstorm one more list: a list of emergencies other than an earthquake for which their list of supplies would be appropriate. Accept all answers and discuss them briefly.

Activity Two: Create a Kit

Materials
- Inexpensive backpack or other ample container with shoulder straps
- Art supplies
- Writing paper and pencils
- Items for the kit (will vary)

Procedure

1. Tell students that they are going to assemble an easy-to-carry kit which can be kept in the classroom for emergencies. Ask them to suggest appropriate containers, or show them an inexpensive backpack obtained for this purpose.

2. Divide the class into teams and assign responsibilities to each team. Roles might include:

a. Decorators: design and produce a logo or other distinctive decoration and fasten it to the kit.

b. Listmakers: copy the class list from the board or overhead (see Part 2, Activity One, Step 5) neatly and with correct spelling, and fasten it to the inside or outside of the container as a checklist. Also provide a copy to the suppliers.

c. Suppliers: decide which items on the list are already in the classroom, which will have to be purchased, and which can be brought from home. With the teacher's help, arrange for supplies to be bought or brought.

Essential items for the kit will include:

    bottled water and cups (Use plastic containers to cut weight, avoid breakage.)
    class roster with students' names and addresses
    first-aid checklist and supplies
    flashlight and spare batteries

Other items might include:

    pocket transistor radio and spare batteries
    paper and pens
    permanent marker
    colored flag to summon aid
    playing cards and pocket games
    hard candy and other compact, durable foods
    trash bags (for raincoats, ground cloths, etc.)

3. Invite the school nurse or someone from the Red Cross or the Fire Department to visit the classroom and discuss first aid procedures. After this visit the students may want to assemble a small medical kit and add it to their emergency supplies.

Teacher Take Note: Discuss the questions in Part 3, Activity One, with the instructor.

4. When the kit is completed, decide where to keep it. Explain that the teacher will carry the kit during evacuation drills or actual evacuations.

Activity Three: Poster Party

Materials for each small group
- Poster board
- Art supplies
- Pencils and scrap paper for rough drafts

Safety Chant

**If inside, drop and cover—
That's where you'll be safe.
If outside, stay outside—
Find an open space.**

Procedure

1. Read the chant to your class. Repeat the chant with the whole class several times, then ask students to create hand motions to accompany it. Suggest combinations of clapping, finger snapping, and patting on legs. As individual students work out their own rhythmic combinations, encourage them to demonstrate to the class so all can learn the same motions.

2. Tell students that now they have learned a great deal about earthquakes and earthquake preparedness, they have a responsibility to share their knowledge. One way of doing this is to make a set of posters and put them in places where they

will be seen. Each poster would feature the word *Earthquake* and a reminder of some quake-safe action. Ask them to suggest appropriate slogans. These might include:

Where's Your Emergency Kit?

Drop and Cover

If Outside, Stay Outside

Keep Calm—Self Control is Contagious

After the Quake, Evacuate

Move Away from Windows, Shelves, and Lights

3. Divide students into small groups, and have each group agree on the slogan they want to illustrate.

4. Distribute materials. Suggest that each group work out a rough version of their poster first, allowing everyone to have input into the design. If necessary, suggest ways for group members to share the execution of the poster: perhaps one student lettering, one sketching the design in pencil, and another painting.

5. When the posters are finished, discuss places to display them other than the classroom. Placing them in the hallways or the cafeteria would spread the message to other grades. Help students make arrangements to display some of the posters in stores, libraries, and other public places.

Extensions

1. Explore with students some ways to make the emergency kit lists available to people who do not have children in school. Perhaps the city government would pay for having copies made, and students could take charge of distribution.

2. Students might write to local businesses or visit them to request donations of the pack itself and the materials for the kit. This would be another way to involve the community beyond the school in earthquake preparedness.

Evacuation Drill

Vocabulary

evacuation
foreshock
aftershock

Content Concepts

1. Students can cope with hazards during evacuation.

2. Students are first responsible for their own safety, but also can help if others are injured.

3. After an earthquake, students can cope with the disturbed environment and their own emotional reactions.

Objectives

Students will

—identify hazards they might find during evacuation.

—describe ways of helping others who are injured during earthquakes.

—describe feelings they might have and dangers they might face after an earthquake.

Learning Links

Language Arts: Writing and reading hazard descriptions, discussing hazards and coping strategies, discussing and writing (older children) about what happens after an earthquake.

Social Studies: Practicing Drop and Cover and evacuation procedures, discussing responsibility for one's own safety in an emergency, and what can be done for others.

Activity One: Get Ready, Get Set

Materials for teacher and students
• Materials and procedure for earthquake drill, Unit V, Level 1, Activity Two
• Overhead projector
• Index cards

Procedure

1. Review classroom earthquake drill procedures with students and have them practice the Drop and Cover routine on Master 42. You may choose to do the drill without using the simulation script this time.

2. Take the class to the cafeteria and school library and discuss quake-safe actions to take in each of these settings. Have the children demonstrate those actions.

3. Tell students that during an earthquake it's important to stay where they are and take immediate quake-safe action. After the ground stops shaking, it is time to evacuate the building. Explain some of the hazards that may exist even after the major quake has passed, including aftershocks, fires, live electrical wires, and fumes.

4. Walk the class through your regular fire drill route to an open area outdoors that you have chosen in advance. Ask students to make mental notes as they go along of things that might become hazards during an earthquake, and share their ideas when you reach your designated site. Write each

Reminders for the Teacher

- **Take cover.**
- **Talk calmly to students.**
- **Give instructions for evacuation or other emergency**

When no Shelter is available

Move to an inside wall. Kneel next to the wall, facing away from windows. Bend head close to knees, cover sides of head with elbows, and clasp hands behind neck. If a coat is available, hold it over your head for protection from flying glass, and ceiling debris.

Earthquake Safety Reminders for Students

If you're outside
- **Stay outside.**
- **Go to an open area away from hazards.**
- **Keep quiet and listen for instructions.**

If you're inside
- **Stay inside.**
- **Take cover immediately under a table, desk, or counter.**
- **Keep quiet and listen for instructions.**
- **Remain in safe position for at least 60 seconds, or until the shaking has stopped and your teacher tells you to leave your shelter.**

e • vac • u • a • tion

Evacuation is the act of emptying completely. When we evacuate a building, we want to leave it quickly, quietly, and safely.

fore • shock

A foreshock is an earthquake which comes before the main quake and is less severe.

af • ter • shock

An aftershock is an earthquake which follows a major quake and is less severe.

Reminder

If you are in a school bus or a car when the quake starts shaking—

- the driver should stop as soon as possible away from buildings, power lines, bridges, and highway overpasses and underpasses.

- passengers should stay in the vehicle and hold on (cars and buses have shock absorbers).

appropriate suggestion on an index card. The list of possible hazards may include:

  power failure (Is there emergency lighting available?)

  halls or stairways cluttered with debris (Are there lockers or trophy cabinets along hallways that could fall and block your path?)

  smoke in the hallway

  an exit door that jams and will not open

  an aftershock (Students should stop walking immediately and begin Drop and Cover.)

  bricks, glass, and debris outside the doorway

  electrical wires fallen on the ground

5. Return to the classroom. Hand one of the students an index card with a description of a hazard. Discuss this hazard and its impact on evacuation. Continue handing out the cards, one at a time, until all the hazards have been discussed. Give students an opportunity to express ideas about how they can cope with the hazards and evacuate safely.

6. Explain to the class that if there is a strong earthquake, each student's first responsibility is his or her own safety. However, every student can learn what to do to help if someone else is injured. Present some "What if" questions for discussion. What would you do if:

  A student or teacher were injured? (If someone is injured and can't walk, don't move the person unless there is immediate danger of fire or flooding. Instead, place a sturdy table carefully above the person to prevent further injury. Then go for help.)

  Someone was cut by shattered glass and is bleeding? (Even the youngest child can learn to apply pressure to the wound.)

  Someone is hit by a falling lamp or a brick? (If the person is conscious and able to walk, take him or her to an individual in charge of first aid. Even if the person appears to be unhurt, have someone stay nearby to report signs of dizziness or nausea.)

Activity Two: Put It All Together

Materials for teachers and students
- Chairs and other objects as needed to simulate earthquake obstacles
- Classroom emergency kit
- Paper and pencils
- Master 62, Drill and Evacuation Checklist

Procedure

1. Tell students that you are going to conduct an evacuation drill. Have them help you devise a way to simulate hazards (fallen lockers/cabinets) along the hallway before the drill.

2. Back in the classroom, library, or cafeteria, call out *Earthquake!* Students (and you) should take quake-safe positions immediately, without any further direction. Remind students that a teacher or other adult may not be with them when an actual earthquake occurs.

3. After 45 seconds, while students remain in quake-safe position, briefly review the evacuation procedure. If it's cold, and students' coats are in the room, instruct them to quietly and quickly pick up their coats before leaving the room. Ask students not to put the coats on until they are outside. If an aftershock occurs along the way, they may need to place them over their heads.

4. Give the instruction *Evacuate!*, and proceed through the building evacuation route. Take along your classroom emergency kit (See Part 2, Activity 2 of this unit).

5. When the class is assembled outside, take roll. Use the Drill and Evacuation Checklist on Master 62 to evaluate the procedure. If errors were made, plan with students to correct them, and repeat the drill if necessary. But remember to emphasize the students' successes, not their shortcomings.

Teacher Take Note: Physical reactions to an actual earthquake may well include nausea and vomiting, or bladder and bowel incontinence. Even the simulation may trigger physical reactions in a few children. You may want to make discreet preparations to deal with this possibility.

Teacher Take Note: Since we never know until the shaking has stopped which quakes are foreshocks or aftershocks and which is the main event, it is essential to begin Drop and Cover at the first sign of a quake.

Teacher Take Note: There is no guarantee that emergency medical or fire personnel will be available to your school immediately after an earthquake. Local emergency teams will be severely overtaxed. It may be 24 to 48 hours before assistance arrives. Anticipating a delay in being reunited with their families and discussing ways of coping will help students deal with their feelings of separation and isolation.

Extensions

1. Distribute copies of Master 62, Home Earthquake Safety checklist. Encourage students to go over the list with their parents.

2. With older children, you may want to spend extra time discussing specific things they could to do to assist in cleanup and repair work after an earthquake. However, be sure you also emphasize the limits to what young people can safety undertake, and the precautions they must observe, such as wearing shoes and sturdy gloves when sweeping up broken glass.

6. If weather permits, continue this activity outdoors; if not, return to the classroom, but ask students to pretend they're still outside. Set the stage:

We have just experienced a strong earthquake. Every one of you knew what to do to protect yourself. Some of us received a few bruises, but no one was seriously hurt. We managed to evacuate the school building. We moved slowly because it was difficult to walk through the debris in the halls [and stairwells]. Now we're safely outside and wondering what will happen next.

7. Lead a discussion with students which includes the following questions and considerations:

Our class is all together in the schoolyard. How do we feel? (It is normal to feel scared, worried, or physically sick, and to feel like crying or laughing. It helps to talk about how we feel.)

What could we do for ourselves and each other to help us feel better? (Take a couple of deep breaths to help ourselves stay calm. Hold hands or hug to comfort each other. Talk softly until we're asked to listen to instructions.)

Because we experienced a strong earthquake, we know there must be a lot of damage within our community. We can hear sirens from police cars, fire trucks, and ambulances. We can also hear horns honking, and imagine traffic jammed up all over town.

It may take a long time for parents to get to school. How would you feel if you had to stay at school for many hours, or even for two or three days? (Children in emergency situations worry about being separated from parents. They're concerned about their parents' safety and that of their friends and pets. Allow students to discuss these concerns.)

What are some things we can do to help care for each other and keep busy? (Older students might want to help take care of younger ones from other classes. Perhaps they can think of appropriate activities.)

When you get home, what are some jobs you can do to help clean up and get things back to normal? (Discuss some of the dangers and how to work safely. Specific guidelines will be up to parents.)

How can we prepare for aftershocks? (Stress the Drop and Cover procedure once again, and review the hazard checks from Part 1 of this unit.)

8. Have students write a story or draw a picture sequence about "What I Did After the Earthquake."

Unit VI. Earthquake Safety and Survival

Materials List

Grades K-6
crayons or colored pencils
backpack
art supplies
items for safety kit
poster board
paper
classroom emergency kit
index cards
overhead projector
transparency markers
pencils or pens

Instructional Resources (Books, maps, pamphlets, slides)

Cazeau, C. J. (1975). *Earthquakes*. Chicago: Follett Corp.

Cazeau, C. J. (1977, February). Earthquake. *Instructor*, 86, pp. 76-82.

Lauber, P. (1972). *Earthquakes*. New York: Random House Inc.

Miklowitz, G. D. (1977). *Earthquake!* New York: Julian Messner

Publications (Single copies free)
Federal Emergency Management Agency, P.O. Box 70274, Washington, DC 20024

Available material:
- *Earthquake Safety Checklist, FEMA #46*. 1985 (pamphlet).
- *Coping with Children's Reactions to Earthquakes and Other Disasters, FEMA #48*. 1986 (8-pp. booklet).
- *Family Earthquake Safety: Home Hazard Hunt and Drill*, FEMA #113. 1986 (8-pp. booklet).
- *Guidebook for Developing a School Earthquake Safety Program, FEMA #88*. 1985 (50-page guide plus appendices that include reprints of FEMA #46, #48 and #113).

References
Bolt, B. A. (1988). *Earthquakes*. San Francisco: W. H. Freeman and Co.
Brownlee, S. (1986, July). Waiting for the big one. *Discover*, 7, pp. 52-71.
Earthquake Country: A Teachers Workshop. (1978, February 25-26). Far Western Section of National Association of Geology Teachers and California Science Teachers Association.

Earthquake Preparedness. (1986). Deerfield, Massachusetts: Channing L. Bete Co.

Getting Ready for a Big Quake. (1982, March). *Sunset,* 168, pp. 104-111.

Living with Our Faults: An Earthquake Preparation Guide. Palo Alto, California: Palo Alto Emergency Services.

MacCabe, M. (1985). *Guidebook for Developing a School Earthquake Safety Program.* Washington, DC: Federal Emergency Management Agency.

Muir, R. (1987). *Earthquakes and Volcanoes: Causes, Effects, and Predictions.* New York: Weidenfeld and Nicolson.

National Oceanic and Atmospheric Administration. (1976). *Catalog of Earthquake Photographs—Key to Geophysical Records,* Documentation No. 7. Boulder, Colorado: National Geophysical Data Center.

Safety and Survival in an Earthquake. (1983). Reston, Virginia: United States Geological Survey.

Schnell, M. L., ed. (1984). *National Earthquake Hazards Reduction Program: Overview Report to The United States Congress.* Reston, Virginia: United States Geological Survey. Circular 918.

Teacher's Package on Earthquake Drills, Book B. Washington, DC: Federal Emergency Management Agency.

Thygerson, A. L. (1979). *Disaster Survival Handbook.* Provo, Utah: Brigham Young University Press.

Yanev, P. (1974). *Peace of Mind in Earthquake Country: How to Save Your Home and Your Life.* San Francisco: Chronicle Books.

Watkins, J. T. (1981, December). The 1906 San Francisco Earthquake. *California Geology.* pp. 260-266.

Fourth Grade Classroom

Name _____

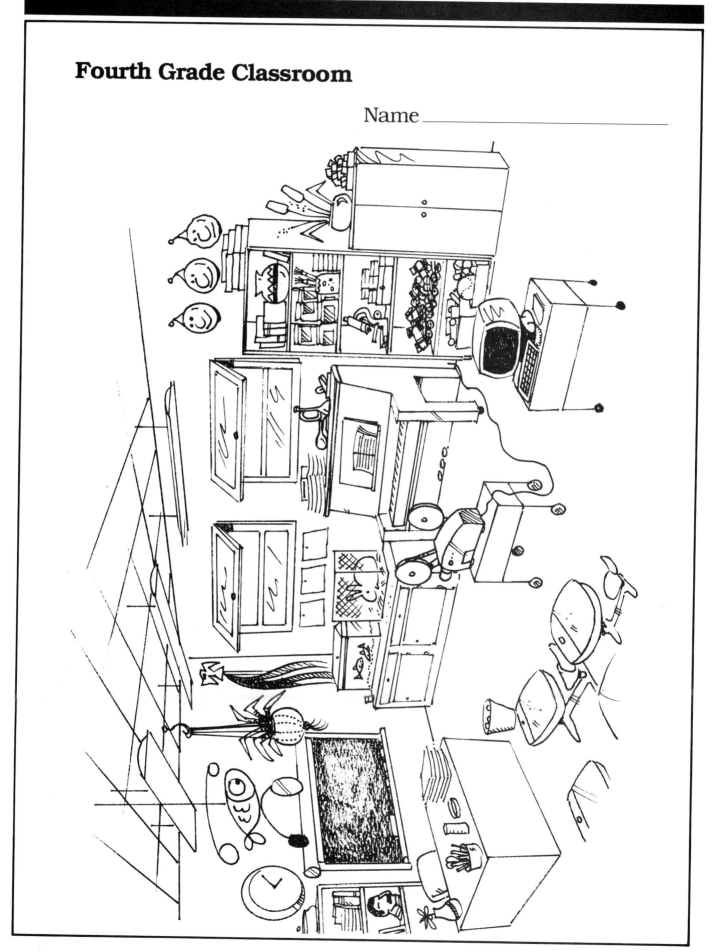

Classroom Hazard Hunt

- Are free-standing cabinets, bookcases, and wall shelves secured to a structural support?

- Are heavy objects removed from shelves above the heads of seated students?

- Are aquariums and other potentially hazardous displays located away from seating areas?

- Is the TV monitor securely fastened to a stable platform *or* securely attached to a rolling cart with lockable wheels?

- Is the classroom piano secured against rolling during an earthquake?

- Are wall mountings secured to prevent them from swinging free or breaking windows during an earthquake?

- Are hanging plants all in lightweight, unbreakable pots and fastened to closed hooks?

Home Hazard Hunt Worksheet

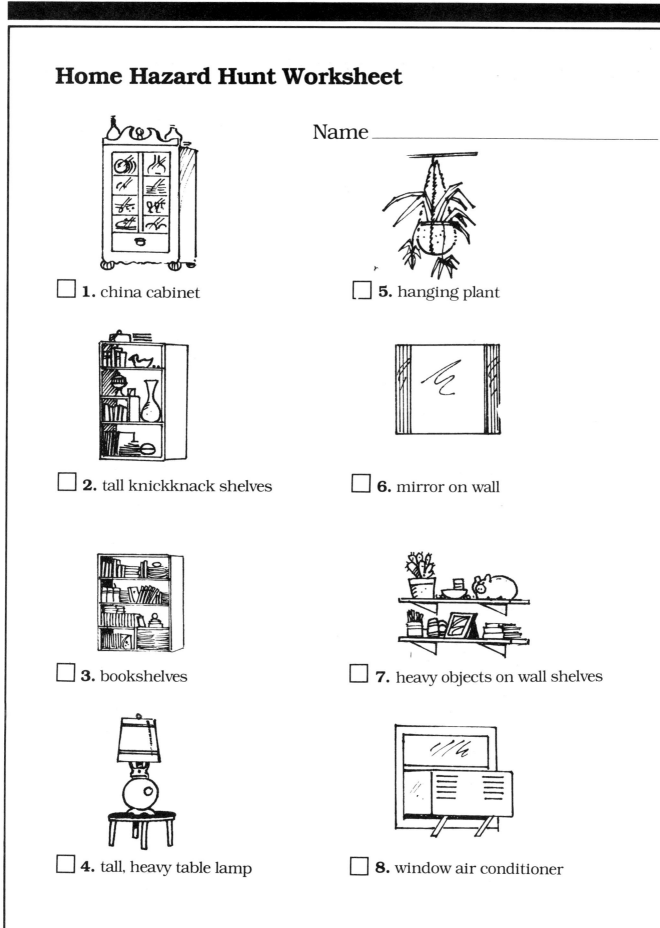

Name _____

☐ **1.** china cabinet

☐ **2.** tall knickknack shelves

☐ **3.** bookshelves

☐ **4.** tall, heavy table lamp

☐ **5.** hanging plant

☐ **6.** mirror on wall

☐ **7.** heavy objects on wall shelves

☐ **8.** window air conditioner

Name _____

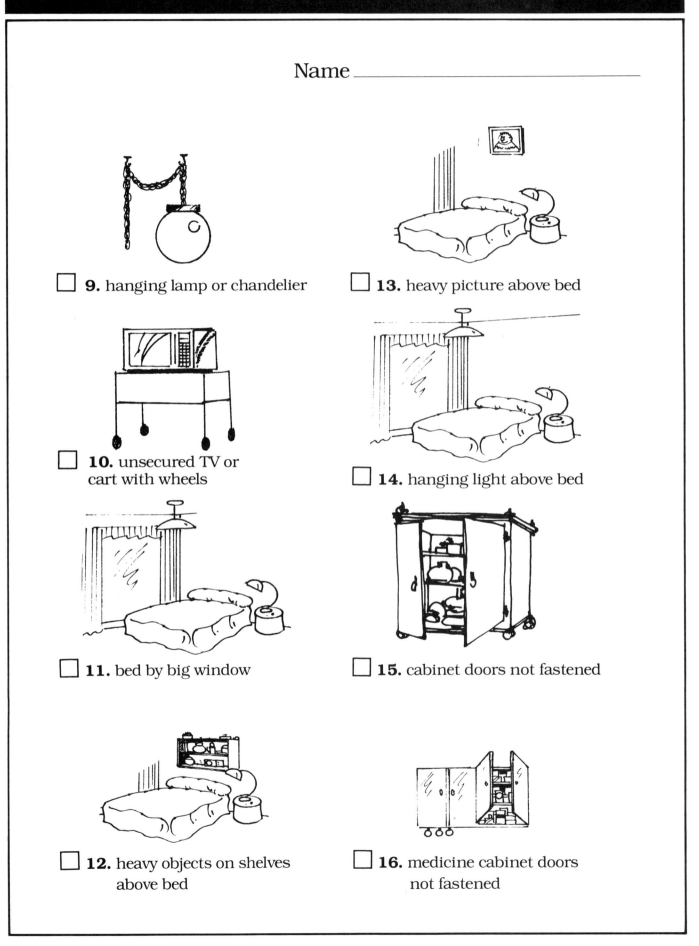

9. hanging lamp or chandelier

10. unsecured TV or cart with wheels

11. bed by big window

12. heavy objects on shelves above bed

13. heavy picture above bed

14. hanging light above bed

15. cabinet doors not fastened

16. medicine cabinet doors not fastened

Name _____

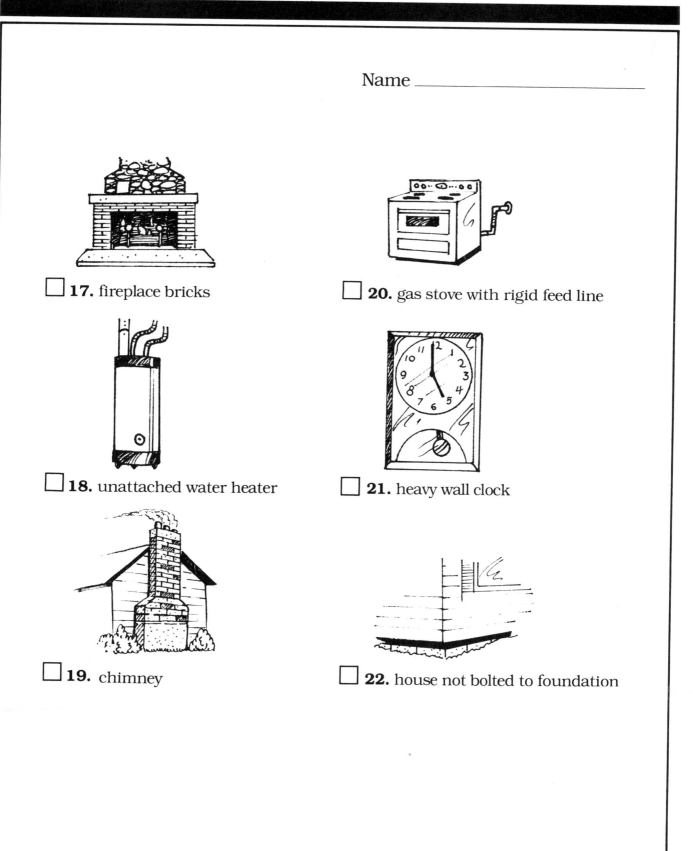

☐ **17.** fireplace bricks

☐ **20.** gas stove with rigid feed line

☐ **18.** unattached water heater

☐ **21.** heavy wall clock

☐ **19.** chimney

☐ **22.** house not bolted to foundation

Quake-Safe Home Checklist

Name _____

- ☐ **1.** Place beds so that they are not next to large windows.
- ☐ **2.** Place beds so that they are not right below hanging lights.
- ☐ **3.** Place beds so that they are not right below heavy mirrors.
- ☐ **4.** Place beds so that they are not right below framed pictures.
- ☐ **5.** Place beds so that they are not right below shelves with lots of things that can fall.
- ☐ **6.** Replace heavy lamps on bed tables with light, nonbreakable lamps.
- ☐ **7.** Change hanging plants from heavy pots into lighter pots.
- ☐ **8.** Use closed hooks on hanging plants, lamps, etc.
- ☐ **9.** Make sure hooks (hanging plants, lamps, etc.) are attached to studs.
- ☐ **10.** Remove all heavy objects from high shelves.
- ☐ **11.** Remove all breakable things from high shelves.
- ☐ **12.** Replace latches such, as magnetic touch latches on cabinets, with latches that will hold during an earthquake.
- ☐ **13.** Take glass bottles out of medicine cabinets and put on lower shelves. (PARENT NOTE: If there are small children around, make sure you use childproof latches when you move things to lower shelves.)
- ☐ **14.** Remove glass containers that are around the bathtub.
- ☐ **15.** Move materials that can easily catch fire so they are not close to heat sources.
- ☐ **16.** Attach water heater to the studs of the nearest wall.
- ☐ **17.** Move heavy objects away from exit routes in your house.
- ☐ **18.** Block wheeled objects so they can not roll.
- ☐ **19.** Attach tall heavy furniture such as bookshelves to studs in walls.
- ☐ **20.** Use flexible connectors where gas lines meet appliances such as stoves, water heaters, and dryers.
- ☐ **21.** Attach heavy appliances such as refrigerators to studs in walls.
- ☐ **22.** Nail plywood to ceiling joists to protect people from chimney bricks that could fall through the ceiling.
- ☐ **23.** Make sure heavy mirrors are well fastened to walls.
- ☐ **24.** Make sure heavy pictures are well fastened to walls.
- ☐ **25.** Make sure air conditioners are well braced.
- ☐ **26.** Make sure all roof tiles are secure.
- ☐ **27.** Brace outside chimney.
- ☐ **28.** Bolt house to the foundation.
- ☐ **29.** Remove dead or diseased tree limbs that could fall on the house.

Neighborhood Hazard Hunt

Name _____

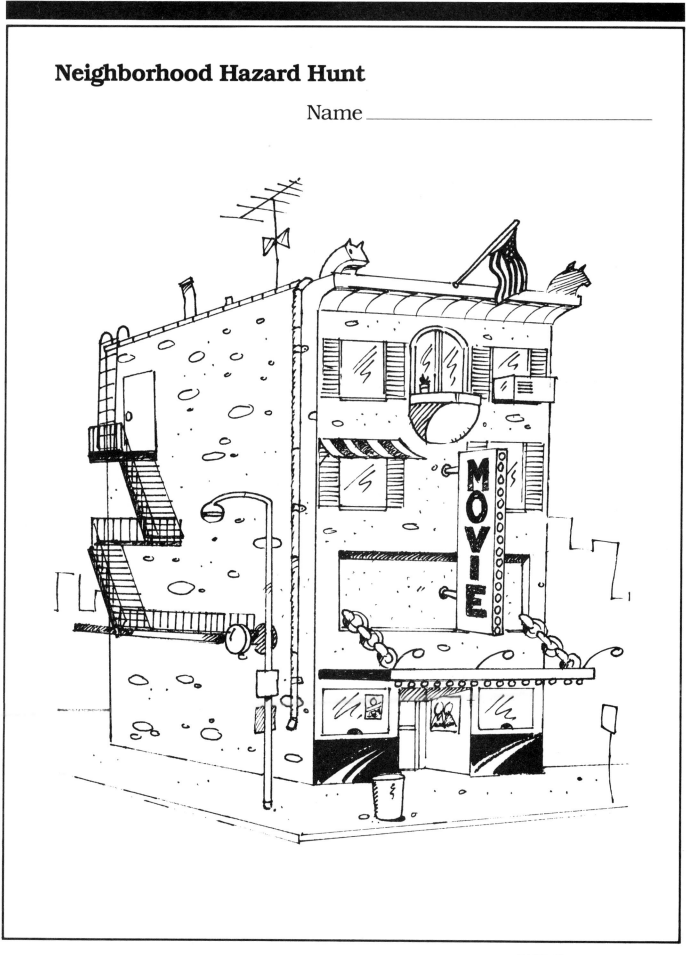

Safety Rules for Shoppers

If an earthquake occurs while you are shopping:

1. Do not rush for exits or doors. Injuries occur when people panic and try to leave all at the same time.

2. Move away from windows.

3. Do not use elevators. The electricity may shut off suddenly.

4. Move away from shelves that may topple or could spill their contents when they fall.

5. Try to move against an inside wall.

6. **Drop and cover:**

   Get under a table, counter, or bench.

   Turn away from the windows.

   Put both hands on the back of your neck.

   Tuck your head down.

   If your shelter moves, hold onto the legs and travel with it.

7. After the shaking has stopped, calmly walk out of the building to a safe area outside, away from buildings.

Community Hazard Hunt

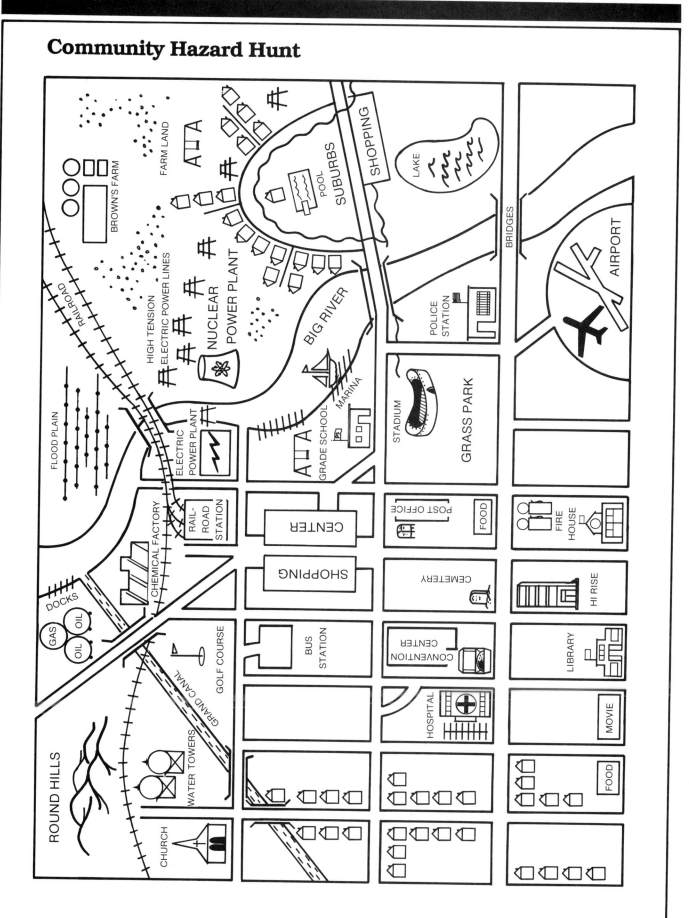

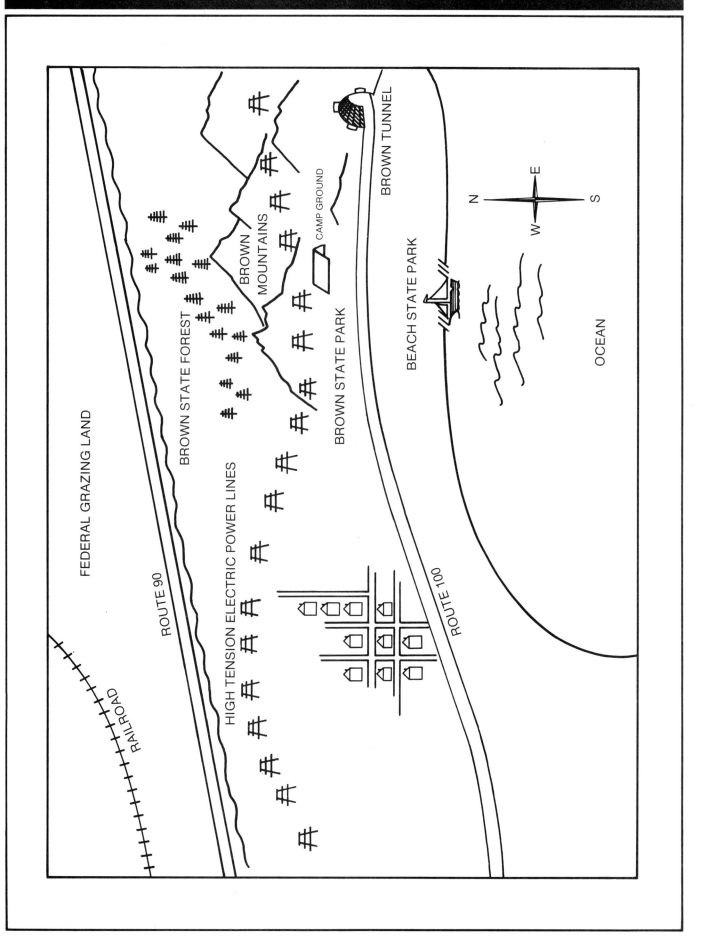

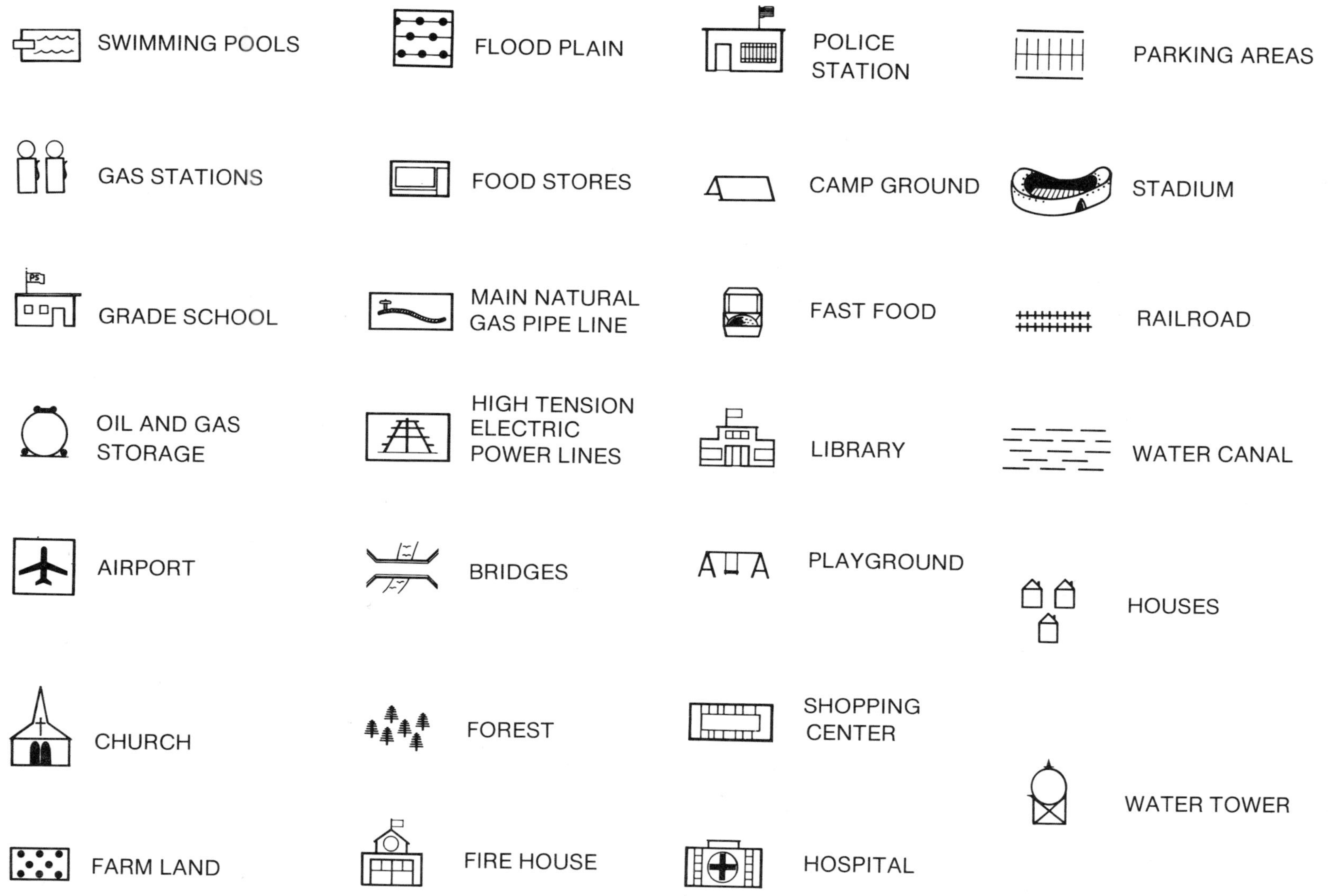

SWIMMING POOLS

GAS STATIONS

GRADE SCHOOL

OIL AND GAS STORAGE

AIRPORT

CHURCH

FARM LAND

FLOOD PLAIN

FOOD STORES

MAIN NATURAL GAS PIPE LINE

HIGH TENSION ELECTRIC POWER LINES

BRIDGES

FOREST

FIRE HOUSE

POLICE STATION

CAMP GROUND

FAST FOOD

LIBRARY

PLAYGROUND

SHOPPING CENTER

HOSPITAL

PARKING AREAS

STADIUM

RAILROAD

WATER CANAL

HOUSES

WATER TOWER

Drill and Evacuation Checklist

1. Did everyone know what to do when told to Drop and Cover?

2. Did everyone follow the procedure correctly?

3. In the classroom, the library, or the cafeteria, was there enough space for all the students under desks, tables, or counters?

4. In the gym or in the hallways, were students able to take shelter away from windows, light fixtures, trophy cases, and other hazards?

5. Do students know how to protect themselves if they are on the playground during an earthquake? If they are in a school bus or a car?

6. Did everyone remain quietly in their safe positions for at least 60 seconds?

7. Did students with special needs participate in the drill and evacuation?

8. Did we remember to take our emergency kit and class roster when we evacuated the classroom?

9. Did everyone go to the safe outdoor area in an orderly way?

10. If we had to change our evacuation route to get to the safe area, did we make wise decisions?

Home Earthquake Safety

1. As a family, determine the safest spots in each room of your home: under heavy pieces of furniture such as tables or desks, in doorways (but be careful of doors slamming shut), and in inside corners.

2. Determine the danger spots in each room. These include any place near:

windows	bookcases
large mirrors	china cabinets
hanging objects	stoves
fireplaces	

   - If you're cooking, remember to turn off the stove before taking cover.

3. Discuss, then practice what to do if an earthquake happens while you're at home. (Children who have practiced safe procedures are more likely to stay calm during an actual earthquake.)

   Drop and cover:
   - Crouch in a safe place (See **1.** above).
   - Tuck your head and close your eyes.
   - Stay covered until the shaking has stopped.

4. Determine an emergency evacuation plan for each room of your home.

   - Keep a flashlight with fresh batteries beside each bed, and shoes to protect feet from glass and other sharp objects.

5. Agree on a safe gathering place outside the house where all family members will meet after an earthquake.

6. Discuss as a family what needs to be done after an earthquake ends.

   Reminders:
   - Stay calm.
   - Be prepared for aftershocks. These may be strong. Take cover if shaking begins again.

   Parents Only:
   - Check for injuries. Apply first aid as needed.
   - Check for fires.
   - Shut off electricity at main power if you suspect damage. Don't turn switches on or off.
   - Shut off gas valves if there is any chance of a gas leak. Detect gas by smell, never by using matches or candles.
   - Shut off water inside and out if breakage has occurred.

Appendix

A. Earthquake Background
B. Book of Legends

Earthquake Background

Earthquake Legends

Ancient peoples experienced the same natural disasters that can affect each of us. Among these were hurricanes, tornadoes, droughts, floods, volcanic eruptions, and earthquakes. Because they did not have scientific explanations for such catastrophes, ancient peoples invented folk narratives, or legends, to explain them. Such legends are part of the literature that we have inherited from many cultures. An examination of legends gives a small insight into the location and frequency of occurrence of major earthquakes.

Defining an Earthquake

Earthquakes are an especially noteworthy type of catastrophe because they strike suddenly, without clear warning, and can cause much panic and property damage in a matter of seconds.

An earthquake is a sudden, rapid shaking of the Earth caused by the release of energy stored in the Earth's crust. An earthquake occurs at a place, called the *focus*, which may be up to about 700 km deep in the Earth. The place on the Earth's surface that is directly above the focus is called the *epicenter* of the earthquake. It has long been known that earthquake epicenters often lie along narrow zones, or belts, of the Earth where mountain building and/or volcanic activity are also present. But earthquakes may also occur in seemingly "stable" areas like the central and eastern United States.

Plate Tectonic Theory and Earthquake Occurrence

According to the recently formulated (late 1960s) theory of plate tectonics, earthquakes occur because of the motion of the pieces of solid crust and upper mantle that form the 100-km-thick, outer rock shell of our planet. This shell, called the *lithosphere*, or rock sphere, is broken into major and minor pieces called *plates*.

There are seven to twelve major plates and a number of smaller ones. From a geophysical perspective the Earth is like a giant spherical jigsaw puzzle with its pieces in constant motion.

The reason for plate motion is unknown. Scientists speculate, however, that the internal heat of the Earth causes convection currents in the semimolten, mantle rock material beneath the plates. They suggest that this convective motion, driven by the Earth's internal heat, drives the plates. Such heat is believed to come from the decay of radioactive minerals in the mantle, which extends to a depth of 2,855 km below the Earth's surface.

Types of Plate Motion

The plates move, relative to one another, at between approximately 2 and 15 cm per year. Three types of plate motion are most important for understanding where and how earthquakes occur. *Divergent plate motion* occurs where the plates are moving apart. Such plate separation most often occurs along the mid-ocean ridges. As the plates separate, new ocean crust forms from mantle material by volcanic eruptions or fissure flows. Many shallow earthquakes result from separation of plates. Because these usually occur in the deep ocean, however, they are rarely of concern to humans.

Plates are moving toward each other in such places as around the Pacific Ocean basin, and the Mediterranean. This is called *convergent plate motion.* Where the leading edge of a plate is made of ocean crust and underlying mantle, the plate tends to sink under the edge of the opposing plate. Such motion is called *subduction.*

An oceanic trench is a common feature at plate boundaries where subduction is occurring, such as along the Pacific side of the Japanese or Aleutian island areas and the Pacific side of South America. As the subducting plate sinks into the mantle, it begins to melt. The resulting molten rock materials gradually rise toward the Earth's surface to form volcanoes and fissure flows of lava. Subduction results in many earthquakes with foci from near the Earth's surface to about 700 km below the surface. Some of these earthquakes are extremely violent.

Where the opposing plates are both made of continental material, their collision tends to raise mountain chains. The convergent motion of the continental masses of India and Southeast Asia began millions of years ago and continues into the present. The result is the Himalayan Mountains, which are still rising slowly and are being subjected to frequent earthquakes as the mountain building process continues.

The conservation of the area of the lithosphere is one of the important concepts that relates to the divergent and convergent activity of plates. That is, a worldwide balance exists between the creation of new lithosphere at the mid-ocean ridges and the destruction of the lithosphere along subduction zones. This allows us to picture the Earth as remaining relatively constant in size. Earlier explanations of folded and thrust-faulted mountain ranges incorrectly required that the Earth shrink in size as it cooled. The mountains were thought to rise as the lithosphere buckled, something like the shriveling of the skin on an apple as it ages.

In the third major type of plate motion, the edges of the plates slip past each other. This is called *lateral* (or *transform*) *plate motion*. The line of contact between the plates is a *fault*. The stresses involved in lateral plate motion actually cause rupturing and movement on faults some distance from the area of contact between the plates. Therefore, it is proper to speak of a *fault zone* when discussing rock movement caused by lateral plate motion.

One of the lateral faults best known in to North Americans is the San Andreas fault of California. The San Andreas and its associated faults extend from the Gulf of California to the Pacific coast north of San Francisco. Earthquakes occur frequently in the San Andreas fault zone. Some of them have caused loss of life and extensive property damage.

Mid-Plate Earthquakes

Many earthquakes occur at places far from plate boundaries. Some of them, like the New Madrid earthquakes of 1811–1812 and the Charleston earthquake of 1886, have been major historical disasters. Explaining such mid-plate earthquakes has been a challenge to the theory of plate tectonics outlined above. Recent research has shown, however, that the zones of instability within plates can produce earthquakes along *intraplate* fault zones which may be hidden at the Earth's surface. Because of the location of these fault zones and their infrequent activity, it is still difficult to assess the hazards they may pose.

Plate Tectonics, Faulting, and Topography

From the previous discussion, the origin of major topographic elements of the ocean floor become more apparent. Among these are the world-circling, 60,000 km-long mid-ocean mountain ranges, or mid-ocean ridges, and the trenches, whose depth below the ocean floor exceeds any chasm found on land. Plate motion also causes the folding and faulting of continental rocks and their uplift into mountains. Thrust faulting may accompany such mountain building. A thrust fault is one in which the upper block of rock slides over a lower block which is separated from it by the fault. Earthquakes occur at and near the fault surface, as the blocks of rock move relative to one another.

Normal faults occur where rock units are pulled apart allowing movement vertically under the influence of gravity. The result of normal faulting, on a continental scale, is the creation of long, deep valleys or the lowering subsidence of large pieces of coastal topography. A normal fault is one in which the upper block *moves downward* relative to the lower block which is separated from it by the fault. As in thrust faulting, earthquakes occur at and near the fault surface as the blocks of rock move relative to one another.

Lateral faults occur where plates are sliding past each other. A lateral fault is one in which the blocks of rock move in a predominantly horizontal direction past each other with the vertical, or near-vertical, fault surface separating them. In the ideal case, lateral faults do not cause much change in the elevation of the opposing blocks of rock. Rather, they move the existing topography to different locations. Earthquakes occur at and near the fault surface as the blocks move relative to one another.

Detecting Earthquakes

When rock units move past each other along normal, thrust, or lateral fault surfaces, or zones, the result is often an earthquake. Vibrations arise at the earthquake focus and travel outward in all directions. The vibrations travel through the upper part of the lithosphere and also penetrate the deeper shells of the Earth's structure. The waves that travel through the upper part of the lithosphere are called *surface waves*. Those that travel within the Earth are called *body waves*.

The two main varieties of surface waves are Love waves, which travel sideways in a snake-like motion, and Rayleigh waves, which have an up-and-down motion. Surface waves from a large earthquake travel for thousands to tens of thousands of square kilometers around the earthquake epicenter. They are primarily responsible for the shaking of the ground and damage to buildings that occur in large earthquakes.

Body waves are either P- (for Primary) waves or S- (for Secondary) waves. Regardless of the nature of the material through which they travel, P-waves are always faster than S-waves. The difference in the arrival times of the two types of body waves allows seismologists to locate the focus of an earthquake.

Instrumental Measurement of Earthquakes

One way to describe an earthquake is in terms of the amount of energy it releases. That energy is indicated by the strength of the surface and body waves that travel away from the earthquake focus. As simple as this principle may seem, it was not until the late 1800s that a machine (seismograph) to detect and record earthquake waves was invented by British scientists working in Japan. The most famous of these early seismographs was invented by John Milne, who returned to Great Britain to establish the field of seismology.

In modern observatories, seismograph instruments can measure the north-south, east-west, and vertical motion of the ground as the various types of seismic waves travel past. Each machine sends an electrical signal to a recorder which produces a highly amplified tracing of the ground motion on a large sheet of paper. This tracing is called a seismogram. Modern seismographs record data digitally, increasing the speed and accuracy of earthquake measurements.

The American seismologist Charles Richter used the amplitude of the body waves shown on seismograms to measure the amount of energy released by earthquakes. The scale which he created in 1935 is called the Richter Scale in his honor. It uses Arabic numerals to rate earthquake magnitudes. The scale is logarithmic and open-ended. That is, there is no lower or upper limit to the magnitude of an earthquake. However, the largest earthquake ever recorded had a Richter magnitude of 8.9. The Richter magnitude of an earthquake also can be measured from the amplitude of its surface waves.

Intensity Measurement of Earthquakes

Even before seismographs came into common use, the effort to classify earthquakes by the damage they produce reached success through the work of the Italian seismologist Giuseppe Mercalli and other European scientists. The 1902 Mercalli scale was modified in 1931 by two American seismologists, H. O. Wood and Frank Neumann. In the Modified Mercalli scale, Roman numerals from I to XII are used to rate the damage, ground motion, and human impact resulting from an earthquake.

The intensity assigned to an earthquake is a relative measure. That is, the Modified Mercalli intensity at a given place depends on the distance from the earthquake epicenter as well as the geological structure of the area. For example, houses built on bedrock will receive less damage than similar houses built on sediment at the same distance from the earthquake epicenter. Poorly built structures will receive more damage than those reinforced to withstand earthquakes.

Location and Earthquake Risk

Earthquakes tend to occur where they have occurred before. There also appears to be some periodicity to the recurrence of earthquakes, that is, some more or less regular interval between major quakes. Unfortunately, human memory and written records do not go back far enough to allow us to predict earthquakes accurately along any known fault. Of course, some faults lie hidden beneath sediment or rock cover and have not been active in recorded time. When an earthquake occurs on such a fault, it may come as a surprise to everyone.

Scientists are developing and refining techniques, such as measuring the change in position of rock along a fault, that may eventually result in an ability to predict the magnitude and date of an earthquake on a known fault. Meanwhile, it is prudent to assume that an earthquake could occur on any fault at any time. Even if an earthquake occurs on a fault that is tens or hundreds of kilometers away, the resulting vibrations could inflict serious damage in your local area.

What Should Be Done To Prepare for an Earthquake?
Weaker structures are more prone to damage than structures built to resist earthquake shaking. Luckily modern houses built with wooden framing are fairly resistant to serious damage in small to medium earthquakes. Most modern commercial buildings are now designed to resist wind forces and earthquake shaking.

Since earthquake shaking is possible almost everywhere in the United States, earthquake safety should be practiced by everyone, whether at home, at school, at work, or on the road.

After personal safety in an earthquake has been attended to, it may be necessary to lead, or join, citizen action groups that are concerned with the safety of the community infrastructure during and after an earthquake. Will the "lifelines"— water, gas, electricity, phone and sewer lines—survive the anticipated earthquake? Will the hospital and other emergency services be operating and adequate to handle emergencies created by the earthquake? Even California, where individuals and governments are sensitive to these questions, the answer seems to be "not completely." What is the status of earthquake preparedness where you live?

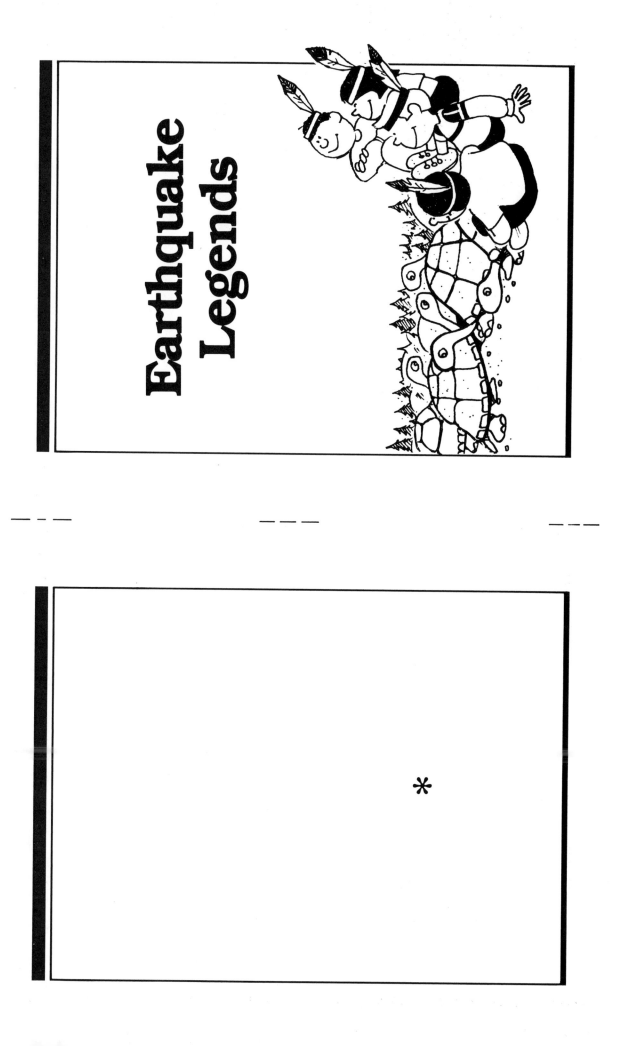

Earthquake Legends

*

1. India

The Earth is held up by four elephants that stand on the back of a turtle. The turtle is balanced in turn on a cobra. When any of these animals moves, the Earth will tremble and shake.

*

20. West Africa

A giant carries the Earth on his head. All the plants that grow on the Earth are his hair, and people and animals are the insects that crawl through his hair. He usually sits and faces the east, but once in a while he turns to the west (the direction earthquakes come from in West Africa), and then back to the east, with a jolt that is felt as an earthquake.

*

2. Assam

(between Bangladesh and China)

There is a race of people living inside the Earth. From time to time they shake the ground to find out if anyone is still living on the surface. When children feel a quake, they shout "Alive, alive!" so the people inside the Earth will know they are there and stop the shaking.

*

19. Romania

The world rests on the divine pillars of Faith, Hope, and Charity. When the deeds of human beings make one of the pillars weak, the Earth is shaken.

*

3. Mexico

El Diablo, the devil, makes giant rips in the Earth from the inside. He and his devilish friends use the cracks when they want to come and stir up trouble on Earth.

*

18. Central America

The square Earth is held up at its four corners by four gods, the Vashakmen. When they decide the Earth is becoming overpopulated, they tip it to get rid of surplus people.

*

4. Siberia

The Earth rests on a sled driven by a god named Tuli. The dogs who pull the sled have fleas. When they stop to scratch, the Earth shakes.

*

17. East Africa

A giant fish carries a stone on his back. A cow stands on the stone, balancing the Earth on one of her horns. From time to time her neck begins to ache, and she tosses the globe from one horn to the other.

*

5. Japan

A great catfish, or *namazu*, lies curled up under the sea, with the islands of Japan resting on his back. A demigod, or *daimyojin*, holds a heavy stone over his head to keep him from moving. Once in a while, though, the daimyojin is distracted, the namazu moves, and the Earth trembles.

*

16. New Zealand

Mother Earth has a child within her womb, the young god Ru. When he stretches and kicks as babies do, he causes earthquakes.

*

6. Mozambique

The Earth is a living creature, and it has the same kinds of problems people have. Sometimes it gets sick, with fever and chills, and we can feel its shaking.

*

15. Scandinavia

The god Loki is being punished for the murder of his brother, Baldur. He is tied to a rock in an underground cave. Above his face is a serpent dripping poison, which Loki's sister catches in a bowl. From time to time she has to go away to empty the bowl. Then the poison falls on Loki's face. He twists and wiggles to avoid it, and the ground shakes up above him.

*

7. Greece

According to Aristotle, (and also to Shakespeare, in the play called *Henry IV, Part I*) strong, wild winds are trapped and held in caverns under the ground. They struggle to escape, and earthquakes are the result of their struggle.

*

14. Colombia

When the Earth was first made it rested firmly on three large beams of wood. But one day the god Chibchacum decided that it would be fun to see the plain of Bogota underwater. He flooded the land, and for his punishment he is forced to carry the world on his shoulders. Sometimes he's angry and stomps, shaking the Earth.

*

8. Belgium

When people on Earth are very, very sinful, God sends an angry angel to strike the air that surrounds our planet. The blows produce a musical tone which is felt on the Earth as a series of shocks.

*

13. Latvia

A god named Drebkuhls carries the Earth in his arms as he walks through the heavens. When he's having a bad day, he might handle his burden a little roughly. Then the Earth will feel the shaking.

*

9. Tennessee, USA

Once a Chickasaw chief was in love with a Choctaw princess. He was young and handsome, but he had a twisted foot, so his people called him Reelfoot. When the princess' father refused to give Reelfoot his daughter's hand, the chief and his friends kidnapped her and began to celebrate their marriage.

The Great Spirit was angry, and stomped his foot. The shock caused the Mississippi to overflow its banks and drown the entire wedding party. (Reelfoot Lake, on the Tennessee side of the Mississippi, was actually formed as a result of the New Madrid earthquake of 1812.)

12. India

Seven serpents share the task of guarding the seven sections of the lowest heaven. The seven of them also take turns holding up the Earth. When one finishes its turn and another moves into place, people on Earth may feel a jolt.

*

10. West Africa

The Earth is a flat disk, held up on one side by an enormous mountain and on the other by a giant. The giant's wife holds up the sky. The Earth trembles whenever he stops to hug her.

*

11. Mongolia

The gods who made the Earth gave it to a frog to carry on his back. When this huge frog stirs, the Earth moves directly above the part of him that moves: hind foot, head, shoulder, or whatever.

*

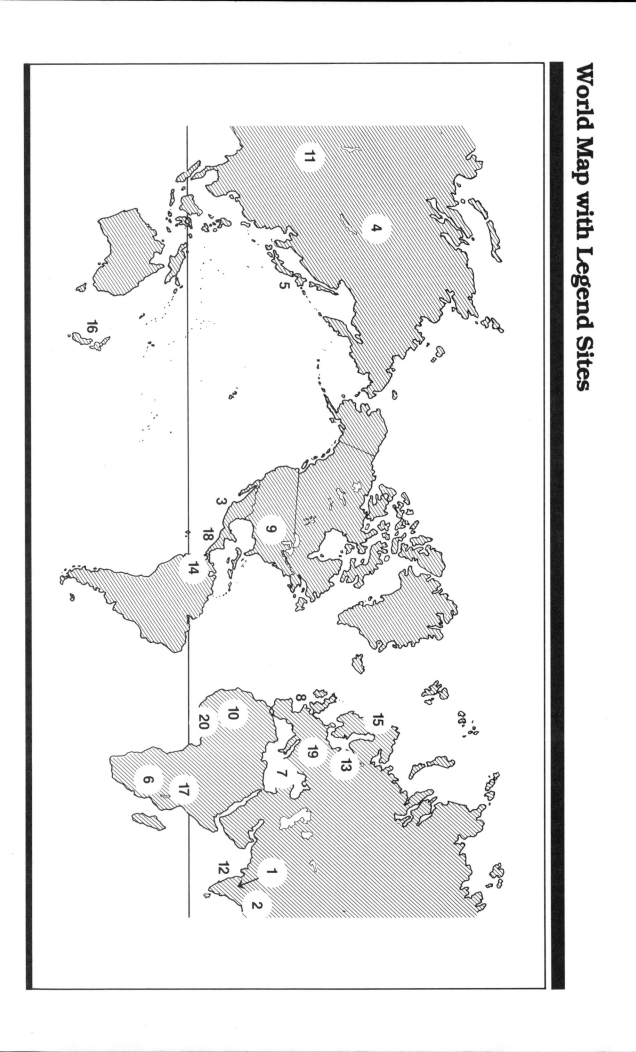